REGENCY SYSTEM

Joe M. Pullis, Ed.D.
Professor, Department of Office Administration
and Business Communication
College of Administration and Business
Louisiana Tech University

Cheryl D. Pullis, M.Ed.
Educational Consultant

Irene Schindler, M.S.
Business Education Department Administrator
Mt. Vernon High School
Mt. Vernon, New York

Glencoe
McGraw-Hill

New York, New York · Columbus, Ohio · Woodland Hills, California · Peoria, Illinois

SPEEDWRITING FOR NOTETAKING AND STUDY SKILLS

Glencoe/McGraw-Hill

*A Division of The **McGraw·Hill** Companies*

Linda Bippen
Contributor

Send all inquiries to:
Glencoe/McGraw-Hill
21600 Oxnard St., Suite 500
Woodland Hills, CA 91367

ISBN 0-02-685155-5

11 12 13 14 15 16 17 18 19 20 DOC/DOC 0 9 8 7 6 5 4

CONTENTS

Introduction

In today's society we live in an age of information. Although computers provide information at lightning speed, the need to capture and share information confronts us constantly in virtually all areas of our lives.

A very important tool for the rapid recording of notes is a comprehensive, scientific notetaking system. *Speedwriting* is precisely that system, and it covers all words in the English language. By studying and practicing the *Speedwriting* principles presented in this text, you will develop an invaluable tool for improving your learning techniques.

The instruction, self-checks, and exercises presented in this text and the accompanying *Student Activity Guide* will provide you not only with *Speedwriting* skills, but with reading, listening, paraphrasing, outlining, and memorization skills as well. Through practice exercises you will learn to select the key points from spoken or written text, as well as how to summarize, record, and organize your notes most efficiently. Additionally, your course in *Speedwriting* is designed to help you learn how to use shortcuts to record lectures, to record notes from reading sources, to take minutes at meetings, and to create outlines for essay examinations. The Learning Circle in Figure 1 illustrates how all of these skills contribute to and are necessary for effective studying and learning.

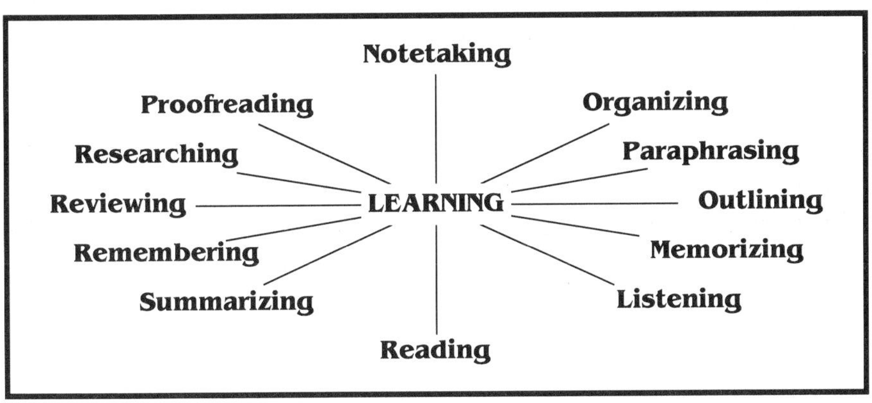

Figure 1: Learning Circle

Another benefit of learning *Speedwriting* is that it will broaden your vocabulary in various fields of interest. For example, words used in medicine, law, science, business, education, and the arts are all covered by the *Speedwriting* principles you will learn in this course.

The *Student Activity Guide* that accompanies this text offers practice in *Speedwriting* and study skills applications. It contains many exercises to help you expand your vocabulary and to reinforce *Speedwriting* principles and notetaking skills. To further sharpen your mastery of *Speedwriting* principles, a series of instruction tapes has been designed to build notetaking speed and accuracy through unit reviews, drills, and sustained dictation. A set of *Speedwriting Vocabulary Builder* cassette tapes is also available.

Although notetaking is a beneficial skill for everyone, it is an invaluable skill for college students who are faced with massive information input. At the college level your notetaking skills will be particularly helpful since much information for examinations is available only from the professors' lectures and not in textbooks. Notetaking is also a profitable skill in the marketplace for students pursuing occupational goals or full- or part-time employment. In short, notetaking skills can provide the extra measure of success in any career that requires capturing and sharing information.

At the completion of this course, you will possess a lifelong skill that will assist you with your college studies and serve you well throughout your career.

PART ONE

What Is *Speedwriting?*

You are about to study *Speedwriting*, a system of writing that is based primarily on what you already know—the alphabet—to represent the sounds that make up our language.

Since you already know the alphabet, you will not spend much time retraining your mind and your hand to write the *Speedwriting* words. Instead, you will concentrate on applying the principles, or rules, of *Speedwriting* to commonly used words. Taking notes, building speed, and transcribing will be accelerated as a result. In a short period of time, you will be writing *Speedwriting* as easily and naturally as you now write longhand, but at a much, much faster rate.

As you study *Speedwriting*, you will also learn techniques for practicing and writing your notes quickly and successfully. Begin today to develop good notetaking and study habits. The dedication you give to learning and practicing *Speedwriting* will help assure success in your career.

BEFORE YOU BEGIN

Your mastery of *Speedwriting* and notetaking skills should begin with the appropriate writing tools. A ball-point pen that glides smoothly across the paper is recommended for taking notes. Use blue or black ink and keep a red pen or pencil easily accessible for making important notations. For example, you will probably want to record due dates for term papers or special assignments in red to flag your attention.

What type of notebook is best? Students have various preferences. Most like a separate spiral notebook for each class subject. If separate notebooks are used, a magic marker should boldly identify each notebook by subject to avoid mix-ups. A three-ring notebook into which dividers are placed is preferred by many students. A great deal of material may be consolidated in a simple three-ring binder. However, please note that it is important to mark individual pages by section numbers in order to facilitate reorganization should the binder come apart.

In order to create a more efficient and motion-saving writing method, some people prefer to draw a vertical line down the middle of their writing page when not using a top-spiral notepad. The hand functions more efficiently within the half page, and this method eliminates the need to lift your hand and return it to the beginning as you must do if you write across the entire page. Still another procedure used by many students when using a left-spiral notebook is to write across the entire right page but leave the back side of each page blank for making special notations or comments about the material on the facing page.

You may prefer to write your textbook assignments and *Speedwriting* drills in a top-spiral notepad and your *Student Activity Guide* exercises in a left-spiral notebook or on separate sheets of paper. Or, all *Speedwriting* exercises could be written in a top-spiral notepad, and all notetaking activities or assignments could be completed in a separate notebook or on separate sheets of paper. Either type of spiral notebook could be used, but the pages of the top-spiral notepad are faster to turn. Follow the directions provided by your instructor. Otherwise, devise your own method and use it consistently.

In order to illustrate the writing of *Speedwriting* on pages with and without vertical center lines, the first document of each lesson's Reading and Writing Exercises is presented without a center line. The remaining documents are presented with center lines. The format selected for your use is a personal preference and need not follow the particular format of the document being written from the text. Where speed of writing is very important, however, the two-column format using the vertical center line is recommended.

Each lecture should be clearly identified and dated. When taking notes from published material, indicate your sources just as clearly.

UNIT

1

Writing with Speed and Ease

What is your present writing speed? It is not surprising if you have no idea how fast or how slow you write.

Here is a brief test to measure your approximate longhand writing rate. While someone times you or you time yourself, write the following sentence as many times as you can in 15 seconds.

Mark said that your plan does look good.

To determine your writing speed, count the total number of words you wrote in 15 seconds and multiply that figure by 4 (the number of 15-second intervals in a minute).

For example, if you wrote the sentence once and finished the word "Mark" on the second writing, you wrote 9 words in 15 seconds. Multiply 9 by 4 for a longhand writing rate of 36 words per minute. Record this speed in your notebook, and after a few *Speedwriting* units, take another test to determine your progress. An average writing speed is between 25 and 35 words per minute. You can look forward to more than doubling your longhand writing rate in only a few weeks by using *Speedwriting,* with even more increases in speed the more you apply your *Speedwriting* skill.

With *Speedwriting* you will learn to streamline letters as you write. Every time you lift your pen to cross a *t* or dot an *i*, you lose valuable time and reduce your speed. *Speedwriting* eliminates extra strokes by avoiding loops, dots, and crosses whenever possible. As you practice, you will become comfortable with this technique, and you will find that streamlining letters makes writing faster, easier, and just as easy to read. Look at these examples:

SPEEDWRITING PRINCIPLES

1. Write what you hear.

The English language contains many silent letters. In longhand, you write h-i-g-h even when you hear only the sound *hi* and k-n-o-w when you hear only *no*. In *Speedwriting* you write what you hear: hi and no. In the following examples, each word is followed by the sounds that are written in *Speedwriting*. This feature is known as *sound-spelling* and will help you to learn and remember *Speedwriting* vocabulary.

fee, f-e fe	tie, t-i ti
free, f-r-e fre	tray, t-r-a tra
say, s-a sa	ate, a-t at
knew, n-u nu	sigh, s-i si

Using this principle, write the following words in *Speedwriting*:

see, s-e se	pay, p-a pa
low, l-o lo	fly, f-l-i fli

2. Drop medial vowels.

Medial sounds are sounds that fall in the middle of a word. In *Speedwriting*, do not write vowels that fall in the middle of a word.

build, b-l-d bld	save, s-v sv
*legal, l-guh-l lgl	*glass, guh-l-s gls
did, d-d dd	bulletin, b-l-t-n bltn
budget, b-j-t bjt	*grade, guh-r-d grd

*In *Speedwriting* the letter for g is pronounced *guh*, so the sound-spelling would be guh-l-s for glass; guh-r-d for grade; l-guh-l for legal.

Using this principle, write the following words in *Speedwriting:*

given, guh-v-n *gvn* said, s-d *sd*

visit, v-z-t *vzt* paper, p-p-r *ppr*

3. Write initial and final vowels, those you hear at the beginning and the end of a word.

office, o-f-s *ofs* easy, e-z-e *eze*

ahead, a-h-d *ahd* ready, r-d-e *rde*

*do, d-u *du* often, o-f-n *ofn*

follow, f-l-o *flo* *view, v-u *vu*

*Note that *u* is used for the long vowel sounds of $\overline{oo}$ and $\bar{u}$.

Using this principle, write the following words in *Speedwriting:*

value, v-l-u *vlu* enough, e-n-f *enf*

open, o-p-n *opn* happy, h-p-e *hpe*

The three principles you have just learned will allow you to write many words you will encounter as you take notes. In the remaining units, you will learn more principles that will enable you to write other sounds quickly and easily. Before going on, practice these additional words. First, read the word aloud and spell it according to its sound: grow, guh-r-o. Then sound-spell the word as you write it: grow, guh-r-o *gro*

deposit, d-p-z-t *dpzt* type, t-p *tp*

news, n-z *nz* *review, re-v-u *rvu*

sell, s-l *sl* knowledge, n-l-j *nlj*

written, r-t-n *rtn* apply, a-p-l-i *apli*

lease, l-s *ls* unit, u-n-t *unt*

benefit, b-n-f-t bnft   *reason, re-z-n rzn

*Since medial vowels are omitted, the word beginning *re* is represented by an r.

PUNCTUATION SYMBOLS

Use quick, distinct symbols to show punctuation in *Speedwriting* notes. To show capitalization, draw a small curved line under the last letter of the word: Bill, bl.

Sue, s-u su   Ed, e-d ed

Dallas, d-l-s dls   Debbie, d-b-e dbe

Ted, t-d td   New Haven, n-u h-v-n nu hvn

To indicate a period at the end of a sentence, write \ .

Let Bill know. lt bl no \

To indicate a question mark, write x .

Does Bill know? dz bl no x

To indicate the end of a paragraph, write > .

Bill does know. bl dz no >

BRIEF FORMS

You will use some words so often that you will find it helpful to write shortened forms for them. These shortened forms are called **brief forms.** Since brief forms are not written in full, you should memorize them. Study and practice the brief forms until you can write them as quickly, easily, and accurately as you write your own name—without hesitation.

More than one word can be represented by the same brief form. When read in context, however, only one meaning will make sense.

a, an ·   we e

will, well l   the ((

it, at / /   is, his))

to, too t   in, not n

PRINCIPLES SUMMARY

1. Write what you hear: know, n-o no.
2. Drop medial vowels: build, b-l-d bld.
3. Write initial and final vowels: office, o-f-s ofs; ready, r-d-e rde.

but no "e" n ofs

WORD CONSTRUCTION

Practice writing these words in *Speedwriting* in your notebook. **Example:** desire, d-z-r dzr

above, a-b-v	abv	travel, t-r-v-l	trvl
loan, l-n	ln	delay, d-l-a	dla
receive, re-s-v		let, l-t	lt
supply, s-p-l-i	spli	held, h-l-d	hld
help, h-l-p	hlp	telephone, t-l-f-n	tlfn
city, s-t-e	ste	offer, o-f-r	ofr

READING AND WRITING EXERCISES

You now know enough *Speedwriting* to write complete sentences. Read the following sentences aloud. When you encounter an unfamiliar *Speedwriting* word, sound-spell the word. If the correct word still does not come to mind, read on to the end of the sentence. The context, or meaning, of the sentence will help you identify the unfamiliar *Speedwriting* word. If you are still unable to read the *Speedwriting* word, look in the printed key that follows the Reading and Writing Exercises.

Series A

1. e hp l se u sn.
2. l u pa . fe x
3. /) . nu fl unt. /) . nu fl unt.
4.) / unt l lt x) / unt l lt x
5. su l n fli l dls. su l n fli l dls

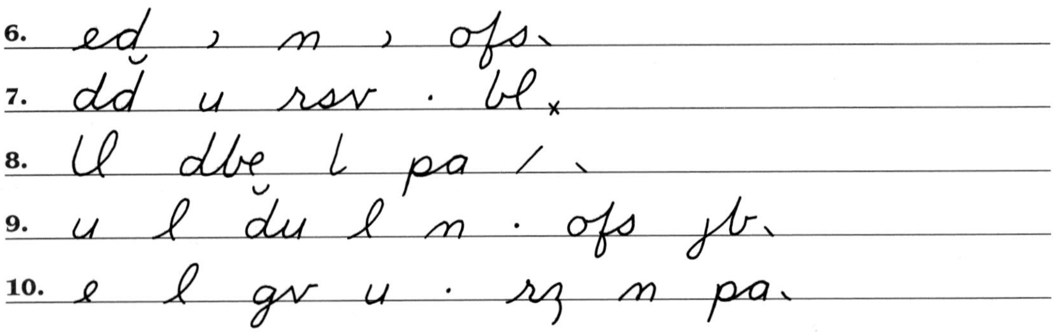

Series B

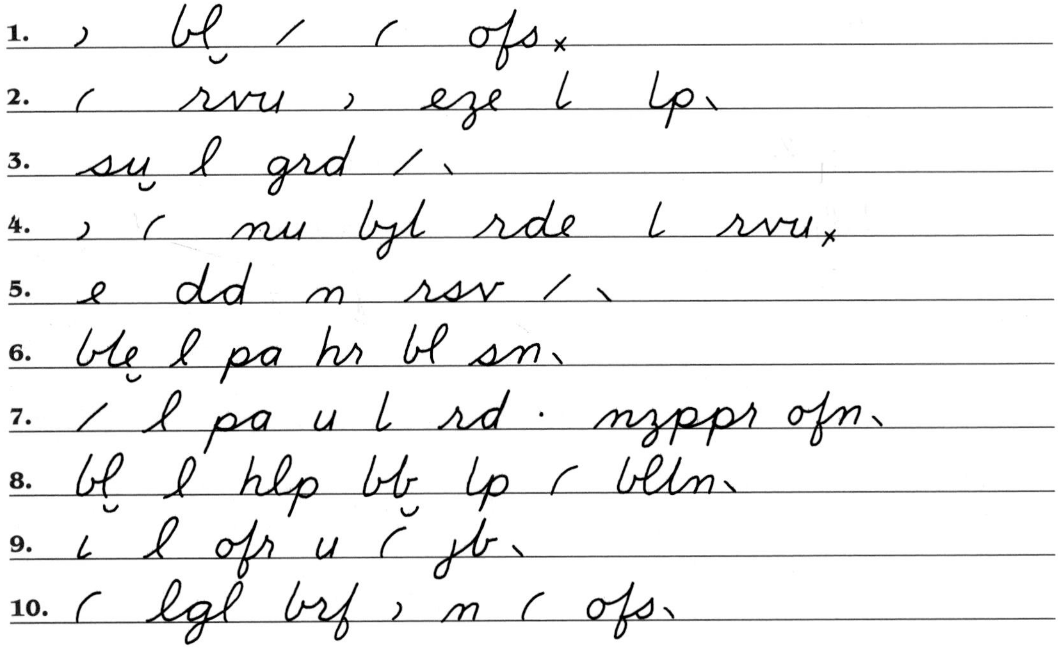

KEY

READING AND WRITING EXERCISES

Series A

1. We hope to see you soon.
2. Will you pay a fee?
3. It is a new file unit.
4. Is the unit too tall?

5. Sue will not fly to Dallas.
6. Ed is in his office.
7. Did you receive a bill?
8. Tell Debbie to pay it.
9. You will do well in an office job.
10. We will give you a raise in pay.

Series B

1. Is Bill at the office?
2. The review is easy to type.
3. Sue will grade it.
4. Is the new budget ready to review?
5. We did not receive it.
6. Betty will pay her bill soon.
7. It will pay you to read a newspaper often.
8. Bill will help Bob type the bulletin.
9. I will offer you the job.
10. The legal brief is in the office.

STUDY PLAN

As you work through each unit, use these steps as a study plan:

1. Study the principles and the words illustrating each principle at the beginning of each unit. Think about how the principle applies to each of the words listed under it.

2. Practice each word listed under the principle. First, say the word aloud: legal. Then sound-spell the word aloud as you would write it in *Speedwriting*: l-guh-l. Then sound-spell and write the word in *Speedwriting*: l-guh-l *lgl* . Write each word two or three times or until you feel comfortable writing the word.

3. Complete the exercises following the presentation of the principles.

4. Read the Reading and Writing Exercises in the textbook until the material can be read easily. If the correct word for the *Speedwriting* does not immediately come to mind, read on to the end of the sentence. The context, or meaning, of the sentence will help you identify the unfamiliar *Speedwriting* words.

   Consult the key if you cannot determine the correct word with the help of sound-spelling and context. Beginning with Unit 3, each document, letter, or memorandum in the key is marked in groups of 20 standard words (28 syllables). Small, raised, consecutive numbers are placed after each group of 20 words. Thus, if while reading you are able to reach the number 4 in one minute, you would be reading at the rate of 80 words per minute (20 × 4). If you reach the number 5, you would be reading at the rate of 100 words per minute. As a general rule, you should be able to read about twice as fast as you expect to write.

5. Write the Reading and Writing Exercises from the key while dictating to yourself.
   a. Read several words from the key.
   b. Write the words while you sound-spell and say each word aloud.
   c. Repeat this procedure until you have written a document completely. Check the *Speedwriting* notes in the textbook for any word that you may not know how to write.
   d. Read back the document from your own *Speedwriting* notes.

UNIT

2

What Is Studying?

Some students define studying as what you do to prepare for a test. This is only a small part of what the word means. Studying is learning for a purpose. You could be reading, listening to someone speak, doing homework, watching a film, practicing a musical instrument, playing sports, or engaging in thinking by yourself. All of these activities are a form of studying.

We are going to look at how to study, particularly when you are doing schoolwork. Acquiring good study habits, as well as efficient notetaking skills, will give you a boost in college and later on the job. In this course, you are gaining notetaking and study skills that can help make learning easier for you, help you get more work done, and help you learn more in a limited period of time.

An important part of studying is keeping a well-organized desk and work environment, but it is one of the keys to efficiency that is easy to neglect. Having a specific plan for your study activities that includes an environment conducive to studying is a positive step toward academic success.

SPEEDWRITING PRINCIPLES

1. Write *c* for the sound of *k*.

copy, k-p-e *cpe*
like, l-k *lc*
package, p-k-j *pcj*

school, s-k-l *scl*
clerk, k-l-r-k *clrc*
desk, d-s-k *dsc*

cpe scl
lc clrc
pcj dsc
Crc

2. Write a capital *C* for the sound of *ch, cha* (pronounced *chay*).

change, chay-n-j 
teach, t-chay 
such, s-chay 
check, chay-k 
chosen, chay-z-n 
church, chay-r-chay 

To write *m* and *w* with ease and speed, streamline the letters.

3. Write  for the sound of *m*.

may, m-a 
much, m-chay 
name, n-m 
my, m-i 
mail, m-l 
same, s-m 

4. Write  for the sounds of *w* and *wh*.

way, w-a 
week, w-k 
when, w-n 
wage, w-j 
what, w-t 
where, w-r 
winner, w-n-r 
which, w-chay 

5. To add *ing* or *thing* as a word ending, underscore the last letter of the *Speedwriting* word.

billing, b-l-ing 
*paying, p-a-ing 
something, s-m-thing 
attaching, a-t-chay-ing 
watching, w-chay-ing 
*saying, s-a-ing 

*Note: Always write long vowels before marks of punctuation.

6. To form the plural of any *Speedwriting* word ending in a mark of punctuation, double the last mark of punctuation.

billings, b-l-ings 
savings, s-v-ings 

7. *Adding s.* Write  to form the plural of any *Speedwriting* word ending in a letter: books, b-k-s 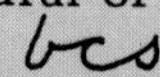. Write  to form possessives: girl's, guh-r-l-s 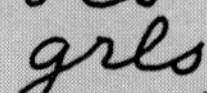. Write  to add s to a verb: runs, r-n-s 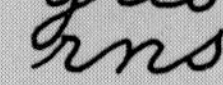. Add  even though the final sound of such words may be z.

checks, chay-k-s 
hopes, h-p-s 
helps, h-l-p-s 
jobs, j-b-s 
Bill's, b-l-s 
gives, guh-v-s 

An  is also used in the writing of proper nouns ending in s, even though the final sound may be z.

James, j-m-s 
Ames, a-m-s 
Burns, b-r-n-s 
Charles, chay-r-l-s 

Practice writing these additional words:

care, k-r 
claim, k-l-m 
games, guh-m-s 
course, k-r-s 
room, r-m 
units, u-n-t-s 
truck, t-r-k 
match, m-chay 
buildings, b-l-d-ings 
each, e-chay 
training, t-r-n-ing 
coverings, k-v-r-ings 

ABBREVIATIONS

Many abbreviations are so common that they come to mind automatically. *Speedwriting* makes use of these abbreviations. Since you already know many of these abbreviations, you will be able to write them quickly from the beginning.

company	co	president	P
information	inf	and	+ [´]
vice president	VP	return	rel [rtn]
catalog	cal		

BRIEF FORMS

are, our	r	can	c
for, full	f	us	s
of, have, very	v		

PRINCIPLES SUMMARY

1. Write c for the sound of *k*: copy, k-p-e cpe.
2. Write a capital C for the sound of *ch, cha*: check, chay-k Cc.
3. Write ⌒ for the sound of *m*: may, m-a ⌒a.
4. Write ‿ for the sounds of *w* and *wh*: way, w-a ‿a; when, w-n ‿n.
5. To add *ing* or *thing* as a word ending, underscore the last letter of the *Speedwriting* word: billing, b-l-ing bl_; something, s-m-thing s⌒_.
6. To form the plural of any *Speedwriting* word ending in a mark of punctuation, double the last mark of punctuation: billings, b-l-ings bl=.
7. Write s to form the plural of any *Speedwriting* word ending in a letter, to form possessives, to add s to a verb: jobs, j-b-s jbs; Bill's, b-l-s bls; gives, guh-v-s gvs; or to write the final s of a proper noun: James, j-m-s Jms.

WORD DEVELOPMENT

Write the following related words in *Speedwriting* in your notebook.

Example: bill bl	-s bls	-ing bl_	-ings bl=
truck trc	-s	-ing	-er
keep cp	-s	-ing	-er
move mv	-s	-ing	-r
follow flo	-s	-ing	-er
time tm	-s	-ing	-r
teach tC	-es	-ing	-er
give gv	-s	-ing	-r
save sv	-s	-ing	-ings

WORD CONSTRUCTION

Practice writing these words in *Speedwriting* in your notebook. **Example:** approaching, a-p-r-chay-ing aprC_

cake, k-k	makes, m-k-s
because, b-k-z	planning, p-l-n-ing
case, k-s	while, w-l
nature, n-chay-r	water, w-t-r
could, k-d	future, f-chay-r
items, i-t-m-s	matter, m-t-r
closing, k-l-z-ing	selling, s-l-ing
needs, n-d-s	coverage, k-v-r-j
caller, k-l-r	medical, m-d-k-l
mailing, m-l-ing	receiving, re-s-v-ing

READING AND WRITING EXERCISES

Series A

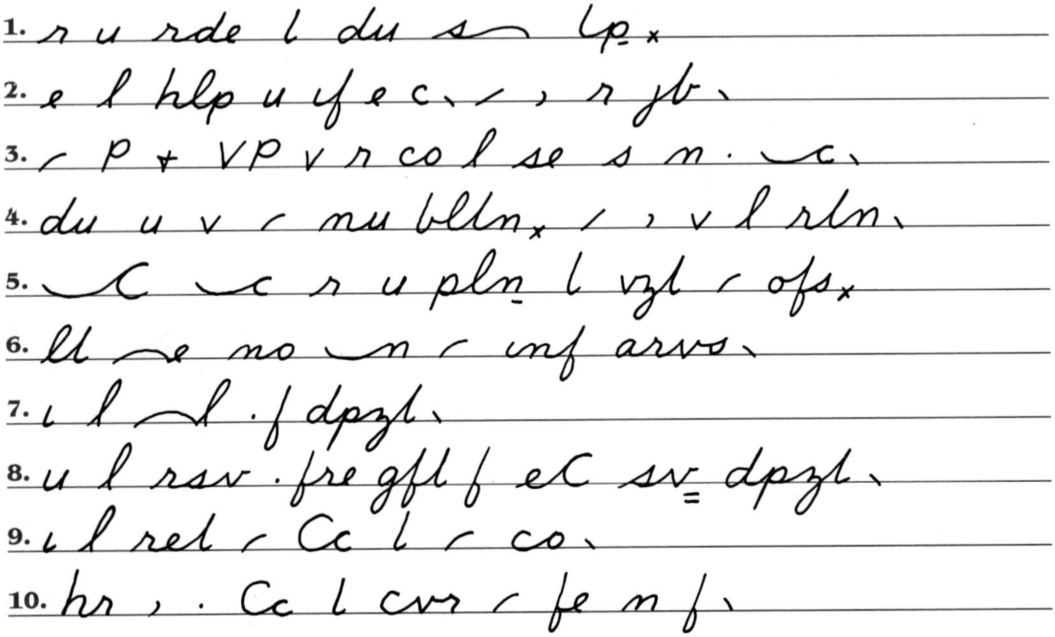

Series B

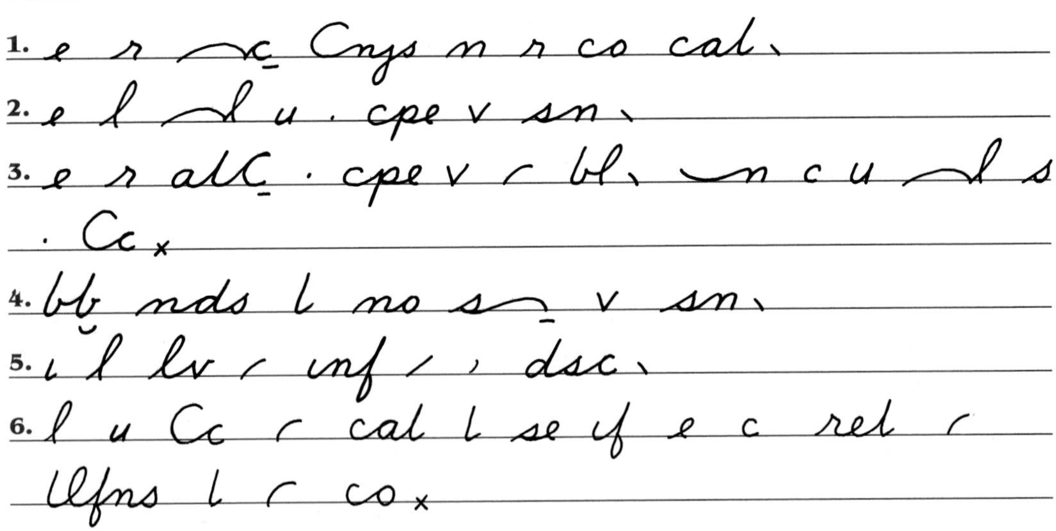

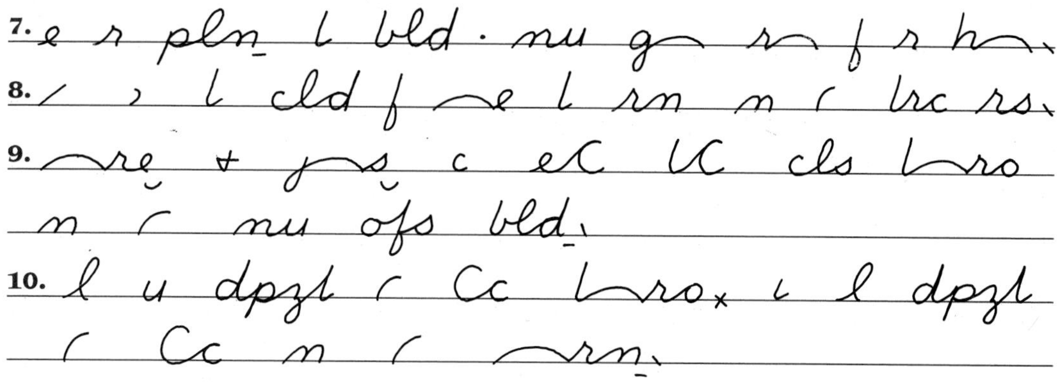

KEY

READING AND WRITING EXERCISES

Series A

1. Are you ready to do some typing?
2. We will help you if we can. It is our job.
3. The president and vice president of our company will see us in a week.
4. Do you have the new bulletin? It is very well written.
5. Which week are you planning to visit the office?
6. Let me know when the information arrives.
7. I will mail a full deposit.
8. You will receive a free gift for each savings deposit.
9. I will return the check to the company.
10. Here is a check to cover the fee in full.

Series B

1. We are making changes in our company catalog.
2. We will mail you a copy very soon.
3. We are attaching a copy of the bill. When can you mail us a check?
4. Bob needs to know something very soon.
5. I will leave the information at his desk.
6. Will you check the catalog to see if we can return the telephones to the company?
7. We are planning to build a new game room for our home.
8. It is too cold for me to run in the track race.

9. Mary and James can each teach class tomorrow in the new office building.

10. Will you deposit the check tomorrow? I will deposit the check in the morning.

UNIT 3

Your Study Environment

An elaborate study area is not necessary, but you do need a specific place you reserve for studying that will be free of distractions.

Make sure your chair is of the right height, encourages good posture, and is comfortable. Your writing surface should be 28 to 29 inches high. Your desk or writing area should be clean and free of clutter. A good light over your work surface is a necessity.

Keeping a good supply of working pens, pencils, and paper readily available is a good study habit. Dictionaries, books, and related materials should all be within easy reach.

Keeping an up-to-date list of assignments and priorities will allow you to concentrate on meeting current deadlines and will also help prevent the feeling of being swamped that results from doing the easiest assignments first and running out of time for the more difficult assignments.

A place away from people, TV noise, telephone interruptions, radios, and other distractions is the most productive setting for study. You should also avoid a study area that is too warm, as high temperatures can make you very sleepy.

SPEEDWRITING PRINCIPLES

1. Write *m* for the blended sounds of *m-m* (*mem* and *mum*). Write *m* also for the blended sounds of *m-n* (*men/min, mon, mun.*)

remember, re-mem-b-r *rmbr*
memory, mem-r-e *mre*
memorize, mem-r-z *mrz*
memo, mem-o *mo*
mumps, mum-p-s *mps*
mental, men-t-l *mll*
menu, men-u *mu*
mineral, min-r-l *mrl*
monetary, mon-t-r-e *mtre*
money, mun-e *me*

2. Write *m* for the word ending *ment.* Write *m* also for the word ending *m-nd, (mand, mend, mind).*

settlement, s-t-l-ment	*sllm*	demand, d-mand	*dm*
replacement, re-p-l-s-ment	*rplsm*	amend, a-mend	*am*
*payment, p-a-ment	*pam*	recommend, r-k-mend	*rcm*
*agreement, a-guh-r-e-ment	*agrem*	remind, re-mind	*rm*

*Always write the final root-word vowel when adding word endings.

3. Write a capital *N* for the sound of *ent, nt* (pronounced *ent*).

sent, s-nt	*sN*	entry, nt-r-e	*Nre*
wants, w-nt-s	*‿Ns*	renting, r-nt-ing	*rN̲*
center, s-nt-r	*sNr*	current, k-r-nt	*crN*

Use *N* to form contractions.

don't, d-nt	*dN*	couldn't, k-d-nt	*cdN*
can't, k-nt	*cN*	doesn't, d-z-nt	*dzN*

Practice these additional words:

maximum, m-x-mum	*⌒xm*	didn't, d-d-nt	*ddN*
minimum, min-mum	*mm*	country, k-nt-r-e	*cNre*
minutes, min-t-s	*mts*	recent, re-s-nt	*rsN*
agent, a-j-nt	*ajN*	merchant, m-r-chay-nt	*⌒rCN*

apparent, a-p-r-nt *aprN* won't, w-nt *wN*

front, f-r-nt *frN* tremendous, t-r-men-d-s *trmds*

PRINCIPLES SUMMARY

1. Write *m* for the blended sounds of *m-m* (*mem* and *mum*): members, mem-b-r-s *mbrs*; mumps, mum-p-s *mps*. Write *m* also for the blended sounds of *m-n* (*men/min, mon, mun*): menu, men-u *mu*; mineral, min-r-l *mrl*; monetary, mon-t-r-e *mtre*; money, mun-e *me*.

2. Write *m* for the word ending *ment*: settlement, s-t-l-ment *stlm*. Write *m* also for the word ending *m-nd* (*mand, mend, mind*): demand, d-mand *dm*; amend, a-mend *am*; remind, re-mind *rm*.

3. Write a capital *N* for the sound of *ent, nt*: sent, s-nt *sN*; and for contractions: don't, d-nt *dN*.

WORD DEVELOPMENT

Write the following related words in *Speedwriting* in your notebook.

pay *pa*	-ing	-ment	-ments
plant *plN*	-s	-er	-ing
agree *agre*	-s	-ing	-ment
place *pls*	-s	re-	-ment
rent *rN*	-al	-ing	-er
settle *stl*	-s	-ing	-ments

WORD CONSTRUCTION

Practice writing these words in *Speedwriting* in your notebook.

event, e-v-nt member, mem-b-r

different, d-f-r-nt documents, d-k-ment-s

assignments, a-s-n-ment-s

central, s-nt-r-l

recommends, r-k-mend-s

pleasant, p-l-z-nt

movement, m-v-ment

print, p-r-nt

memorizing, mem-r-z-ing

remembers, re-mem-b-r-s

READING AND WRITING EXERCISES

1

Fearing Change

ppl r ofn afrd v Cnj. / , eze l fr
—l e dN no bcz e cN se ahd.
/ crN —vm n lcnlje , cz —jr
Cnjs n fctres + ofss acrs / cNre.
s— ppl fr lz jbs bcz v / Cnjs,
/ dm f nu jbs , gro + me adlts
r ret l scl f clss —C l hlp n
lrn lcncl scls + ern btr ujs. e
v ltl rzn l fr Cnj if / l rzlt
n . btr lf f s.

2

mo l —lvn crlr

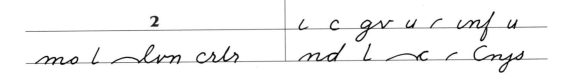

l c gv u / inf u
nd l —c / Cnjs

n r sls pln, l
v . cpe v c nu
pln ⌣C gvs f
dlls, / c crN
L r ofs, cp
. v bze scjl, e
r ~c plns f
s~ bq evNs f
c ⌣cs ahd,
n cs u lri l
rC ~e / ~u
ofs l l lv c
cpes u nd / c
frN dsc, fl fre
l cl ~e f hlp n
c fCr if u nd /.

3

mo l jde jcsn ~u
mo, l rm u v r
plns l hld bjl hr
n c nr fCr, c
rzn f c hr, l rvu
nu bjl ls + c
me e l nd l pa
f sC Nres, e r
~c . scjl f eC
ofs, u l rsv .
nls asn u . dfnl
L, if u v nu
ls or rplsms
pln l gv . brf
s~re v eC / chr.

KEY

READING AND WRITING EXERCISES

1

Fearing Change

People are often afraid of change. It is easy to fear what we don't know because we can't see ahead. The[1] current movement in technology is causing major changes in factories and offices across the country.[2] Some people fear losing jobs because of the changes.

The demand for new jobs is growing, and many adults are[3] returning to school for classes which will help in learning technical skills and earning better wages. We have little[4] reason to fear change if it will result in a better life for us. (93)

2

MEMO TO: Melvin Carter

I can give you the information you need to make the changes in our sales plan. I[1] have a copy of the new plan which gives full details.

At the current time, our office is keeping a very busy[2] schedule. We are making plans for some big events for the weeks ahead. In case you try to reach me at my office,[3] I will leave the copies you need at the front desk.

Feel free to call me for help in the future if you need it.[4] (80)

3

MEMO TO: Judy Jackson

My memo is to remind you of our plans to hold budget hearings in the near future.[1]

The reason for the hearings is to review new budget items and the money we will need to pay for such[2] entries. We are making a schedule for each office. You will receive a notice assigning you a definite[3] time.

If you have new items or replacements, plan to give a brief summary of each at the hearing. (78)

UNIT 4

Putting Your Skill to Work

Start using *Speedwriting* whenever you take notes. You now know several hundred words that can be written according to the *Speedwriting* principles you have learned. Be sure to use the brief forms and abbreviations to help you write faster and more efficiently. The more automatic your writing becomes, the easier it will be for you to concentrate on what is being said. The more you use *Speedwriting*, the more automatic it will become. Use it daily!

You will take notes for a longer period of time without tiring if you maintain correct posture. Sit with both feet firmly on the floor. Keep your back straight. Your writing space should be cleared of unnecessary items and your writing arm given a comfortable position. Write with one hand placed on the top of your notebook to steady it while holding your pen in a relaxed grip.

Another good way to put your skill to work is to visualize words in *Speedwriting* that you see in print—books, magazines, pictures, signs, advertisements. When you are listening to a newscast or any program with dialogue on radio or television, listen and discover how many words you can visualize in *Speedwriting* and jot them down.

SPEEDWRITING PRINCIPLES

1. Write  for the sound of *ish* or *sh*.

finish, f-n-ish 

machine, m-ish-n 

should, ish-d 

show, ish-o 

wish, w-ish 

issuing, i-ish-u-ing 

2. Write a capital  for the sound of *ad* or *al* at the beginning of a word (pronounced *add, all,* or *al*).

admit, ad-m-t a—l

advise, ad-v-z avz

admire, ad-m-r a—r

advice, ad-v-s avs

also, al-s-o aso

album, al-b-m ab—

If a word begins with the letters *a-d* or *a-l* but does not form the blended sounds of *ad* or *al* in the same syllable, write the word according to the sound.

adopt, a-d-p-t adpl

align, a-l-n aln

3. Write n for the initial sound of *en* or *in* (pronounced *n*).

anything, en-e-thing ne̲

indent, in-d-nt ndN

involve, in-v-l-v nvlv

engine, en-j-n nyn

engineers, en-j-n-r-s nynrs

intent, in-t-nt nlN

BRIEF FORMS

from f—

manage —j

firm fr

on, own o

part, port pl

letter L

would d

perhaps Ph

market —r

your u

BRIEF FORM DEVELOPMENT

Use brief forms and abbreviations to build related words. For instance:

Brief Form: *for*

form, for-m f—

inform, in-for-m nf—

formal, for-m-l f—l

Brief Forms: *can* and *not*

cancel, can-s-l csl

cannot, can-not cn

Abbreviation: *company*

formula, for-m-l-a	fmla	accompanying, a-company-ing	aco
fortune, for-chay-n	fCn	accompaniment, a-company-ment	acom

To avoid possible misinterpretations in reading and transcribing, write some *Speedwriting* words according to the rule rather than as derivatives of brief forms.

William, w-l-y-m	wlym	mechanical, m-k-n-k-l	mkncl

NEW BRIEF FORM DEVELOPMENT

management	mgm	yours	us
manager	mgr	wouldn't	dN
managing	mg	report	rpl
marketing	mk	depart	dpl
letters	Ls	letterhead	Lhd

ABBREVIATIONS

Mr.	mr	Ms.	ms
Mrs.	mrs	Miss	M

SALUTATIONS

Dear Mr. Gray	d mr gra	Dear Ms. Miller	d ms mlr
Dear Mrs. Chase	d mrs Cs	Dear Miss Temple	d M tmpl
Dear Ed	d ed	Dear Sue	d su

COMPLIMENTARY CLOSES

Sincerely yours	su	Very truly yours	vtu
Cordially yours	cu	Yours truly	ut
Sincerely	s	Yours very truly	uvt
Cordially	c	Respectfully yours	ru

PRINCIPLES SUMMARY

1. Write A for the sound of *ish, sh*: show, ish-o Ao .
2. Write a capital a for the word beginnings *ad* and *al*: advice, ad-v-s Avs ; also, al-s-o Aso .
3. Write n for the initial sound of *en* or *in*: entire, en-t-r ntr .

WORD DEVELOPMENT Write the following related words in *Speedwriting* in your notebook.

encourage ncrj	-s	-ing	-ment
inform nfm	-s	-ing	-ant
furnish frnA	-es	-ing	-ings
short Art	-s	-age	-ages
shop Ap	-s	-ping	-per
report rpt	-s	-ing	-er

WORD CONSTRUCTION Practice writing these words in *Speedwriting* in your notebook.

shown, ish-n	efficient, e-f-ish-nt
support, s-port	brochure, b-r-ish-r
advising, ad-v-z-ing	efforts, e-for-t-s
increase, in-k-r-s	she, ish-e
any, en-e	afford, a-for-d
entire, en-t-r	publishing, p-b-l-ish-ing

READING AND WRITING EXERCISES

1

Dreaming of Owning a Home

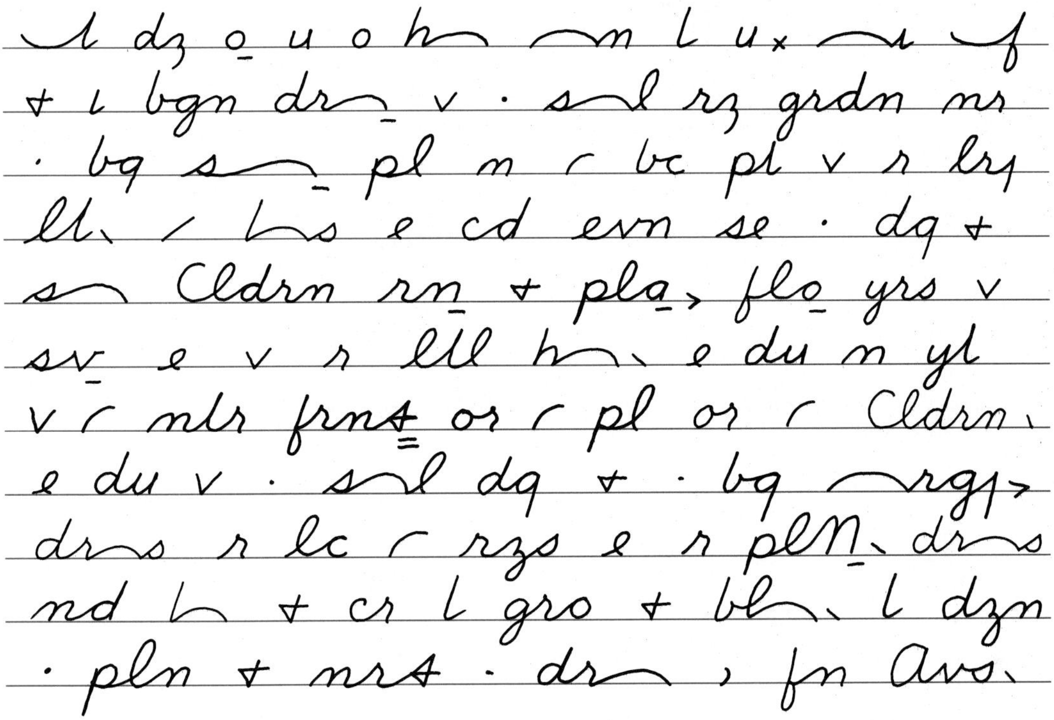

2

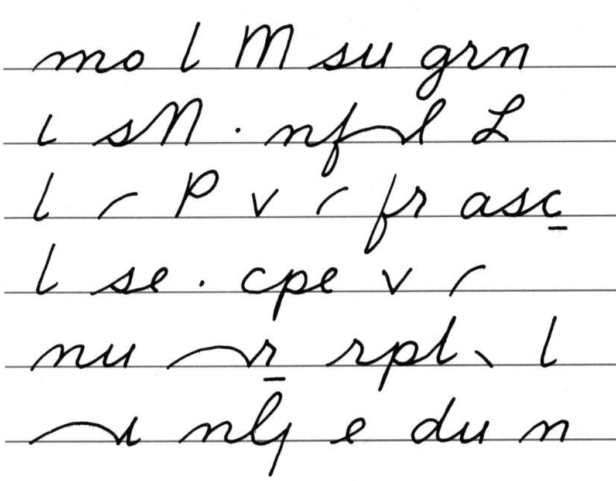

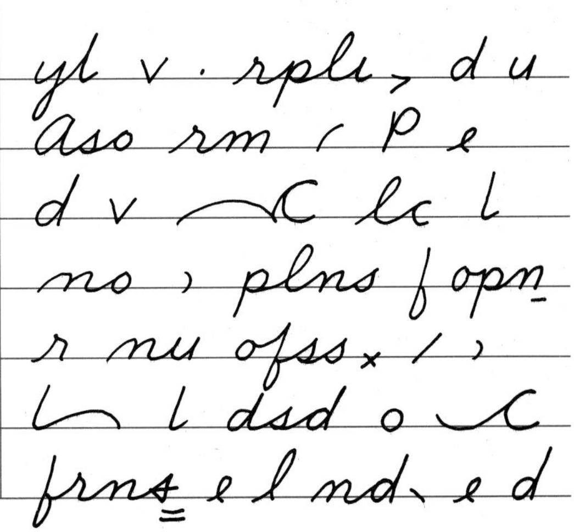

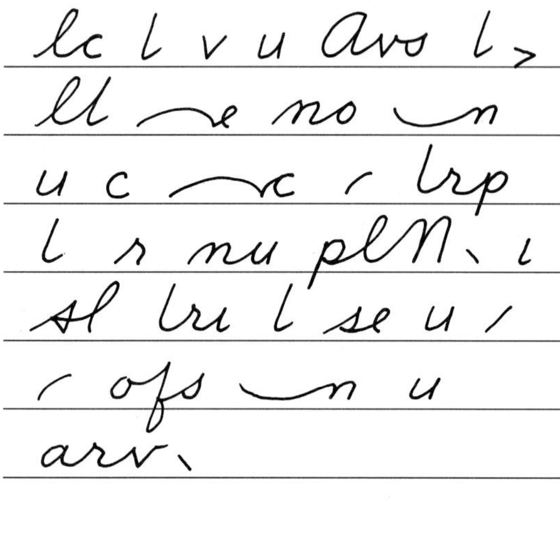

3

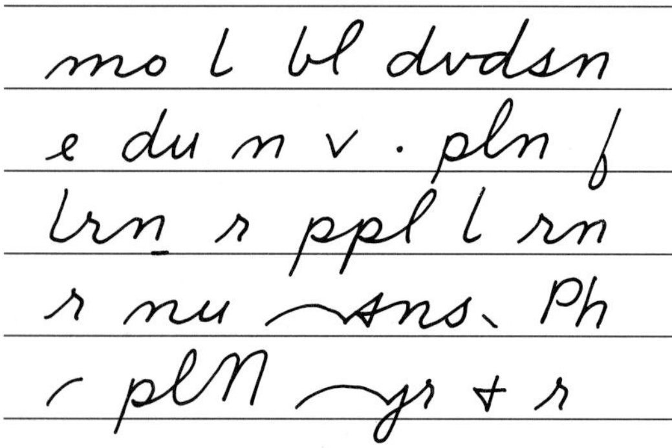

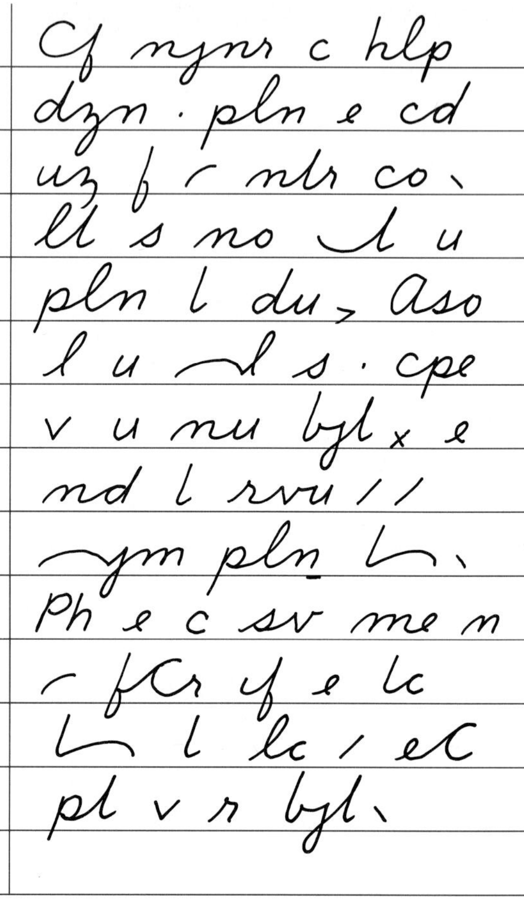

KEY

READING AND WRITING EXERCISES

1

Dreaming of Owning a Home

What does owning your own home mean to you? My wife and I began dreaming of a small rose garden near a big[1] swimming pool in the back part of our large lot. At times we could even see a dog and some children running and playing.[2]

Following years of saving we have our little home. We do not yet have the entire furnishings or the pool or[3] the children. We do have a small dog and a big mortgage.

Dreams are like the roses we are planting. Dreams need time and[4] care to grow and bloom. To design a plan and nourish a dream is fine advice. (94)

2

MEMO TO: Miss Sue Green

I sent an informal letter to the president of the firm asking to see a copy[1] of the new marketing report. To my knowledge, we do not yet have a reply.

Would you also remind the[2] president we would very much like to know his plans for opening our new offices? It is time to decide[3] on which furnishings we will need. We would like to have your advice too.

Let me know when you can make the trip to our[4] new plant. I shall try to see you at the office when you arrive. (91)

3

MEMO TO: Bill Davidson

We do not have a plan for training our people to run our new machines. Perhaps the[1] plant manager and our chief engineer can help design a plan we could use for the entire company. Let us[2] know what you plan to do.

Also, will you mail us a copy of your new budget? We need to review it at[3] management planning time. Perhaps we can save money in the future if we take time to look at each part of our[4] budget. (81)

UNIT 5

Building Your Writing Speed

The 18 *Speedwriting* words below make up more than one-third of all word occurrences in the English language, and you have already learned the English words they represent. Practice these high-frequency *Speedwriting* words until you can write them without hesitation:

the		are, our		it, at	
and		for, full		I	
of, have, very		can		will, well	
in, not		a, an	·	is, his	
to, too		would		we	
you, your		on, own		from	

By using these shortcuts every time you write one of these words, you will soon be able to write them automatically and increase your writing speed. Brief forms and abbreviations are great aids to building your writing speed. Not only do they occur frequently in written and spoken communication, but they are often the basis for developing many additional words.

You will not have to change your basic handwriting style for *Speedwriting*. However, it is important to develop writing habits that clearly distinguish one *Speedwriting* word from another.

Take a moment now to review your writing style. Do you omit unnecessary loops, crosses, dots, and initial and final strokes where appropriate? Compare the following examples with the *Speedwriting* words you have written so far.

Streamlining *m* and *w*: Write *m* and *w* with a swift, smooth sweep of the pen.

m		me	
w		way	

Loops and Solid Lines: Write *l* with a clearly defined loop; write *t* with a solid stem. Your stroke for *t* should be clearly taller (about twice the height) than your *i*. The same is true for *l* and *e*, *nt* and *n*, *chay* and *k*.

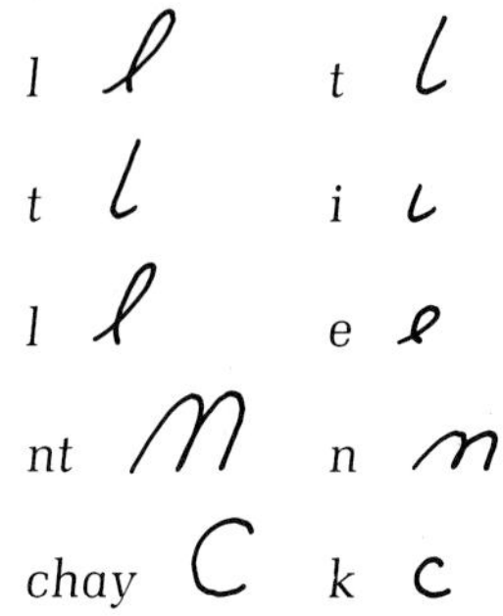

Closed Circles: It is important to close the circles in *s*, *d*, *p*, *guh*, and *a*.

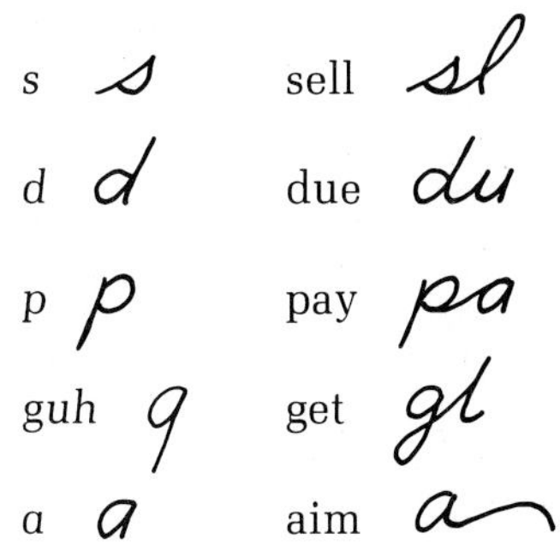

Stems on Tall Letters: Develop the habit of writing the stem long enough to distinguish *d* from *a*.

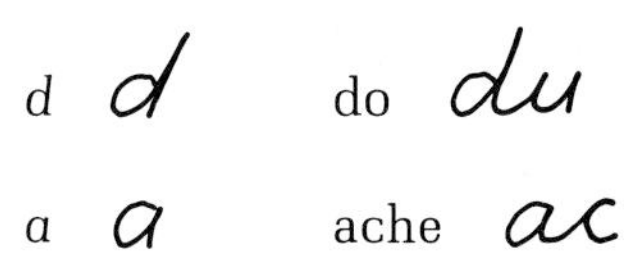

Writing *s, ish, and* (ampersand): Develop a curve in the *s* to distinguish it clearly from the *ish*.

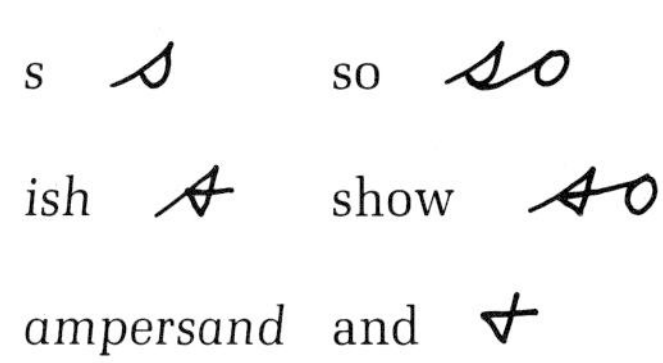

Streamlining Letters: Omit loops and upward strokes for *h*, *t*, *b*, *f*, *u*, and *i* when these letters occur at the beginning of a *Speedwriting* word. Omit tails at the end of a *Speedwriting* word.

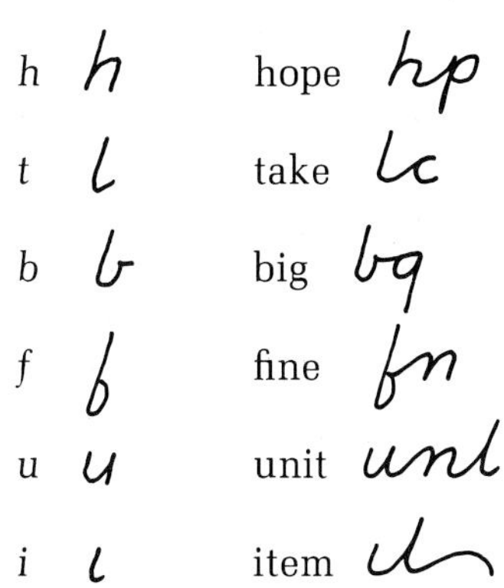

Writing *v* and *u*: The letter *v* ends with a brief tail at the top; *u* ends in a swift downward stroke. Write *v* with a sharp point to distinguish it from *u*.

v	v	save	sv
u	u	view	vu

Final *guh* and *j*: These end in a swift, solid downward stroke.

guh	g	dog	dg
j	j	judge	jj

Final *o*: This ends at the top of the circle; *a* ends in a downward stroke.

o	o	low	lo
a	a	say	sa

SPEEDWRITING PRINCIPLES

1. Write o for the sound of *ow* (ou). Always write this sound in a *Speedwriting* word.

allow, a-l-ow	alo	doubt, d-ow-t	dot
now, n-ow	no	out, ow-t	ot
proud, p-r-ow-d	prod	town, t-ow-n	ton

2. Write a printed capital S (joined) for the word beginnings *cer, cir, ser, sur* (pronounced *sir*).

certain, cer-t-n	Stn	serve, ser-v	Sv
survey, sur-v-a	Sva	certificate, cer-t-f-k-t	Stfct
service, ser-v-s	Svs	sermon, ser-mun	Sm
circle, cir-k-l	Scl	surprise, sur-p-r-z	Sprz

SALUTATIONS

Gentlemen	j	Dear Sir	dS
Ladies	l	Dear Sir or Madam	dS
Ladies and Gentlemen	lj		

PUNCTUATION SYMBOLS

Write ! to indicate an exclamation mark:

What happy news we have for you! l hpe nz e v f u!

Write = to indicate a hyphen:

Will you recommend a well-known book? l u rcm . l=nnbc x

Write ═ to indicate a dash:

We do not know the reason—do you? e du n no r rzn═du u x

To indicate solid capitalization, double the curved line underneath the last letter of the *Speedwriting* word.

MONEY MANAGEMENT, mun-e manage-ment me mjm

To indicate an underlined title, draw a solid line under the *Speedwriting* word.

<u>Newsweek</u>, n-z-w-k <u>nzwc</u>

PRINCIPLES SUMMARY

1. Write o for the sound of *ow* (ou): allow, a-l-ow alo.
2. Write a printed capital S (joined) for the word beginnings *cer, cir, ser, sur* (sir): certain, cer-t-n Stn.

WORD DEVELOPMENT

Write the following related words in *Speedwriting* in your notebook.

out ol	-side	-line	-lines
research rSC	-es	-ing	-er
doubt dol	-s	-ing	-less
survey Sva	-s	-ing	-or
allow alo	-s	-ing	
surprise Sprz	-s	-ing	

WORD CONSTRUCTION

Practice writing these words in *Speedwriting* in your notebook.

how, h-ow	down, d-ow-n
warehouse, w-r-h-ow-s	services, ser-v-s-s
power, p-ow-r	circuit, cir-k-t
search, ser-chay	outfit, ow-t-f-t
outlook, ow-t-l-k	serving, ser-v-ing
certificates, cer-t-f-k-t-s	downtown, d-ow-n-t-ow-n

READING AND WRITING EXERCISES

1

A Career in Human Services

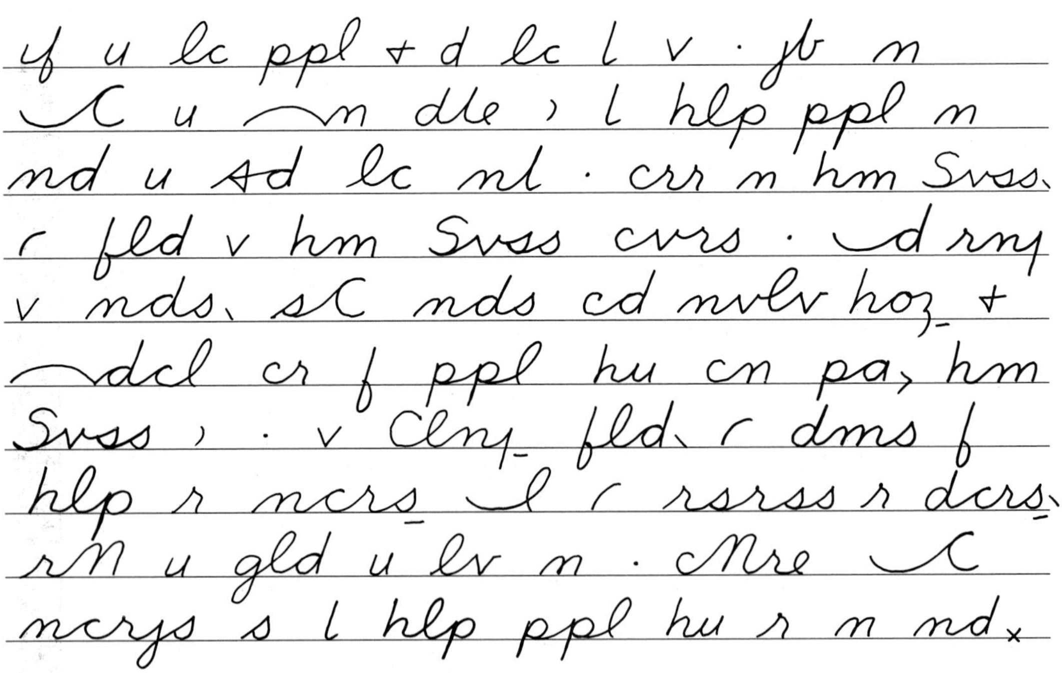

2

dS⌒ r u pa̲ hi rN
+ yl v v lll l so
f/ₓ Ph u d lc l
o u o h⌒ yl cn
s⌒ l sv enf
me f (don pam,
yf so e c hlp u.
e r no ofr̲. nu
h⌒ pam pln
⌣C l alo u l
pls . lo don pam
o u nu h⌒. e
Aso v . byl pln
f hos pams. yf
u lc ol . ln f⌒
s no u c scyl
u pams ne ⌣a
u ⌣s, gv s .
ml v u l⌒ +
e l so u . eze
pam pln f u
hoshld. ci

3

1 e r rel̲ (cpe̲
⌒sn e bl f⌒ u
fr. s⌒d⌒s (
⌒sn l n prN.
⌣n / dz prN (
cpes r n clr, e
v ⌒d me cls n
SC v . ajN hu
Svss u ⌒sns.
nn c gl (pls
e nd f rprs,
e hp u c ofr s
. ⌒sn ⌣C gvs
blr Svs. l u ll
s no ⌣l u pln
l du ₓ su

KEY

READING AND WRITING EXERCISES

1

A Career in Human Services

If you like people and would like to have a job in which your main duty is to help people in need, you should[1] look into a career in human services. The field of human services covers a wide range of needs. Such needs[2] could involve housing and medical care for people who cannot pay.

Human services is a very challenging[3] field. The demands for help are increasing while the resources are decreasing. Aren't you glad you live in a country[4] which encourages us to help people who are in need? (91)

2

Dear Sir or Madam:

Are you paying high rent and yet have very little to show for it? Perhaps you would like to[1] own your own home, yet cannot seem to save enough money for the down payment.

If so, we can help you. We are now[2] offering a new home payment plan which will allow you to place a low down payment on your new home. We also[3] have a budget plan for house payments. If you take out a loan from us now, you can schedule your payments any way[4] you wish.

Give us a minute of your time, and we will show you an easy payment plan for your household. Cordially[5] yours, (101)

3

Gentlemen:

We are returning the copying machine we bought from your firm. Sometimes the machine will not print. When[1] it does print, the copies are not clear.

We have made many calls in search of an agent who services your machines.[2] None can get the parts we need for repairs.

We hope you can offer us a machine which gives better service. Will you[3] let us know what you plan to do? Sincerely yours, (69)

UNIT

6

Paraphrasing and Notetaking

Students sometimes believe that the more lengthy their class notes, the more successful they will be in preparing for examinations with these notes. Although class notes should always be thorough, there is danger in trying to record everything the instructor says in a lecture. Selective notetaking requires listening carefully to a lecture and paying special attention to the major points of the presentation. Rather than attempting to record everything the instructor says, it is generally much better to paraphrase the major points of the lecture.

Paraphrasing is a restatement of the essential ideas from written or spoken material. Paraphrasing for notetaking means that you restate the main facts or ideas from readings, lectures, or speeches in your own words. The process of putting information into your own words while the notes are being recorded helps you learn and makes subsequent studying even more effective.

When you paraphrase notes during a lecture, you are actually able to take more comprehensive notes since you are concerned with identifying the most important points of the lecture. You are thus able to devote your attention and energy to being certain each of these important points is included in your notes. Later when you are studying or reviewing your notes, you will find that such notes are a much more efficient study source because they were selectively paraphrased when they were recorded and therefore contain the most significant information of the particular lecture being reviewed or studied.

SPEEDWRITING PRINCIPLES

1. To form the past tense of any regular verb, write a hyphen after the *Speedwriting* word (pronounced *duh* or *ed*).

used, u-z-duh *uz-*

copied, k-p-e-duh *cpe-*

helped, h-l-p-duh *hlp-*

received, re-s-v-duh *rsv-*

finished, f-n-ish-duh *fns-*

limited, l-m-t-ed *lmt-*

WRITING NUMBERS

Write figures to indicate cardinal numbers.

someone	s 1	12 pairs	12 prs
anyone	ne 1	two girls	2 grls

ABBREVIATIONS

north	N	west	W
south	S	corporation	corp
east	E	enclose, enclosure	enc

ABBREVIATED WORD DEVELOPMENT

northern	Nrn	eastern	Ern
*southern	Srn	western	Wrn

*Note: Word beginnings and endings may be added to brief forms and abbreviations to form derivatives, even though the pronunciation of the derivative may differ from the root word.

BRIEF FORMS

be, but, been, buy, by	b	accept	ac
during	du_	after	af
necessary	nes	appropriate	apo
why	y	determine	dt

PRINCIPLES SUMMARY

1. To form the past tense of any regular verb, write a hyphen after the *Speedwriting* word: used, u-z-duh uz- .

WORD DEVELOPMENT

Write the following related words in *Speedwriting* in your notebook.

attach aTC	-es	-ing	-ed
involve nvlv	-d	-s	-ment
place pls	-ing	-d	re-

apply *apli*	-ies	-ing	-ied
ask *asc*	-s	-ing	-ed
agree *agre*	-d	-ing	-ment

WORD CONSTRUCTION

Practice writing these words in *Speedwriting* in your notebook.

cashed, k-ish-duh

increased, in-k-r-s-duh

marked, m-r-k-duh

issued, i-ish-u-duh

furnished, f-r-n-ish-duh

insured, in-ish-r-duh

scheduled, s-k-j-l-duh

signed, s-n-duh

based, b-s-duh

informed, in-for-m-duh

allowed, a-l-ow-duh

amended, a-mend-ed

READING AND WRITING EXERCISES

1

Hot Summers

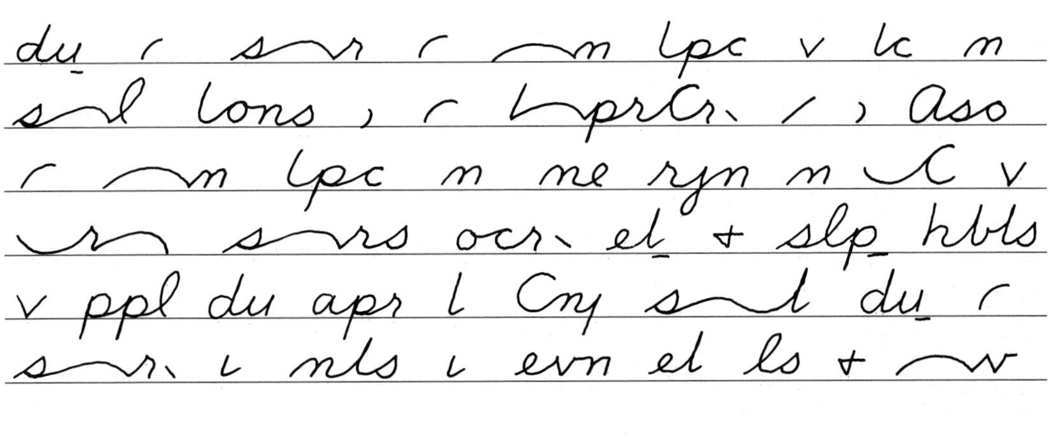

/ . slor spd, no I lcs l du olsd
Crs wn r sn, hl. i du v I olsd
Cr wC hlps me ndr r smr.
smho i mq l ft evn wn i v
no nrje l cl r grs or pN r
hos.

2

dS f . bnt- ln
e l ofr I wcs
fre vzl l r clys
b r se. if u ac /
l n b nes f u l
pa ne f u r m +
mls, du u vzl
e l so u nu +
uz- mdl clys
wC u ma b o r
eze pam pln b
dN dla. y n cl
no + dl . ln f u
fre wC x, e d lc
l so u ho hpe lf
c b / clys b r se.
su

3

dS i d lc l b . cpe
v u nu bc ho l
ncrs rll sls. af
rd . rsN rvu v
r bc i blv / l
hlp n . cly crs
n wC i v nrl-.
bcz clss v bgn i
nd r bc no. cd
u r4 . cpe l mi

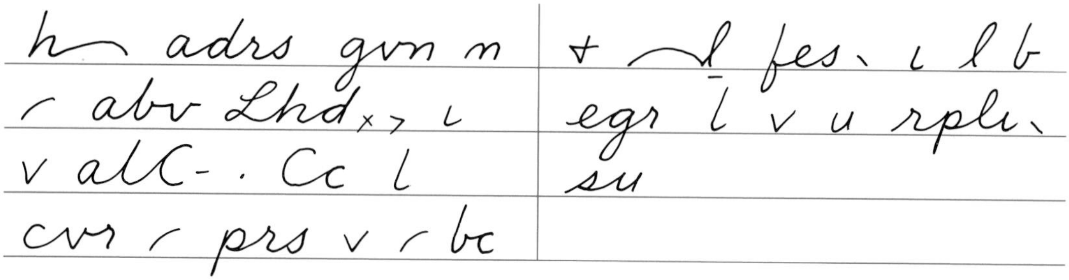

KEY

READING AND WRITING EXERCISES

1

Hot Summers

During the summer the main topic of talk in small towns is the temperature. It is also the main topic[1] in any region in which very warm summers occur. Eating and sleeping habits of people do appear to[2] change somewhat during the summer. I notice I even eat less and move at a slower speed.

No one likes to do[3] outside chores when the sun is hot. I do have one outside chore which helps me endure the summer. Somehow I manage[4] to fish even when I have no energy to cut the grass or paint the house. (94)

2

Dear Sir:

For a limited time, we will offer one week's free visit to our Cottages by the Sea. If you[1] accept, it will not be necessary for you to pay anything for your room and meals.

During your visit we will[2] show you new and used model cottages which you may buy on our easy payment plan, but don't delay. Why not call[3] now and determine a time for your free week?

We would like to show you how happy life can be at Cottages by[4] the Sea. Sincerely yours, (84)

3

Dear Sir:

I would like to buy a copy of your new book, *How to Increase Retail Sales.* After reading a recent[1] review of the book, I believe it will help in a college course in which I have enrolled. Because classes have begun,[2] I need the book now. Could you rush a copy to my home address given in the above letterhead?

I have[3] attached a check to cover the price of the book and mailing fees. I will be eager to have your reply. Sincerely[4] yours, (81)

UNIT
7

Review and Reinforcement

You now know enough *Speedwriting* to write most of the words used in typical written as well as oral communication. This unit reviews the principles you've studied so far. No new principles will be introduced in this unit. Instead, use this opportunity to check your progress.

1. The following words illustrate principles you studied in Units 1–6:

view, v-u vu	package, p-k-j pcj
build, b-l-d bld	much, m-chay mC
easy, e-z-e eze	while, w-l wl
billing, b-l-ing bl	jobs, j-b-s jbs
billings, b-l-ings bl	Ted's, t-d-s tds
something, s-m-thing sm	helps, h-l-p-s hlps
member, mem-b-r mbr	she, ish-e se
money, mun-e me	wish, w-ish ws
remind, re-mind rm	advice, ad-v-s avs
settlement, s-t-l-ment sllm	also, al-s-o aso
patient, p-ish-nt psN	certain, cer-t-n Stn
engineers, en-j-n-r-s njnrs	surplus, sur-p-l-s Spls
house, h-ow-s hos	copied, k-p-e-duh cpe-

2. Following are the brief forms you have studied. Write the *Speedwriting* brief form for each of these words in your notebook.

are	r	of	v	is	)
at	/	very	v	for	f
a	·	too	t	in	n
the	⌒	not	n	us	s
will	l	his	)	full	f
can	c	it	/	have	v
our	r	well	l	to	t
an	·	we	e	from	f⌒
during	du_	firm	fr	your	u
part	pt	perhaps	Ph	own	o
letter	L	port	pt	on	o
market	⌒r	would	d	manage	⌒j
be	b	after	af	buy	b
why	y	but	b	determine	dt
by	b	appropriate	apo	been	b
accept	ac	necessary	nes		

3. Write in your notebook these brief form derivatives that are developed from some of the above brief forms:

haven't	vN	yours	us	cancel	csl
welfare	lfr	manager	⌒jr	formal	f⌒l
report	rpt	forgotten	fgtn	cannot	cn
forgive	fgv	informing	nf⌒_	letters	Ls

4. The following *Speedwriting* words represent the abbreviations you have studied. How quickly can you read them?

READING AND WRITING EXERCISES

1
Job Training

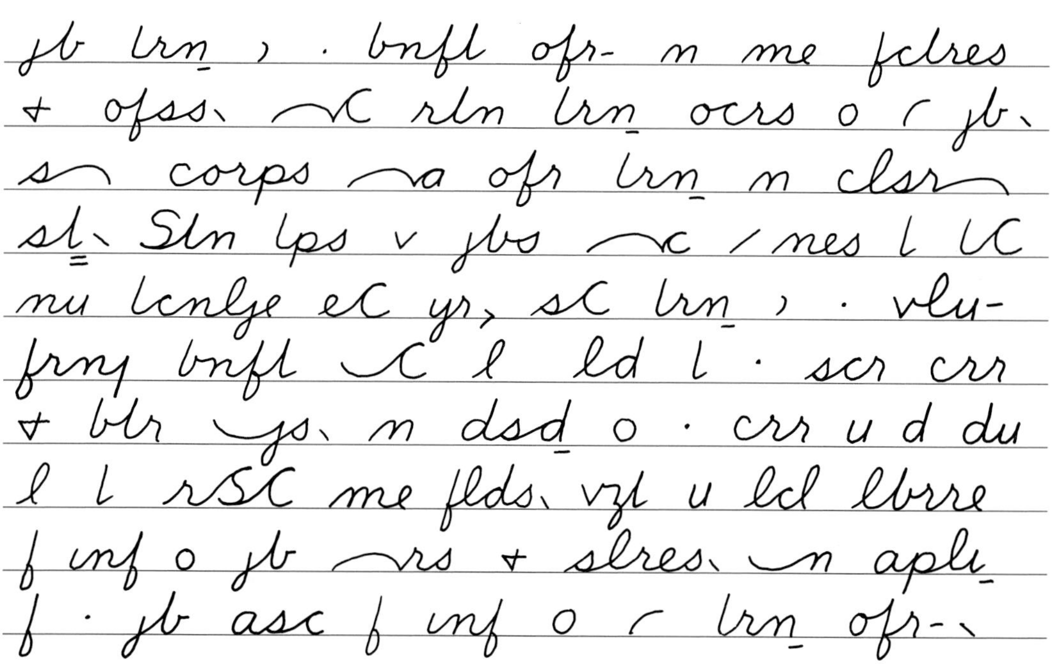

2

dS Ph u v fgln u
pam , du. d u
lc . ml l ⌒l s
. Cc x > e v b psN
b e du n no f u
v rsv- r Ls rm
u l ⌒c u pam o
⌐ . ⌒N u cl s x
(, n nes l pa
u bl n f . f u cn
⌒y l pa (ntr
bl e l ac pl v (>
f (crN pln , l
⌒C f u bjl y n
vzl r ln ofs x r
ajN ⌒a b v hlp
l u . uvl

3

d rCrd no , (
⌐ l pln r
s⌒r sl . me
rll ⌒yrs hld
lry sls du dfrN
⌐s v (yr . y
dN e bri s⌒
nu + dl . ⌐ f
1 bq s⌒r evN x
e c brn (ntr
sp sNr nl .
⌒yr sdc sl >
i d lc l se (
sl rn f . f ⌒c .
Ph e cd cp (sps
opn af rglr clz
⌐s > f u agre
i l lc l (
⌒rCNs + ll u
no ⌒l , dsd- .
ul

KEY

READING AND WRITING EXERCISES

1

Job Training

Job training is a benefit offered in many factories and offices. Much routine training occurs on[1] the job. Some corporations may offer training in classroom settings. Certain types of jobs make it necessary[2] to teach new technology each year.

Such training is a valued fringe benefit which will lead to a secure[3] career and better wages. In deciding on a career, you would do well to research many fields. Visit your[4] local library for information on job markets and salaries. When applying for a job, ask for[5] information on the training offered. (106)

2

Dear Sir:

Perhaps you have forgotten your payment is due. Would you take a minute to mail us a check?

We have been[1] patient, but we do not know if you have received our letters reminding you to make your payment on time. Won't you[2] call us? It is not necessary to pay your bill in full. If you cannot manage to pay the entire bill, we[3] will accept part of it.

If the current plan is too much for your budget, why not visit our loan office? Our agent[4] may be of help to you. Yours very truly, (89)

3

Dear Richard:

Now is the time to plan our summer sale. Many retail managers hold large sales during different[1] times of the year. Why don't we try something new and determine a time for one big summer event? We can turn the[2] entire shopping center into a major sidewalk sale.

I would like to see the sale run for a full week. Perhaps[3] we could keep the shops open after regular closing times.

If you agree, I will talk to the merchants and let[4] you know what is decided. Yours truly, (87)

Listening and Making Notetaking Decisions

PART TWO

Among the many skills that can contribute to making you successful, listening is one of the most essential. Effective listening increases your productivity by helping you understand the needs, desires, and ideas of the persons you work with. It helps you respond more quickly and efficiently and reduces the amount of time you spend solving problems.

Effective listening differs from hearing. Listening is an active process. Good listeners do not just sit and let listening happen. During a conversation, they participate in the communication process by focusing on what the speaker is saying, and they think about how they will respond. While taking notes, effective listeners are constantly evaluating the presentation and deciding what to incorporate in their notes.

Taking selective notes is a function of attentive listening. Effective notetaking is a continuous process of deciding what notes to record, and active listening is necessary for making good decisions regarding what to include in your notes as well as what to exclude from your notes. The advantage of taking selective notes is that it is much less likely that major points of a presentation will be omitted while you are recording less important or less significant information. The greater number of major concepts you are able to incorporate in your notes, the more useful your notes will prove to be. Being certain to include the major points in your notes, however, often means excluding less significant information from your notes. Active listening is therefore necessary for identifying the major and minor points of any presentation.

Some guidelines for becoming a better listener include the following:

1. Show interest in what the speaker is saying by maintaining eye contact.
2. Keep your attention focused on the speaker. When your thoughts start to drift or when you begin to daydream, immediately concentrate on the speaker again.
3. Search for the speaker's thoughts and ideas rather than focusing on just the speaker's words.
4. Summarize the speaker's message or theme, separate the major points from the minor ones, and note the specific facts that support the theme.

UNIT 8

Outlining Your Study Notes

Outlining is a method of organizing and listing ideas and information. You will more likely use outlining with written material than when taking notes from oral presentations or lectures. If a lecturer is extremely well organized and the topic is suited to an outline type of format, then the use of outlining initially for notetaking might be feasible; however, you will most likely take lecture notes in presentation sequence or in "major sections." You will use outlining to a greater extent if you are the person making an oral presentation or speech than if you are the one taking notes on an oral presentation.

To create a study outline of printed material, first determine what the main ideas of the material are. Below the main ideas, list the important details that relate to the main ideas. The following suggestions may be helpful when outlining.

1. Read a section of printed material for which you are taking notes and decide what the main ideas are.

2. Main topics will reflect ideas, general statements, and conclusions. A good author will present the main idea of a chapter or major section first and label it clearly. If the book or written material is unorganized, you may have to read very carefully to pinpoint the main ideas before writing them in your own words.

3. In outlining printed material for study purposes, your headings may be in the form of single words, brief phrases, complete sentences, or a combination of these forms.

4. Use Roman numerals to indicate main ideas.

5. Read carefully for supporting ideas and note these supporting details in your outline. Supporting details or subdivisions are the various segments or parts that make up the main idea. Supporting material contains definitions, examples, illustrations, and explanations that support the main idea.

6. Use capital letters to designate the supporting details.

7. List sub-details (further information regarding the supporting details) with regular Arabic numbers.

SPEEDWRITING PRINCIPLES

1. Write *l* for the sound of *ith* or *th*.

them, ith-m *lm*	health, h-l-ith *hll*
then, ith-n *ln*	methods, m-ith-d-s *mlds*
growth, guh-r-ith *grl*	although, al-ith-o *alo*

2. Write *l* for the word ending *ly* or *ily* (pronounced *lee* or *uh-lee*).

family, f-m-ly *fml*	easily, e-z-ly *ezl*
yearly, y-r-ly *yrl*	recently, re-s-nt-ly *rsNl*
certainly, cer-t-n-ly *Slnl*	rapidly, r-p-d-ly *rpdl*

3. Write a capital *D* for the word beginning *dis*.

display, dis-p-l-a *Dpla*	disturb, dis-t-r-b *Dlrb*
dismay, dis-m-a *Dma*	dislike, dis-l-k *Dlc*
discuss, dis-k-s *Dcs*	distant, dis-t-nt *DlN*

4. Write a capital *M* for the word beginning *mis*.

mistake, mis-t-k *Mlc*	mislay, mis-l-a *Mla*
mislead, mis-l-d *Mld*	misfit, mis-f-t *Mfl*

misplaced, mis-p-l-s-duh Mpls-
misgivings, mis-guh-v-ings Mgv

Word beginnings, word endings, and sound blends that can also be individual words can be used to express those words.

add a
all a
missing M
*men m

*Remember that *man* is written ⌒m .

Practice writing these additional words:

discover, dis-k-v-r Dcvr
evidently, e-v-d-nt-ly evdNl
really, r-l-ly rll
nearly, n-r-ly nrl
gladly, guh-l-d-ly gldl
either, e-ith-r elr
these, ith-z lz
this, ith-s ls
there, their, ith-r lr
misprint, mis-p-r-nt MprN

BRIEF FORM DEVELOPMENT

Use the principles you have learned in this unit to develop new *Speedwriting* words from brief forms.

necessarily nesl
appropriately apol
partly pll
reportedly rpl-l
willingly ll
firmly frl

VOCABULARY STUDY

marketing ⌒r — Those activities involved in getting a product from the producer to the consumer, such as advertising, promoting, and selling.

yearly report yrl rpl — A summation of the activities of a department, division, or entire corporation over a 12-month period.

PRINCIPLES SUMMARY

1. Write *l* for the sound of *ith* or *th*: them, ith-m *lm*; growth, guh-r-ith *grl*.
2. Write *l* for the word ending *ly* (lee) or *ily* (uh-lee): family, f-m-ly *fml*.
3. Write a capital *D* for the word beginning *dis*: discuss, dis-k-s *Dcs*.
4. Write a capital *M* for the word beginning *mis*: mistake, mis-t-k *Mlc*.

WORD DEVELOPMENT

Write the following related words in *Speedwriting* in your notebook.

play *pla*	dis-	-ed	-ing
short *Arl*	-s	-ly	-age
take *lc*	mis-	-s	-ing
clear *clr*	-ly	-ed	-ing
time *lm*	-d	-ing	-ly

WORD CONSTRUCTION

Practice writing these words in *Speedwriting* in your notebook.

therefore, ith-r-for	mistaken, mis-t-k-n
through, ith-r-u	only, on-ly
whether, w-ith-r	disclose, dis-k-l-z
misprints, mis-p-r-nt-s	than, ith-n
accordingly, a-k-r-d-ing-ly	discussed, dis-k-s-duh

WRITING ASSIGNMENT

Write the following sentences in *Speedwriting in your notebook.*

1. Do you have plans for retirement? We have a new policy which pays very well.

2. The agent sent us a memo reminding us to mail our payment.
3. We are paying too much money for the policy. May we look for a new agent?
4. We could file a new claim. We will let you know if we reach a settlement.
5. We are seeing a high demand for the new policy.

READING AND WRITING EXERCISES

1

Healthy Families

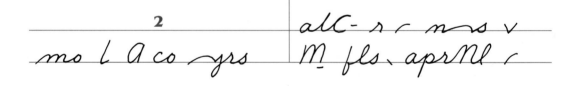

. hlle fml unl alos Cldrn l gro
n . hpe h—. / aso ncrys Cldrn
+ ls prNs l gro + lrn lglr n .
scr nvrnm. a v s du bls —n e
r alo- l —c Mlcs + r ncry-
l lrn f— l—, me v c vlus e
lrn- f— r flrs + —lrs r—n .
pl v s f r nlr lvs. Cldrn r sd
l du bls n —y- c lry isus n lf
—n sC isus r Dcs- opnl. f—ls
hu Dcs isus opnl c lrn lglr.

2

mo l a co —yrs

alC- r c —s v
M- fls. aprMl c

fls v b Mpls-, d
eC v u lc lru u
pprs l se f r M
fls cd v b Mla-
o u dsc? me v r
fldrs r old + v
Mld Uls. ls Mlcs
c ezl b —d.

3

d—rs —lsn i
—N l U u ho
—C i lc r nu
hll fd Dplas u
v n u fr—se. / ,
ncry l se r grl
n hll fds n ls
sle. i U u d lc
l se r enc-
arlcl —C Dcss
s— rzns e r
se sC . rpd Cny
n r hll fd —r.
Ph / l ncry u l
cp a l u Dpla.
s

KEY

WRITING ASSIGNMENT

1. du u v plns f rlrm? e v . nu plse —C pas v l.
2. r ajN sN s . mo rm s l —l r pam.
3. e r pa l —C me f r plse. —a e lc f . nu ajN?

4. e cd fl . nu cl, e l lt u no if e rC . stlm.

5. e r se . hi dm f r nu plse.

READING AND WRITING EXERCISES

1

Healthy Families

A healthy family unit allows children to grow in a happy home. It also encourages children[1] and their parents to grow and learn together in a secure environment. All of us do better when we are[2] allowed to make mistakes and are encouraged to learn from them.

Many of the values we learned from our fathers and[3] mothers remain a part of us for our entire lives. Children are said to do better in managing the large[4] issues in life when such issues are discussed openly. Families who discuss issues openly can learn[5] together. (101)

2

MEMO TO: All Company Managers

Attached are the names of missing files. Apparently the files have been[1] misplaced. Would each of you look through your papers to see if the missing files could have been mislaid on your desk?

Many of[2] our folders are old and have misleading titles. Thus, mistakes can easily be made. (55)

3

Dear Mrs. Wilson:

I want to tell you how much I like the new health food displays you have in your pharmacy. It[1] is encouraging to see the growth in health foods in this city. I thought you would like to see the enclosed article[2] which discusses some reasons we are seeing such a rapid change in the health food market. Perhaps it will[3] encourage you to keep adding to your display. Sincerely, (70)

UNIT

9

Are You Listening?

There is no communication skill more important than the ability to listen, especially since we spend so much of our time participating in this activity. Most people spend more than 50 percent of their communicating time listening. The ability to listen is one of the most important factors for success in school, on the job, and in personal life.

Studies have shown that the average person listening to a 20-minute oral presentation will remember approximately half of what was said immediately after the talk is over. Within 48 hours, the average listener will have forgotten another 50 percent of what was covered. This leaves a retention rate of only about 25 percent. These facts reinforce the importance of taking good notes.

Has anyone ever told you that you weren't listening, even when you know you heard every word spoken? We do hear far more sounds than we listen to. Sometimes we concentrate on just one sound and other sounds around us disappear. At other times we block out all sounds—even the ones we should be listening to. This sometimes happens in school or on the job when we daydream, often causing us to miss important information. Full concentration on listening and taking notes in the classroom or at work can help you retain a greater amount of what you are meant to hear and understand.

SPEEDWRITING PRINCIPLES

1. Retain beginning or ending vowels when building compound words.

When you combine two words to make one word, you are building a compound word. If one of these words begins or ends in a vowel, keep the vowel in the *Speedwriting* word: payroll = pay + roll *parl*

headache, h-d + a-k *hdac* teenage, t-n + a-j *tnaj*

seaside, s-e + s-d *sesd* highway, h-i + w-a *hi‿a*

2. Retain the first and final root-word vowel when adding prefixes and suffixes. When a prefix contains a long vowel followed by a root-word vowel, omit the prefix vowel.

disappear, dis-a-p-r	Dapr	misuse, mis-u-z	Muz
payment, p-a-ment	pam	disallow, dis-a-l-ow	Dalo
reapply, re-a-p-l-i	rapli	readmit, re-ad-m-t	rA—t

MORE ABOUT NUMBERS

An ordinal number shows the sequence of an item in a set: *third* child, *fifth* day. Write ordinal numbers in the following way:

42nd	42d	53rd	53d
85th	85l		

ABBREVIATIONS

credit	cr	number	No
total	tol	percent	%
amount	a—t	attention	atl

BRIEF FORMS

as, was	z	great, grate	gr
general	jn	were, with	◡
hospital	hsp	that	la
arrange	ar		

BRIEF FORM DEVELOPMENT

Use your new brief forms to develop other *Speedwriting* words.

within	◡n	generally	jnl
greatly	grl	without	◡ol
arrangements	arms		

VOCABULARY STUDY

reassess *rass* — To re-evaluate, or to determine a new value of property as a basis for taxation.

minimum payment *mm pam* — The least amount of money required at specific dates on a credit purchase.

PRINCIPLES SUMMARY

1. Retain beginning and ending vowels when building compound words: payroll = pay + roll *parl*.
2. Retain the initial and final root-word vowel when adding prefixes and suffixes: reopen, re-o-p-n *ropn*; payment, p-a-ment *pam*.

WORD DEVELOPMENT

Write the following related words in *Speedwriting* in your notebook.

amount *a-d*	-s	-ed	-ing
number *No*	-s	-ed	-ing
total *tol*	-s	-ed	-ing
any *ne*	-how	-where	-way
apply *apli*	re-	-ies	-ing

WORD CONSTRUCTION

Practice writing these words in *Speedwriting* in your notebook.

arranged, arrange-duh	lower, l-o-r
herewith, h-r-with	payroll, p-a-r-l
higher, h-i-r	greater, great-r
highly, h-i-ly	lowering, l-o-r-ing
throughout, ith-r-u-ow-t	photograph, f-t-o-guh-r-f

WRITING ASSIGNMENT

Write the following sentences in *Speedwriting* in your notebook.

1. We recommend using our new checks.
2. We will print new checks for you. Do you want us to mail the checks to you at home?
3. You will have to pay a minimum fee and make a deposit if you want to use our new checks.
4. The president wants a copy sent to each of the board members.
5. The desk clerk will return the deposit to you.

READING AND WRITING EXERCISES

1
Making a Will

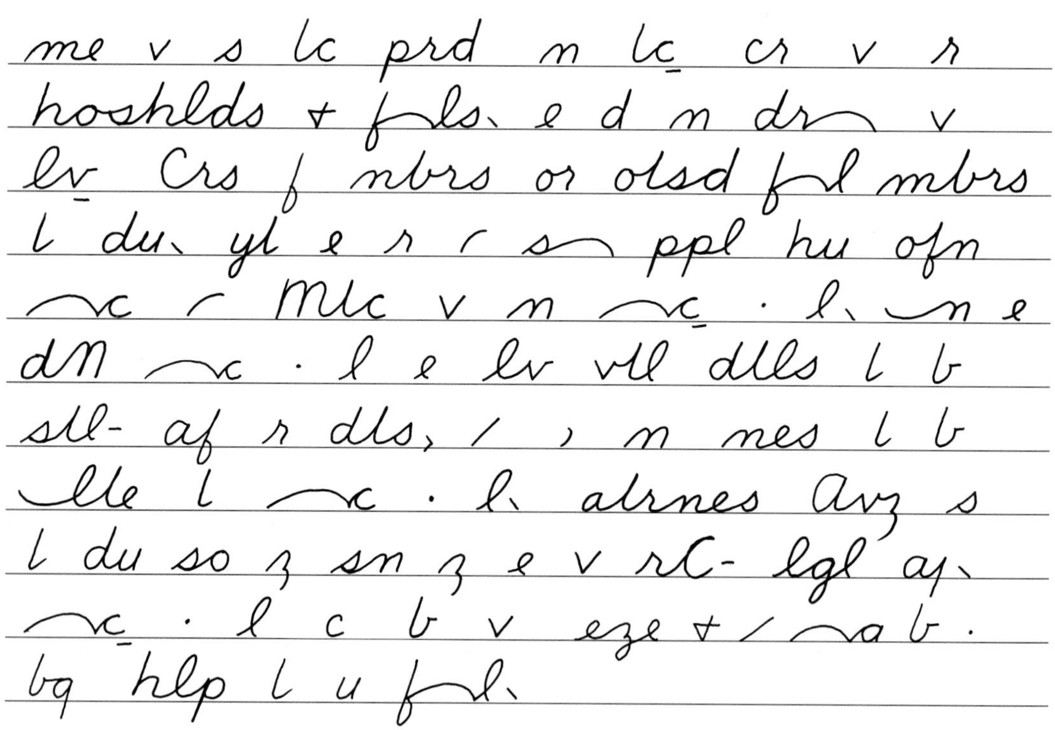

2

mo l a cls
yrs z hd v ls
corp i z v hpe
l lrn l . gr jb
u r a du. . No v
ppl v rln l sa
la lr cls gvn
v fn all. ol .
dol a v u dzrv
cr f u pl n gv ls
co . gr n.

3

1 e rsv- u L nf
s la r sesd cl l
b rass- o r 14l.
r L M o l sa
la r vlu v ls
hos ncrs- grl=
b 25%= n r nu
hea z bll, e r
sre b u v d .
Mlc. r hea
C rns nr r
bC hos, n nu.
if ne r, old +
bdl n nd v rpr.
r hea z bll . fu
yrs af e bl r
bC hos. l r nlf
r rd z nvr rpr-
af r z bll, e hp
la u ofs l lc . blr
lc r la hea. if r
hos, rass- e d
lc l se apo rprs
d o r rd. vlu

KEY

WRITING ASSIGNMENT

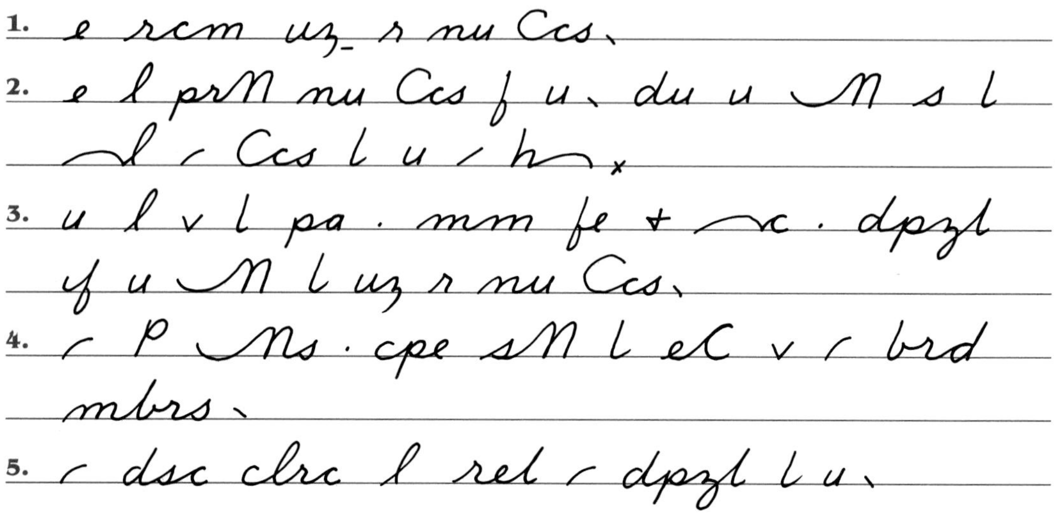

READING AND WRITING EXERCISES

1

Making a Will

Many of us take pride in taking care of our households and families. We would not dream of leaving chores for[1] neighbors or outside family members to do. Yet, we are the same people who often make the mistake of not[2] making a will. When we don't make a will, we leave vital details to be settled after our deaths.

It is not[3] necessary to be wealthy to make a will. Attorneys advise us to do so as soon as we have reached legal[4] age. Making a will can be very easy, and it may be a big help to your family. (96)

2

MEMO TO: All Claims Managers

As head of this corporation, I was very happy to learn what a great job[1] you are all doing. A number of people have written to say that their claims were given very fine attention.[2] Without a doubt, all of you deserve credit for your part in giving this company a great name. (57)

3

Gentlemen:

We received your letter informing us that our seaside cottage will be reassessed on the 14th.[1] The letter went on to say that the value of this house increased greatly—by 25 percent—when the[2] new highway was built.

We are sorry, but you have made a mistake. The highway which runs near our beach house is not new.[3] If anything, it is old and badly in need of repair. The highway was built a few years after we bought our[4] beach house. To our knowledge, the road was never repaired after it was built.

We hope that your office will take a better[5] look at that highway. If our house is reassessed, we would like to see appropriate repairs made on the road.[6] Very truly yours, (124)

UNIT 10 Listening for Notetaking

You can use your *Speedwriting* shortcuts to support your lecture notes. Many instructors will assist you in organizing your notes by putting an outline of the lecture on the chalkboard before class or as the lecture is progressing. Other instructors will demonstrate varying degrees of organizational ability in their presentations. When taking lecture notes from a very organized instructor who presents a lecture outline, you can use the outline as a starting point for your notes and then add supporting details as you are listening.

The following are some listening suggestions to help make your notetaking more productive.

1. Sit at the front. Your listening ability is much better when you are close to the lecturer. Being close helps you to be more attentive by allowing fewer distractions.
2. Concentrate on the lecture. This sounds obvious, but it isn't. Make a conscious effort to pay attention to the lecture. You will be surprised at how often you will digress and find yourself drawing doodles, counting ceiling tiles, or daydreaming.
3. Listen for major ideas and write them down.
4. Listen for information that supports the major ideas and include this information in your notes.
5. If time is available during the lecture, make a mental summary and review what has been said. The practice of summarizing and reviewing will help you focus on the lecture and avoid mind-wandering.
6. Don't get offended if you disagree with something being said. Learn to listen with your mind, not your emotions.
7. Focus on what is being said, not on a speaker's appearance, voice, or mannerisms.
8. Be extra alert during the first and the last five minutes of a class or lecture. At these times, a lecturer usually gives an overview and a summary.

9. Use your *Speedwriting* techniques and shortcuts to ease the writing burden and allow extra energy and time for attentive listening.

10. Highlight important ideas, concepts, and instructions by underlining with a pen or colored marker.

SPEEDWRITING PRINCIPLES

1. Write a capital P (disjoined from other letters) for the word beginnings *per* and *pur*.

person, per-s-n Psn	per P
personnel, per-s-n-l Psnl	purchase, pur-chay-s PCs
permit, per-m-t Pmt	purpose, pur-p-s Pps

Write a capital P also for the word beginnings *pre, pro,* and *pro* pronounced as *prah.*

preview, pre-v-u Pvu	produce, pro-d-s Pds
prefer, pre-f-r Pfr	proposal, pro-p-z-l Ppzl
prevent, pre-v-nt PvNt	problem, prah-b-l-m Pblm
provide, pro-v-d Pvd	proper, prah-p-r Ppr

2. Write g for the word ending *gram.*

program, pro-gram Pg	telegram, t-l-gram tlg

VOCABULARY STUDY

proposal Ppzl — A plan of action, usually presented in writing.

out-patients ot=psNs — Patients receiving treatment at a hospital without being admitted for overnight stays.

building permit bld P–t	A legal document authorizing an organization or individual to begin construction of a building.

PRINCIPLES SUMMARY

1. Write a disjoined capital P for the word beginnings *per, pur, pre, pro,* and *pro* (prah): person, per-s-n Psn; prepare, pre-p-r Ppr; produce, pro-d-s Pds; problem, prah-b-l-m pbl–
2. Write g for the word ending gram: program, pro-gram Pg

WORD DEVELOPMENT

Write the following related words in *Speedwriting* in your notebook.

purchase PCs	-ing	-d	-s
proceed Psd	-s	-ing	-ed
produce Pds	re-	-ing	-s
profit Pft	-s	-ed	-ing
progress Pgrs	-ed	-ing	-ive

WORD CONSTRUCTION

Practice writing these words in *Speedwriting* in your notebook.

programs, pro-gram-s	procedure, pro-s-j-r
prepared, pre-p-r-duh	telegrams, t-l-gram-s
purposes, pur-p-s-s	providing, pro-v-d-ing
personally, per-s-n-l-ly	process, prah-s-s
problems, prah-b-l-m-s	proposed, pro-p-z-duh

WRITING ASSIGNMENT

Write the following sentences in *Speedwriting* in your notebook.

1. We will admit you to the hospital as soon as we can arrange it.
2. We are increasing the amount of your credit. The new total of your loan is shown below.
3. We are offering this chair at 20 percent less than the regular price.
4. Did you know that a great number of teenage drivers are insured with our firm?
5. In general, the training class went well even though there was a great deal of disagreement.

READING AND WRITING EXERCISES

1

Safety in the Sun

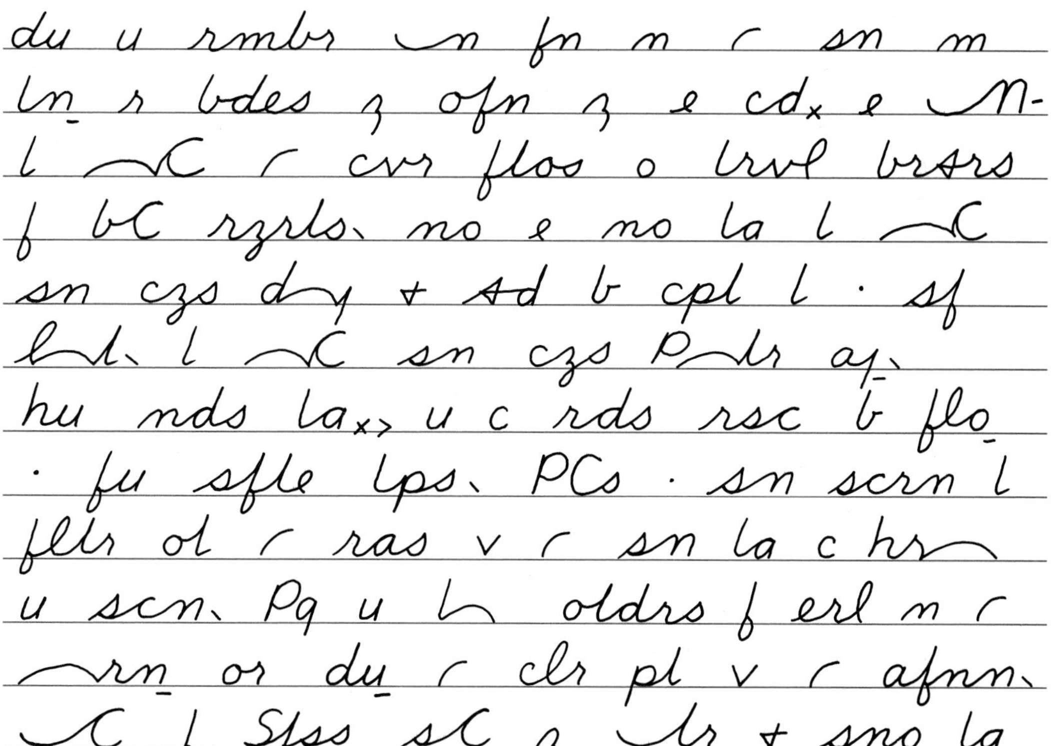

gv of A- ras. rmbr la snbrns
c Aso ocr evn du clode ~r.

2

mo l ~r rbrl
Lpl n ~u Ppzl
f (nu hsp i pln
l Pvd . dzn f (
bld z l z jn inf
nd- l gl . bld
P~l. y dN u Ppr
. nz rls gv dlls
v (Ppzl, rzdNs
v ls sle sd no la
r hsp l ofr me
nu Pgs ~C l
bnfl ol=psNs z
l z n=psNs,
e v rsv- ~C
all f (nzppr
rsNl du l ncrs-
hsp fes. ls d s~
l b . apo L l
ll ppl no r plns
l ncrs Svss.

3

1 (Pps v ls L, l
dl y e v n rsv-
(crds e PCs-f
u co. ~n e dsd-
l b (crds u ~
Sln la e d v L
ahd v L. z l
rcl e asc- la (
crds b rs-. u
ajN asr-s la lr
d b no PbL du
ls L v (yr. e v
b psN b 3 ~cs v
gn b + e v n

rsv- r crds, e	f no o / d b apo
hp la / l n b nes	f u l nf s v
l csl b af ls c	dlas b llq. ul
e l n ac r crds.	

KEY

WRITING ASSIGNMENT

1. e l a-d u l r hsp z sn z e c ar /.
2. e r ncrs r a-d v u cr. r nu lol v u ln, sn blo.
3. e r ofr ls Cr / 20% ls ln r rglr prs.
4. dd u no la . gr No v lna drvrs r nsr- r fr?
5. n jn r lrn cls N l evn lo lr z . gr dl v Dagrem.

READING AND WRITING EXERCISES

1

Safety in the Sun

Do you remember when fun in the sun meant tanning our bodies as often as we could? We wanted to match the[1] cover photos on travel brochures for beach resorts. Now we know that too much sun causes damage and should be kept[2] to a safe limit. Too much sun causes premature aging. Who needs that?

You can reduce risk by following a[3] few safety tips. Purchase a sun screen to filter out the rays of the sun that can harm your skin. Program your time[4] outdoors for early in the morning or during the cooler part of the afternoon. Watch for surfaces such as[5] water and snow that give off added rays. Remember that sunburns can also occur even during cloudy[6] weather. (121)

2

MEMO TO: Mr. Robert Temple

In my proposal for the new hospital, I plan to provide a design[1] for the building as well as general information needed to get a building permit. Why don't you prepare[2] a news release giving details of the proposal? Residents of this city should know that our hospital will[3] offer many new programs which will benefit out-patients as well as in-patients.

We have received much attention[4] from the newspaper recently due to increased hospital fees. This would seem to be an appropriate time[5] to let people know our plans to increase services. (109)

3

Gentlemen:

The purpose of this letter is to determine why we have not received the cards we purchased from your[1] company. When we decided to buy the cards, you were certain that we would have them ahead of time. As I[2] recall, we asked that the cards be rushed. Your agent assured us that there would be no problem during this time of the[3] year. We have been patient, but three weeks have gone by and we have not received the cards.

We hope that it will not be[4] necessary to cancel, but after this week we will not accept the cards. From now on, it would be appropriate[5] for you to inform us of delays by telegram. Yours truly, (110)

UNIT 11 What's Worth Noting

There is always one question that should be asked regarding any information you read or hear: Is it worth saving? To be able to decide whether something is or is not worth noting requires your answering some other questions.

1. *Do you need the information?* An ideâ, fact, or supporting detail of any kind may be interesting, but is it important enough to put in your notes? Be sure to write down the main topic and then decide on the importance of all supporting information.
2. *Does the information relate to the topic?* Be sure to determine the specific topic. Put this in your notes and decide what information is definitely relevant to the topic.
3. *Is what you read or hear a fact?* There are facts that are indisputable, like the fact that there are seven days in a week. This type of fact can go into your notes without any more detail. However, the majority of facts will be ones backed by evidence. You will need to take down the proof of these additional facts.
4. *Is what you read or hear an opinion?* Listen closely and be alert to clues that signal opinions. Such qualifying words as *it may be, many people believe, possibly, in all likelihood, this theory, to my way of thinking,* and other similar expressions often lead to statements of opinion rather than fact. Remember that anything people believe without proof is an opinion, not a fact. Label opinion as such in your notes.

An organized lecturer will make the job easier for you to determine what is important and provide you with clues as the lecture progresses. A lecture is usually organized into a beginning, a middle, and an end.

The beginning of a lecture gives an overview, states the main idea, clarifies terminology, fills in necessary background, and reveals the lecturer's point of view. The middle of a lecture supplies supporting details for the main idea or ideas; sub-details that amplify the supporting details; and arguments, examples, and evidence. The end of a lecture may repeat the main points, link the lecture to a reading or other lectures, or set the scene for an assignment.

Listen for phrases that will help you decide what is important. Phrases such as *First, let me point out that; Secondly, a good example of this would be; Let me stress the importance of; Some examples of this are;* and *Let me sum up* are tips that what follows is something worth noting.

Listen for important facts and concepts and write only what is worth noting. Write your notes in words, phrases, or short sentences using your *Speedwriting* for all known words.

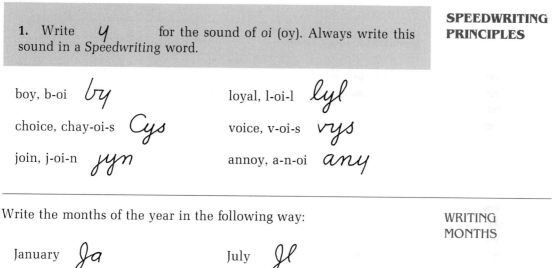

SPEEDWRITING PRINCIPLES

1. Write y for the sound of *oi* (oy). Always write this sound in a *Speedwriting* word.

boy, b-oi	by	loyal, l-oi-l	lyl
choice, chay-oi-s	Cys	voice, v-oi-s	vys
join, j-oi-n	jyn	annoy, a-n-oi	any

WRITING MONTHS

Write the months of the year in the following way:

January	Ja	July	Jl
February	Fb	August	ag
March	Mr	September	Sp
April	ap	October	Oc
May	Ma	November	Nv
June	Jn	December	Dc

ABBREVIATIONS

department	dpt	insurance	ins
envelope	env	regard	re
invoice	inv		

BRIEF FORMS

between	bln	participate	pp
ship	ꞩ	property	prp
situate	sil	refer	rf
those	loz	respond, response	rsp
operate	op	suggest	sug
point	py		

BRIEF FORM DEVELOPMENT

leadership	ldrꞩ	situated	sil-
operator	opr	shipment	ꞩm
appointment	apym	disappoint	Dapy

PRINCIPLES SUMMARY

1. Write y for the sound of *oi* (oy): boy, b-oi by

WORD DEVELOPMENT

Write the following related words in *Speedwriting* in your notebook.

point py	ap-	-ed	-s
avoid avyd	-s	-ed	-ing
regard re	-s	dis-	-ing
join jyn	-ed	-s	-ing
member mbr	-s	-ship	-ships

WORD CONSTRUCTION

Practice writing these words in *Speedwriting* in your notebook.

soil, s-oi-l

suggested, suggest-ed

enjoyed, en-j-oi-duh

shipments, ship-ment-s

noise, n-oi-z	joint, j-oi-nt
oil, oi-l	referred, refer-duh
joy, j-oi	responding, respond-ing

WRITING ASSIGNMENT

Write the following sentences in *Speedwriting* in your notebook.

1. The total amount was due by the 12th. Your attention to this matter would be a great help.
2. There were as many men as there were women in the total number of people on the payroll.
3. You will receive your new credit card without delay.
4. As soon as the matter was brought to my attention, I asked that new arrangements be made.
5. We were happy to learn that sales are generally doing very well in the East.

READING AND WRITING EXERCISES

1

Modern Man

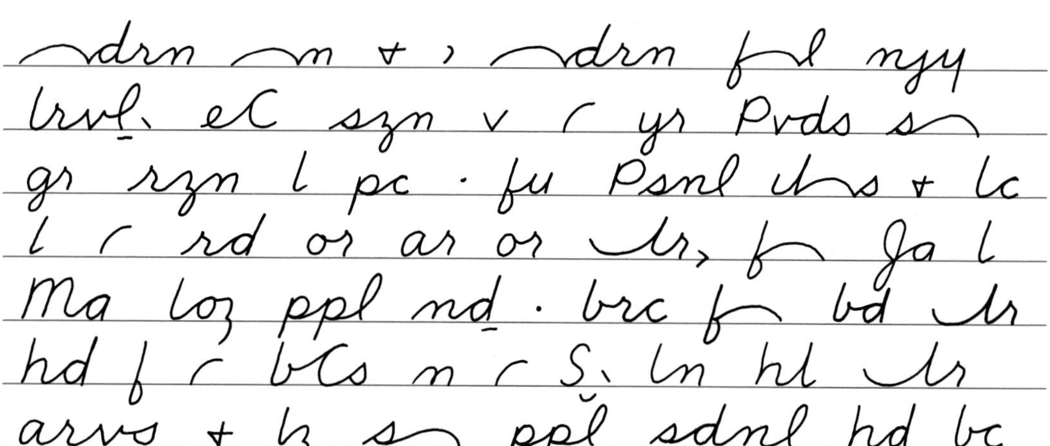

l r N n SC v clr ar. s—s / s—s la rels v l e v e fl r ury l lc f s— dfrN, c—p , . v pplr pst— du Jl + āq. slp n lns + cc — opn frs Pvd . rfr4 Cny. —drn —n —a n b so —drn af a.

2

1 n u L v ap 13 u rf- l . dla n r Ja 4m v ofs splis. e r sre f ne Pbls cz- b r dla b r cpe v r inv 4os la u splis — 4- z sn z pam z rsv-. —a e sug ls —ld f gl u 4m v envs o h, u c avyd dla b —l u Cc b Ma 30. u envs l b 4- o Jn 7 or r flo —c, f u flo ls pln f fCr PCss e c Pvd u — blr Svs. su

3

dS dd u no la u —a b pa bln 15 + 20% l —C f u ins, dd u aso no la loz plses —a n cvr r crN vlu v u h— + Psnl

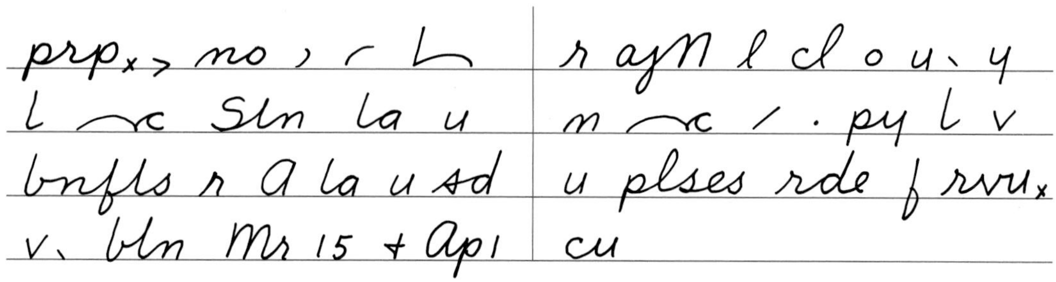

KEY

WRITING ASSIGNMENT

1. 

2. 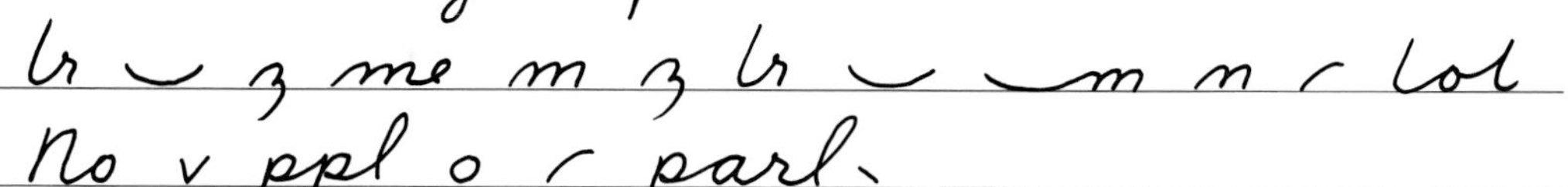

3. 

4. 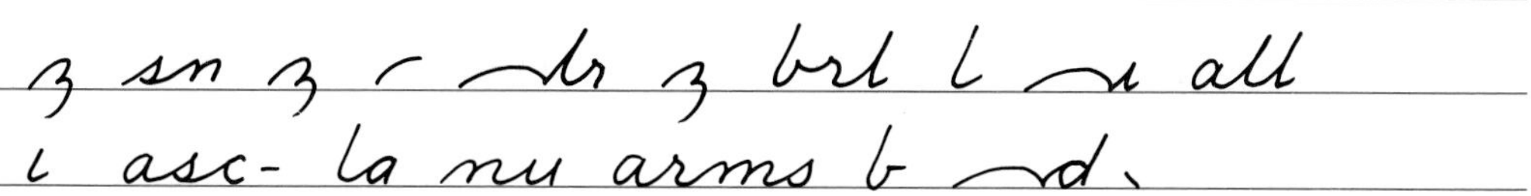

5. 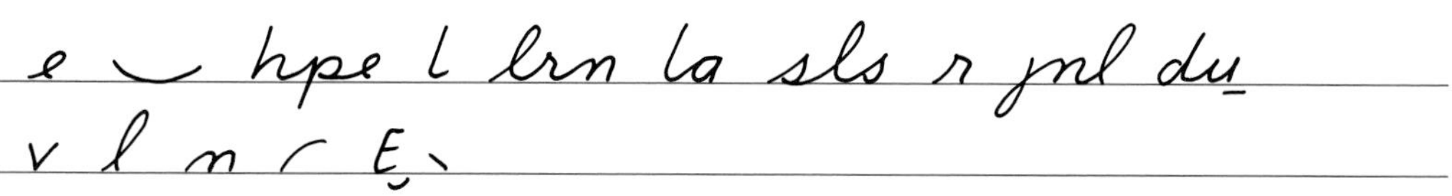

READING AND WRITING EXERCISES

1

Modern Man

Modern man and his modern family enjoy traveling. Each season of the year provides some great reason to[1] pack a few personal items and take to the road or air or water.

From January to May those people[2] needing a break from bad weather head for the beaches in the South. Then hot weather arrives, and these same people[3] suddenly head back to the North in search of cooler air. Sometimes it seems that regardless of what we have, we feel the[4] urge to look for something different.

Camping is a very popular pastime during July and August.[5] Sleeping in tents and cooking with open fires provide a refreshing change. Modern man may not be so modern after[6] all. (121)

2

Gentlemen:

In your letter of April 13, you referred to a delay in our January shipment of[1] office supplies. We are sorry for any problems caused by the delay, but our copy of the invoice shows that[2] your supplies were shipped as soon as payment was received. May we suggest this method for getting your shipment of[3] envelopes on time? You can avoid delay by mailing your check by May 30. Your envelopes will be shipped on[4] June 7 or the following week.

If you follow this plan for future purchases, we can provide you with better[5] service. Sincerely yours, (104)

3

Dear Sir:

Did you know that you may be paying between 15 and 20 percent too much for your insurance? Did[1] you also know that those policies may not cover the current value of your home and personal property?[2]

Now is the time to make certain that your benefits are all that you should have. Between March 15 and April 1,[3] our agent will call on you. Why not make it a point to have your policies ready for review? Cordially yours,[4] (80)

UNIT **12**

Taking Textbook Notes

A requirement for most college classes is the reading of a course text or texts upon which much of the class lecture is based. Instructors will seldom cover everything in these textbooks in class, but they will expect you to be thoroughly prepared on all the material for lectures and exams. These assignments should be completed promptly, and good notes should be taken as you read.

Assignments may be made periodically or all together at the beginning of the course. Keeping up with the assignments is a necessity and will require careful management of your available time. The following tips suggest ways to read a textbook and take notes.

1. *Survey Your Textbook.* Go over the table of contents; see how the book is organized. Is there an index? Look for special features at the end of the book—special vocabulary, formula charts, or the like. Get an overview as to what the book is about and what it contains. Also, look at pictures, tables, graphs, and other illustrative material and read the captions beneath them.

2. *Decide on the Notetaking Method You Will Use.* Will it be paragraphing by sequence, paraphrasing by sections, outlining, or a combination of these and other methods? The use of diagrams, divisional charts, circular pie charts, graphs, and other types of schematics may also prove beneficial for certain types of illustrations or information. However, these aids will rarely be used by themselves as the main method for taking notes. You have already discovered that taking notes helps you learn as you read and provides you with a record for later use. Are you going to use one notebook for class lectures and a separate one for textbook notes, or a combination of the two? Whichever method you choose, be consistent by adhering to your system.

3. *Survey Your Specific Assignment.* Go through the chapter or chapters, read all headings and subheadings, and read the summary paragraphs usually found at the end of chapters.

4. *Read and Take Good Notes.* Start at the beginning and read a section at a time, taking notes as you go along. Note the main topics, the subtopics, and the reinforcement ideas and examples for these topics. Don't look for a quick answer or shortcuts by taking notes *only* on chapter summaries. These wrap-up statements seldom contain the details you will need for an examination.

5. *Be Alert for Special Vocabulary.* Every course has its special vocabulary, and you will need to know what these words mean. Looking up words in the dictionary is the best way to clarify certain words. Another way to learn unfamiliar words before using a dictionary is to try to figure out their meanings from context clues. Sometimes you will read a word you think you know very well, but it seems to have taken on a new meaning. That new meaning is what you must write down and learn.

6. *Review and Review.* Review your notes on your assignment as soon as you have finished writing them and relate them to lectures and to the course outline. As you review, ask yourself such questions as *What is important for me to learn from this material? Is there anything here I don't understand? How will I learn it?* Review your notes periodically and before a test.

SPEEDWRITING PRINCIPLES

1. For words ending in a long vowel + *t* (*ate, ete, ite, ote, ute/oot*), omit the *t* and write the vowel.

rate, r-ate ra	right, write, r-ite ri
late, l-ate la	might, m-ite mi
greet, guh-r-ete gre	wrote, r-ote ro
cheat, chay-ete Ce	boat, b-ote bo
cute, k-ute cu	suit, s-oot su

*The word *note* is written nl in order to distinguish it from the word know, written no

Practice writing these additional words:

locate, l-k-ate lca   delighted, d-l-ite-ed dli-

hesitate, h-z-t-ate *hzla*	white, w-ite *i*
receipt, re-s-ete *rse*	fight, f-ite *fi*
defeated, d-f-ete-ed *dfe-*	vote, v-ote *vo*
invite, in-v-ite *nvi*	promoted, pro-m-ote-ed *Po-*

REVIEWING PROPER NAMES

You have already learned how to write proper names. As a brief review exercise, write the following names. Each name is written according to the principles you have learned.

Janet, j-n-t *jnt*	William, w-l-y-m *ly*
Pamela, p-m-l-a *pla*	David, d-v-d *dvd*
Elizabeth, e-l-z-b-ith *elzbl*	Ronald, r-n-l-d *rnld*
Claire, k-l-r *clr*	Martin, m-r-t-n *rtn*
Shelley, ish-l-e *sle*	Jim, j-m *j*
Barbara, b-r-b-r-a *brbra*	Jeremy, j-r-m-e *jre*

PRINCIPLES SUMMARY

1. For words ending in a long vowel + *t*, omit the *t* and write the vowel: rate, r-ate *ra*

WORD DEVELOPMENT

Write the following related words in *Speedwriting* in your notebook.

date *da*	-s	-ing	-d
duplicate *dplca*	-ing	-d	-s
meet *e*	-s	-ing	-ings
separate *spra*	-s	-d	-ing
locate *lca*	-ing	-d	-s

WORD CONSTRUCTION

Practice writing these words in *Speedwriting* in your notebook.

freight, f-r-ate	site, s-ite
sheet, ish-ete	united, u-n-ite-ed
writing, r-ite-ing	treatment, t-r-ete-ment
light, l-ite	related, re-l-ate-ed
regulate, r-guh-l-ate	eliminate, e-l-min-ate

WRITING ASSIGNMENT

Write the following sentences in *Speedwriting*.

1. Although we have no jobs open at this time, we advise you to reapply when the new hospital opens. We will make arrangements to discuss your letter at that time.
2. We will add a total of 20 new men to the payroll. We will need that many to help build the new highway.
3. As a rule, our company does not lay off people. Rather than release men and women from their jobs, we reassign them to new duties. I believe that we will reassign a great number this year.
4. In general, our company offers better benefits than any large firm in town. I have been with this corporation for 11 years now, and I know that this is true.
5. We will be happy to readmit you in our classes. You will receive full credit for the courses you took earlier.

READING AND WRITING EXERCISES

1

Telephones and Telegrams

l cre · s⌒pl ⌒sj b hrs or bo×
bf llfns ⌣ nvN- llgs ⌣ uz-
f brf + urjN ⌒sjs, llgs Pvd-
· gr Svs f · No v yrs + r
Pfr- evn no f Sln Ppss, ni Ls
r uz- f s⌒ ⌒sjs bcz lz c b
sN / · Cpr ra, (llq / 1 h⌒
Pvd- · gr Svs b rN u gld la
u lv du (aj v (llfn ⌣n u
nd l cl · cb×

2

d edlr brns e ⌣
dli- ⌣ (gr cvrj
u gv r fl crnvl,
e cd n v hp- f·
blr rsp ln e rsv-,
e r no nvi u l pp
n · evN e v b pln
f 2 yrs, ls evN l
b cl- (vlj bo so,
(bos l b Dpla-
n r vlj sp sNr,
ri no / lcs z lo
e ⌒a v s⌒ rlr
lrj bos hr, y nes
loz bos l b lca- n
(E prc ll, e r
pln l v bln 20 +
30 bos o Dpla f
1 ⌣c n Ap, l u
pln l ri · arlcl l
rn du (⌣c v (

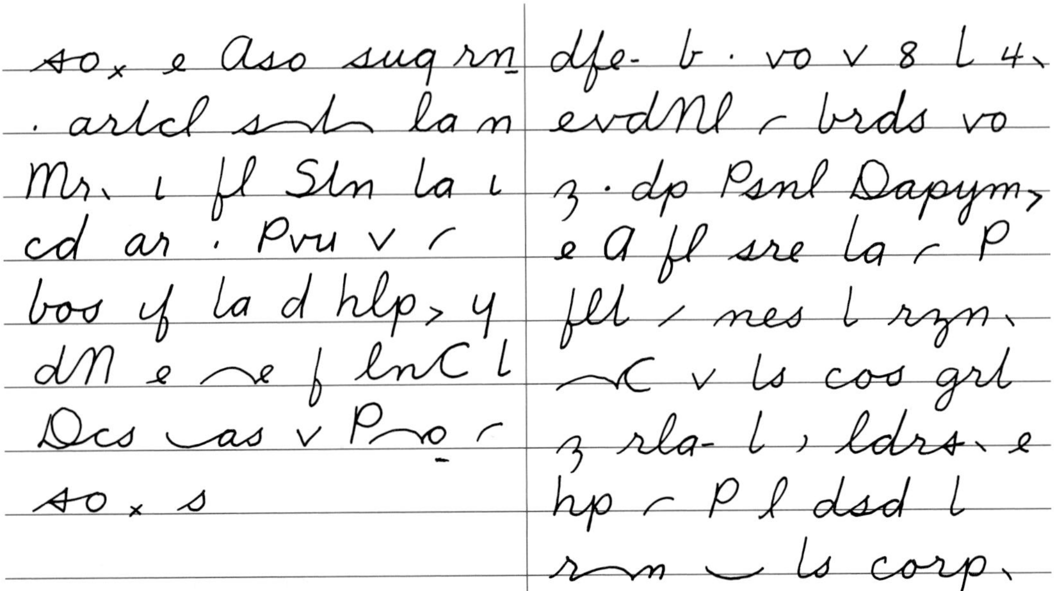

3

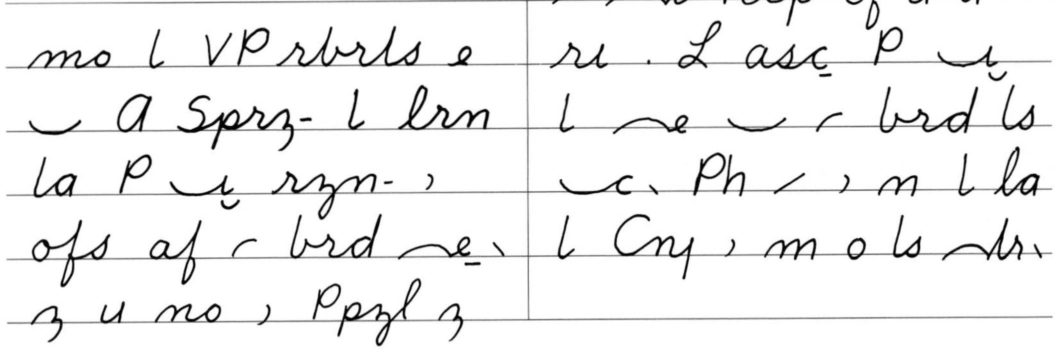

KEY

WRITING ASSIGNMENT

1.

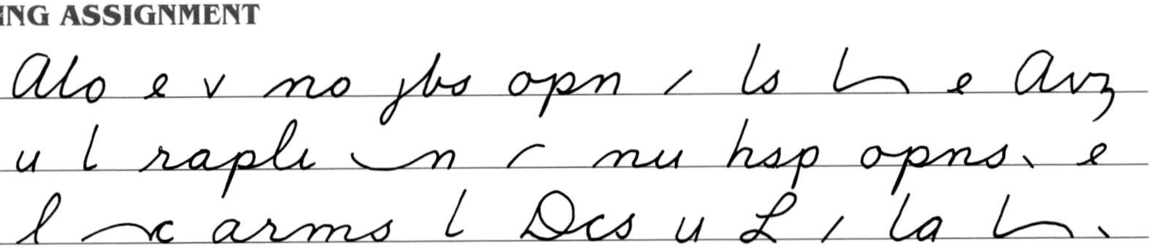

2.

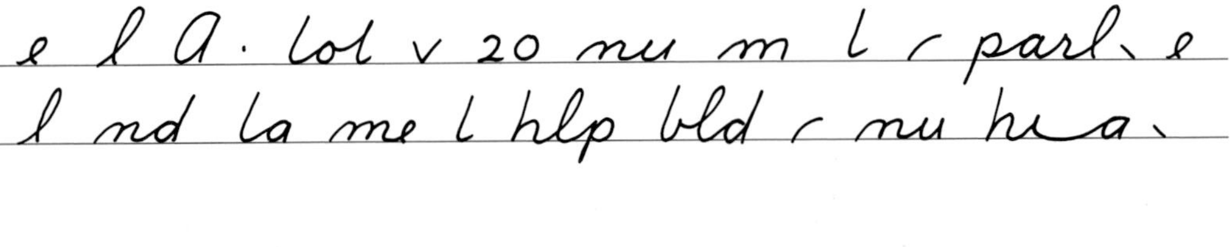

3. z . rl r co dz n la of ppl. rlr ln rls m + ◡m f lr jbs e rasn l l nu dles. i blv la e l rasn . gr No ls yr.

4. n jn r co ofrs blr bnfls ln ne lry fr n lon. i v b ◡ ls corp f 11 yrs no + i no la ls , tru.

5. e l b hpe l rA-d u n r clss. u l rsv f cr f r crss u lc erlr.

READING AND WRITING EXERCISES

1

Telephones and Telegrams

How did anyone manage to live without telephones? Have you thought of how much time it would have taken to[1] carry a simple message by horse or boat? Before telephones were invented, telegrams were used for brief and[2] urgent messages.

Telegrams provided a great service for a number of years and are preferred even now for[3] certain purposes. Night letters are used for some messages because these can be sent at a cheaper rate. The[4] telegram at one time provided a great service, but aren't you glad that you live during the age of the telephone[5] when you need to call a cab? (105)

2

Dear Editor Burns:

We were delighted with the great coverage you gave our fall carnival. We could not have hoped[1] for a better response than we received.

We are now inviting you to participate in an event we have[2] been planning for two years. This event will be called the Village Boat Show. The boats will be displayed in our village shopping[3] center. Right now it looks as though we may have some rather large boats here. If necessary, those boats will be located[4] in the east parking lot.

We are planning to have between 20 and 30 boats on display for one week[5] in April.

Will you plan to write an article to run during the week of the show? We also suggest running[6] an article sometime late in March. I feel certain that I could arrange a preview of the boats if that would help.[7]

Why don't we meet for lunch to discuss ways of promoting the show? Sincerely, (154)

3

MEMO TO: Vice President Roberts

We were all surprised to learn that President White resigned his office after[1] the board meeting. As you know, his proposal was defeated by a vote of 8 to 4. Evidently, the board's[2] vote was a deep personal disappointment.

We all feel sorry that the president felt it necessary to[3] resign. Much of this company's growth was related to his leadership. We hope the president will decide to[4] remain with this corporation. It might help if you would write a letter asking President White to meet with the[5] board this week. Perhaps it is not too late to change his mind on this matter. (113)

UNIT

13

Varying Your Speed of Reading

You will need to vary your reading speed depending on the type of material you are reading. Many students read everything from comic books to scientific texts at the same speed. This practice results in an unproductive use of time and effort.

Some students feel that the answer to keeping up with their reading assignments is to apply speed reading techniques. Research has shown that although speed reading may work well with easy or familiar material, speed readers retain less of more difficult material.

If you need to understand and retain difficult material, it is best to read that material at an average or even slower pace. A flexible reading speed, based on the nature of the material, should produce the best results.

Taking notes as you read is slower than not taking notes as you read, but the learning benefits are well worth the added effort of notetaking. Effective notetaking while reading includes the following benefits:

1. Forces careful reading
2. Improves retention
3. Increases reading efficiency
4. Decreases study time
5. Improves understanding
6. Discourages mind-wandering
7. Gives insight into the subject
8. Provides excellent review material.

SPEEDWRITING PRINCIPLES

1. Write *a* for the word beginning *an*.

answer, an-s-r *asr*

anticipate, an-t-s-p-ate *alspa*

antique, an-t-k alc	analyze, an-l-z alz

2. Write q for the medial or final sound of any vowel + *nk* (*ank, enk, ink, onk, unk*).

bank, b-ank bq	length, l-enk-ith lql
blank, b-l-ank blq	rank, r-ank rq
thank, ith-ank lq	link, l-ink lq

ABBREVIATIONS

junior jr	second, secretary sec
senior sr	

BRIEF FORMS

am, more	go, good g
charge	he, had, him h
doctor, direct dr	they ly

PHRASING

Some word combinations, such as *we are* and *to be*, are used so often that they are usually spoken and read as a group. In *Speedwriting*, we take advantage of this natural association by joining words together. This practice is called *phrasing*.

we are er	to be lb

The pronouns *I*, *we*, and *you* followed by a verb and the word *to* followed by a verb can be easily written and recognized as phrases.

I am	you are ur
I can ic	you can uc

we are	er	to be	lb
we can	ec	to go	lq

With experience in *Speedwriting*, phrases will occur to you naturally as you write. The context, or meaning, of the sentence will help you read the phrase correctly when you see it in your notes.

Practice reading and writing the following phrases:

I am	im	you are	ur
I can	ic	you can	uc
I had	ih	you have	uv
I have	iv	you know	uno
I will	il	you will	ul
I will be	ilb	you would	ud

we are	er	to be	lb
we can	ec	to go	lq
we have	ev	to have	lv
we hope	ehp	to have you	lvu
we would	ed	to have your	lvu
we would be	edb	to know	lno
		to pay	lpa

WRITING CONTRACTIONS

When writing contractions that might be read back as a phrase, use an apostrophe to avoid confusion.

I will	il	I'll	i'l
you will	ul	you'll	u'l
we are	er	we're	e'r

HIGH-FREQUENCY PHRASES

A few word combinations occur together so frequently that certain words within the combinations may be omitted from your *Speedwriting* notes. Three such high-frequency phrases are *thank you for, thank you for your,* and *thank you for your letter*. In the following examples, the words in bold have been omitted in the *Speedwriting* phrases.

thank **you** for lqf   thank **you** for **your** lqf

thank **you** for **your** letter lqfL

PRINCIPLES SUMMARY

1. Write a for the word beginning *an*: answer, an-s-r asr.
2. Write q for the medial or final sound of any vowel + *nk*: bank, b-ank bq.

WORD DEVELOPMENT

Write the following related words in *Speedwriting* in your notebook.

bank bq	-s	-ed	-ing
link lq	-s	-ed	-ing
length lql	-s	-en	-ening
analyze alz	-d	-ing	-s
anticipate alspa	-s	-d	-ing

WORD CONSTRUCTION

Practice writing these words in *Speedwriting* in your notebook.

thinking, ith-ink-ing	thanks, ith-ank-s
ago, a-go	directly, direct-ly
answering, an-s-r-ing	charges, charge-s
you're, u-'-r	anxious, a-ank-ish-s
we'll, we-'-l	going, go-ing

WRITING ASSIGNMENT

Write the following sentences in *Speedwriting*.

1. Our new offices will be situated on the property between our main plant and the old office building.
2. Our plant will not operate between January 28 and February 15. We will use those weeks to situate furnishings in the new building. All of our people will participate in the move.
3. During those weeks, we suggest that all shipments be referred to our main plant. All invoices should be referred to our shipping department.
4. In regard to your recent memo, our move will be covered by insurance. A copy of our policy is enclosed in the attached envelope.
5. Can you suggest changes in this schedule? When may I have your response to these plans?

READING AND WRITING EXERCISES

Watch for phrases beginning with the words *I*, *we*, *you*, and *to*.

1

Abraham Lincoln

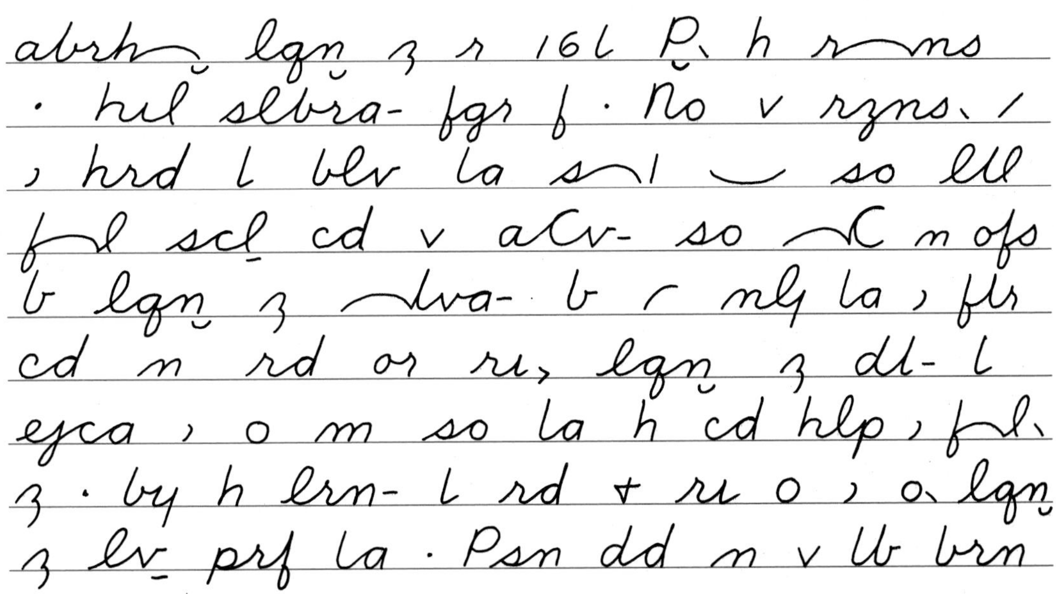

rC l lv n r hos. r lf v
abrh lgn gv s me lsns l lv
b. lgn , rmbr- f ln plLcl
ldr. h gv s vlus.

2

dM adrsn lqf L
re jbs f hi scl
srs. u grds du
ndd rq u / r lp
v u cls. edb gld
lvu apli. enc
. co blln C l
spli me v r asrs
u nd, Alo jnl e
nd secs o . f=L
bss e s v . fu
pl=L opn f hi scl
jrs + srs, bl gra
, . sr hu , fn ,
sec yr r fr. l
sug la u lc h.
uc Aso gl inf
f r Psnl yr rc
lc. if u cn se h Psnll
, sec l gv u r apo
fs l fl ol. vlu

3

ddr a s l M u
lno la lc f
alc frn f u
ofs. lca- . dsc
+ Cr C l lq ul
lc b afrd la
r lql v r dsc ,
n ri f u ofs. l
d b . q L f u l lc
/ / x, l Aso no v

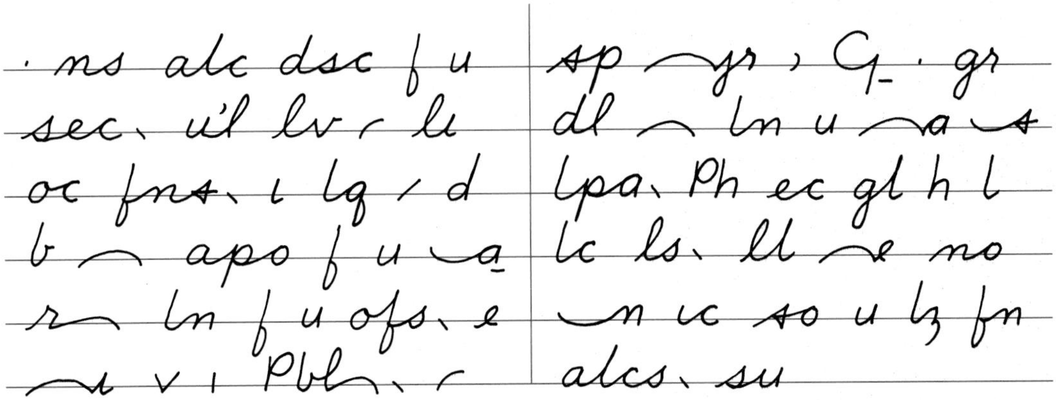

KEY

WRITING ASSIGNMENT

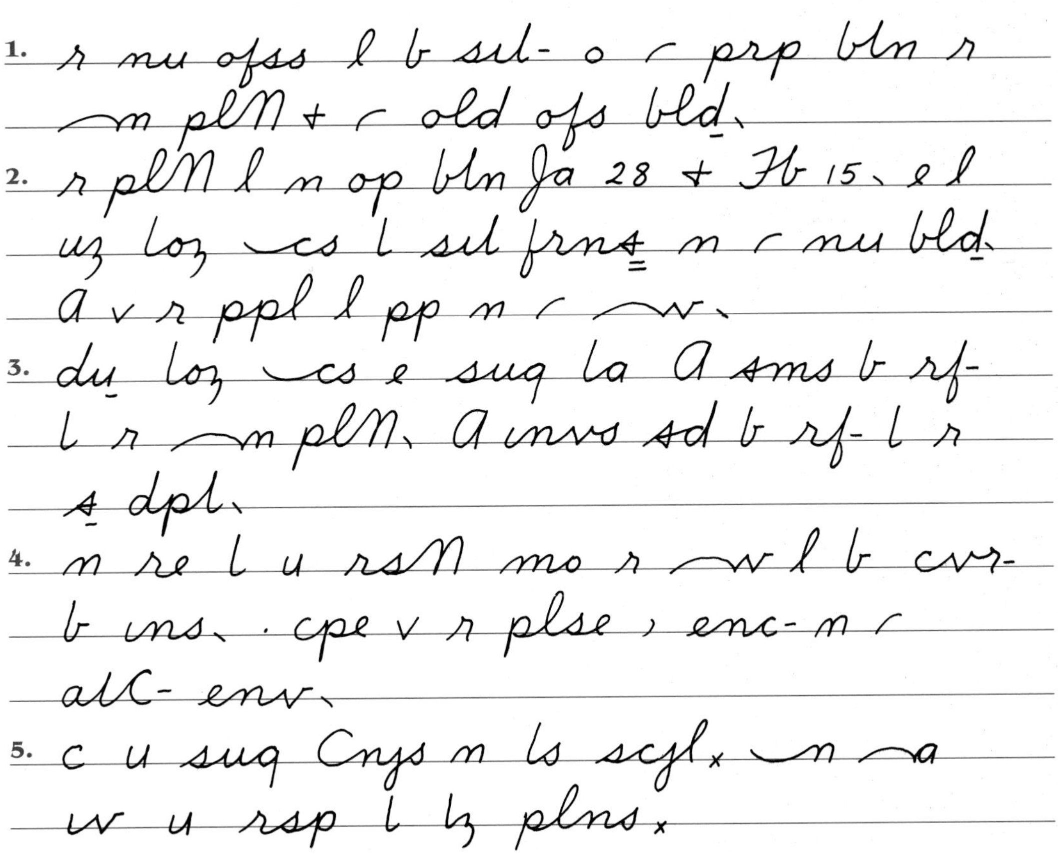

READING AND WRITING EXERCISES

1

Abraham Lincoln

Abraham Lincoln was our 16th President. He remains a highly celebrated figure for a number[1] of reasons. It is hard to believe that someone with so little formal schooling could have achieved so much in office,[2] but Lincoln was motivated by the knowledge that his father could not read or write.

Lincoln was determined[3] to educate his own mind so that he could help his family. As a boy he learned to read and write on his own.[4] Lincoln was living proof that a person did not have to be born rich to live in the White House. The life of Abraham[5] Lincoln gave us many lessons to live by. Lincoln is remembered for more than political leadership.[6] He gave us values. (124)

2

Dear Miss Anderson:

Thank you for your letter regarding jobs for high school seniors. Your grades do indeed rank you at[1] the top of your class. We would be glad to have you apply. I am enclosing a company bulletin which will[2] supply many of the answers you need.

Although generally we need secretaries on a full-time basis,[3] we sometimes have a few part-time openings for high school juniors and seniors.

Bill Gray is a senior who is[4] finishing his second year with our firm. I suggest that you talk with him. You can also get more information from[5] our personnel manager, Mark Lee. If you cannot see him personally, his secretary will give you the[6] appropriate forms to fill out. Very truly yours, (129)

3

Dear Dr. Ames:

I want you to know that I am looking for more antique furnishings for your office. I have[1] located a desk and chair which I think you will like, but I am afraid that the length of the desk is not right for your[2] office. What would be a good time for you to look at it?

I also know of a nice antique desk for your[3] secretary. You'll love the light oak finish. I think it would be more appropriate for your waiting room than for your[4] office. We might have one problem. The shop manager is charging a great deal more than you may wish to pay. Perhaps we[5] can get him to take less. Let me know when I can show you these fine antiques. Sincerely yours, (116)

UNIT 14 Review and Reinforcement

1. Here are the word beginnings you studied in Units 8–13:

dis D

mis M

per, pur P

an a

pre, pro, pro *(prah)* P

2. The following word endings were also presented:

long vowel + t

ly l

*a*te a

gram q

ete e

ite i

ote o

ute/oot u

3. The following words illustrate all of the principles you studied in Units 8–13:

dismay, dis-m-a Dma

person, per-s-n Psn

mistake, mis-t-k Mtc

purpose, pur-p-s Pps

recently, re-s-nt-ly rsNl

prevent, pre-v-nt PvN

rate, r-ate ra

program, pro-gram Pq

health, h-l-ith hll

loyal, l-oi-l lyl

reapply, re-a-p-l-i *rapli*	payroll, p-a-r-l *parl*
answer, an-s-r *asr*	bank, b-ank *bg*

4. Months of the year are written this way:

January *Ja*	July *Jl*
February *Fb*	August *Ag*
March *Mr*	September *Sp*
April *Ap*	October *Oc*
May *Ma*	November *Nv*
June *Jn*	December *Dc*

5. Can you automatically write these brief forms in your notebook? If you are unsure of any brief form, practice writing the word in your notebook until you can write it without hesitation.

that	arrange	were
participate	between	ship
response	great	as
was	with	hospital
those	situate	general
refer	property	operate
respond	suggest	am
more	direct	doctor
charge	go	he
good	had	they
him	point	

6. Write these brief form derivatives in your notebook.

arrangement	generally	operators
within	without	wasn't
greatly	referred	shipping

7. How quickly can you read the following abbreviations?

cr	*No*	*ins*
re	*all*	*a-l*

%   env   dpl
inv   lol   jr
sr   sec

READING AND WRITING EXERCISES

1

Memory Banks

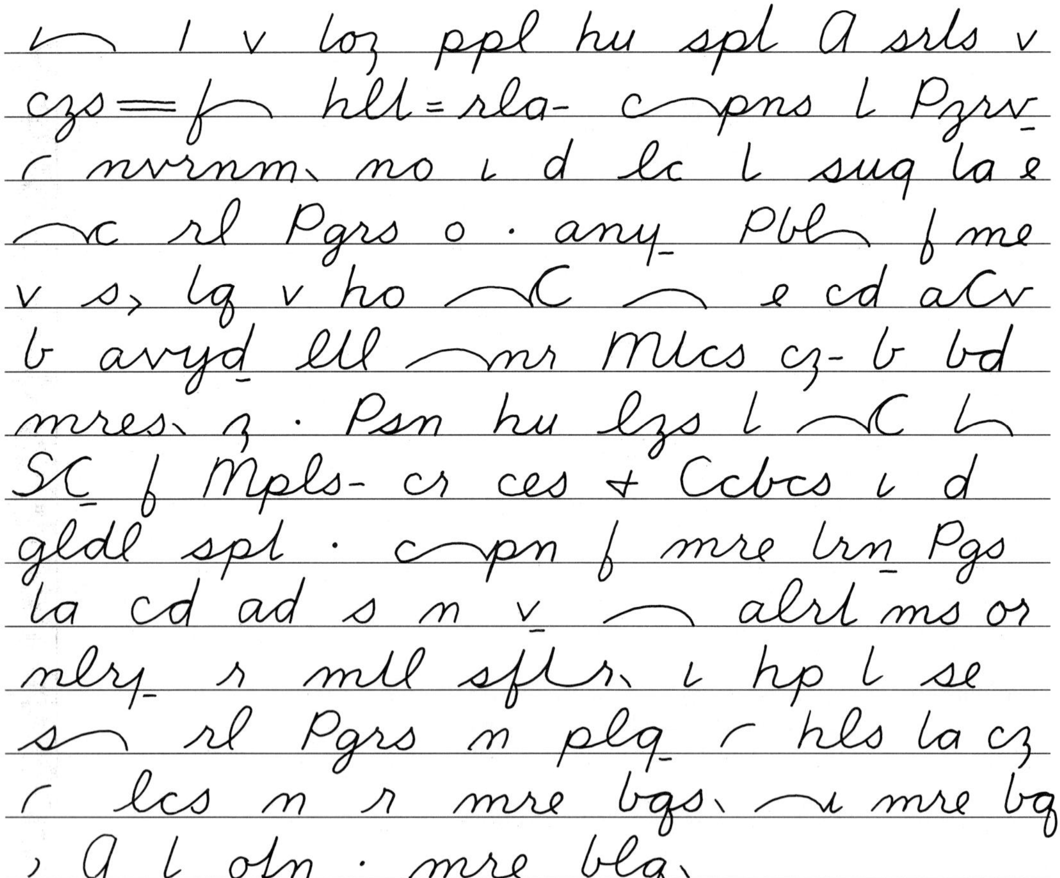

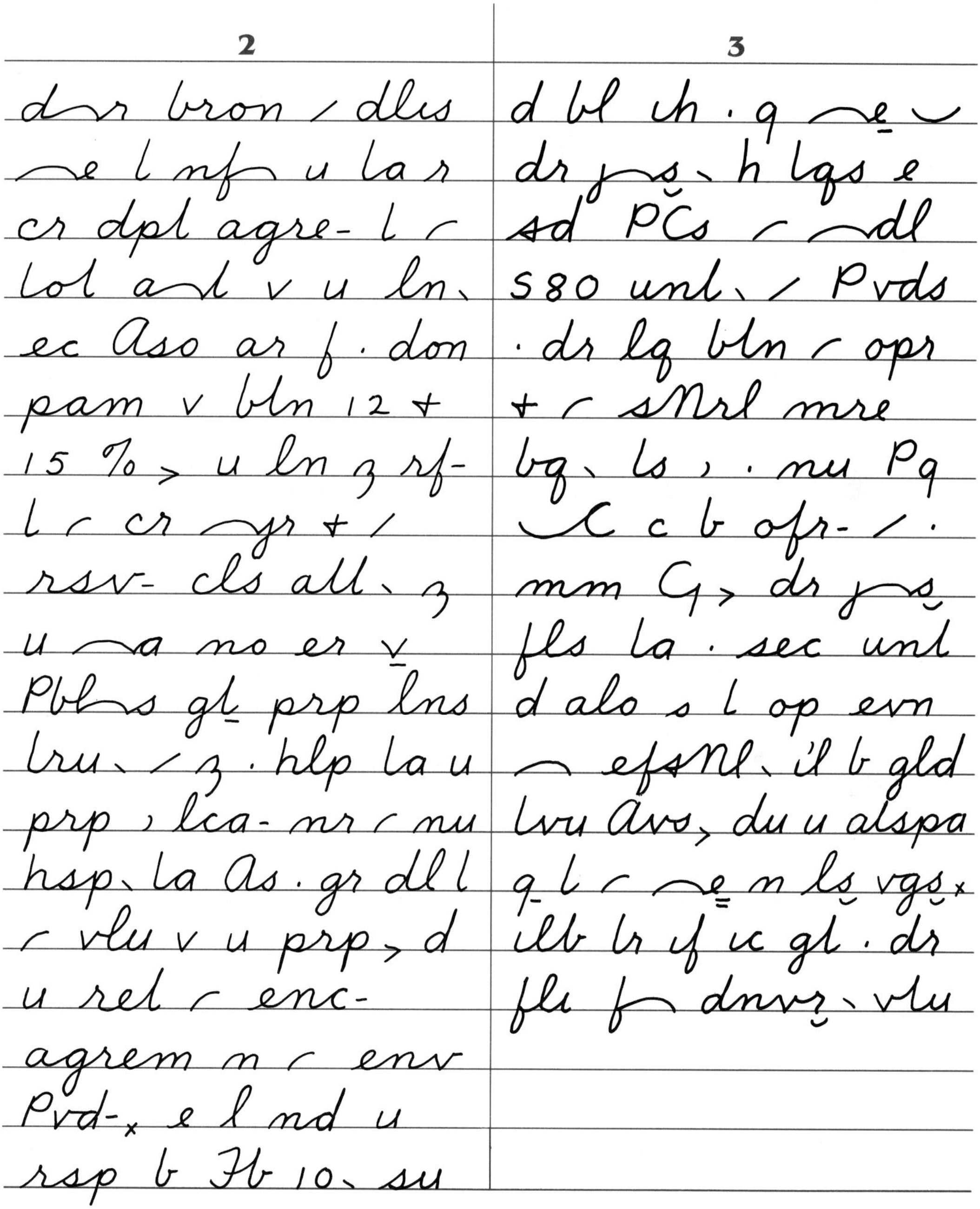

KEY

BRIEF FORMS

la	ar	⌣
pp	bln	s̵
rsp	gr	3
3	⌣	hsp
loz	sil	jn
rf	prp	op
rsp	sug	⌢
⌢	dr	dr
G	q	h
q	h	ly
h	py	

BRIEF FORM DERIVATIVES

arm	jnl	oprs
⌣n	⌣ol	3N
grl	rf-	s̵̲

ABBREVIATIONS

credit	number	insurance
regard	attention	amount
percent	envelope	department
invoice	total	junior
senior	second, secretary	

READING AND WRITING EXERCISES

1

Memory Banks

I am one of those people who support all sorts of causes—from health-related campaigns to preserving the[1] environment. Now I would like to suggest that we make real progress on an annoying problem for many of[2] us.

Think of how much more we could achieve by avoiding little minor mistakes caused by bad memories. As a[3] person who loses too much time searching for misplaced car keys and checkbooks, I would gladly support a campaign for[4] memory training programs that could aid us in having more alert minds or enlarging our mental software.[5] I hope to see some real progress in plugging the holes that cause the leaks in our memory banks. My memory bank is[6] all too often a memory blank. (126)

2

Dear Mr. Brown:

It delights me to inform you that our credit department agreed to the total amount of[1] your loan. We can also arrange for a down payment of between 12 and 15 percent.

Your loan was referred to[2] the credit manager, and it received close attention. As you may know, we are having problems getting property[3] loans through. It was a help that your property is located near the new hospital. That adds a great deal to[4] the value of your property.

Would you return the enclosed agreement in the envelope provided? We will[5] need your response by February 10. Sincerely yours, (110)

3

Dear Bill:

I had a good meeting with Dr. James. He thinks we should purchase the model S80 unit. It[1] provides a direct link between the operator and the central memory bank. This is a new program which can[2] be offered at a minimum charge.

Dr. James feels that a second unit would allow us to operate even[3] more efficiently. I'll be glad to have your advice.

Do you anticipate going to the meetings in Las[4] Vegas? I will be there if I can get a direct flight from Denver. Very truly yours, (96)

PART THREE

What Will *Speedwriting* Do for You?

Speedwriting is a skill that will help launch and then advance your career. Why? *Speedwriting* gives you a special skill that makes you a more versatile individual. In the business world, your employer will know that you had the ambition and the ability to learn this skill, and it is a skill you will be able to use every day in your professional as well as personal life.

Here are some facts about *Speedwriting* and what it can do for you. *Speedwriting* enables you to begin at higher levels in the business and professional world, which in turn leads to advancement in other areas. You will find that *Speedwriting* is helpful at any level—either for taking notes, recording minutes of meetings, summarizing published material, or creating your own dictation material. Your *Speedwriting* skill will also help you get a good job. Advancement from there will depend on your ambition, career goals, and performance.

You can use *Speedwriting* in many ways at any job level. *Speedwriting* makes you a more productive student and employee. Whether you are doing research for a special project, composing a memo or letter, taking notes in a classroom or in a meeting, or recording telephone messages, *Speedwriting* saves time and allows faster completion of tasks. Your ability to increase your productivity will help you earn respect as a student or as a valuable employee.

As you have seen, *Speedwriting* is an alphabetic system of writing that can be learned quickly and easily. With more experience, your speed and accuracy will continue to improve.

UNIT 15

Taking Notes from Required Readings

Novels, plays, and short stories will sometimes be at least part of your required reading. When reading and taking study notes from fiction, make sure your notes include the following information.

1. *Title of Work and Author's Name.* Write this information at the top of your first page of notes and in a briefer form at the top of each succeeding page.
2. *Date and Country in Which the Work was Written.* This information will help you understand the influences of the period and the locale upon the author.
3. *Any Other Important Facts Regarding the Author.*
4. *Notes on the Introduction.* Don't bypass the Introduction. The author often includes important information in the Introduction, especially in works of fiction.
5. *Main Characters of a Story or Play.*
6. *Notes on the Plot—Ideas and Details.* Fill in enough detail and include all the important scenes so that your summary of the story will be useful for later review.
7. *Symbolism.* Writers often use symbols to represent ideas or qualities. Indicate in your notes how a theme of a story or a play is expressed through symbolism.
8. *Thoughts and Possible Questions on the Reading.* Write in your notes any special thoughts you have about the story immediately after reading your assignment. Also, ask yourself questions on the material and formulate your answers while the story is fresh in your mind. This practice will enable you to anticipate possible test questions.

The next time you need to take notes on a fiction assignment, you may find these suggestions helpful. Always use as much *Speedwriting* as possible to ease your notetaking tasks.

Use both underlining and highlighting judiciously. If a book does not belong to you, of course, you should not deface it in any way. Avoid an elaborate practice of underlining or highlighting in several colors, unless the color coding is being used to designate or reflect different levels of concepts. Although selective highlighting is beneficial, the fanciest underlining will not help you remember as much as efficient notetaking. You may find yourself relying on another person's judgment if previous underscoring in a text has occurred. That person could have been an unsuccessful student, so determine for yourself what needs to be noted.

SPEEDWRITING PRINCIPLES

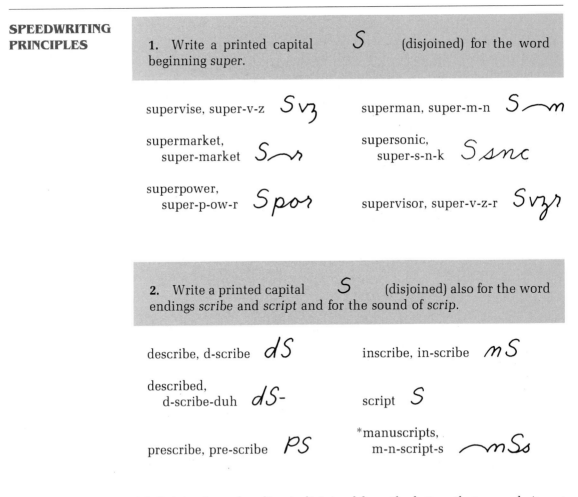

1. Write a printed capital  (disjoined) for the word beginning *super*.

supervise, super-v-z 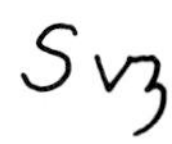

superman, super-m-n 

supermarket, super-market 

supersonic, super-s-n-k 

superpower, super-p-ow-r 

supervisor, super-v-z-r 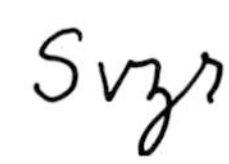

2. Write a printed capital  (disjoined) also for the word endings *scribe* and *script* and for the sound of *scrip*.

describe, d-scribe 

inscribe, in-scribe 

described, d-scribe-duh 

script 

prescribe, pre-scribe 

*manuscripts, m-n-script-s 

*A disjoined word ending is disjoined from the letters that precede it, not from those that follow it.

3. Write *el* for the word beginning *electr.*

electric, electr-k	*elc*	electrical, electr-k-l	*elcl*
electronic, electr-n-k	*elnc*	electronically, electr-n-k-ly	*elncl*

MORE ABOUT PHRASES

In Unit 13, you learned to write phrases beginning with *I, we, you,* and *to.* You can also write other very common word groups as phrases.

I could	*lcd*	will be	*lb*
I hope	*lhp*	would be	*db*
to see	*lse*	it is	*s*
for the	*f*	it's (contraction)	*'s*
of the	*v*	its (possessive)	*s*
that you	*lau*	that your	*lau*

VOCABULARY STUDY

supermarket chain
S⁀r Cn
A group of large grocery stores owned by the same individual or corporation.

programming
Pg-
Providing a computer with programs, which are sets of coded instructions.

PRINCIPLES SUMMARY

1. Write a printed capital *S* (disjoined) for the word beginning *super*: supervise, super-v-z *S vz*.

2. Write a printed capital *S* (disjoined) for the sound of *scrip* and the word endings *scribe* and *script*: describe, d-scribe *dS*; manuscripts, m-n-script-s *mnSs*.

3. Write *el* for the word beginning *electr*: electric, electr-k *elc*.

WORD DEVELOPMENT

Write the following related words in *Speedwriting* in your notebook.

super S	-vise	-vises	-vised
describe dS	-s	-ing	-d
inscribe nS	-s	-ing	-d
electric elc	-al	-ally	
electron eln	-s	-ic	

WORD CONSTRUCTION

Practice writing these words in *Speedwriting* in your notebook.

superbowl, super-b-l

manuscript, m-n-script

prescribing, pre-scribe-ing

supersede, super-s-d

ascribes, a-scribe-s

its, it-s

it's, it-'-s

supermarkets, super-market-s

supervisory, super-v-z-r-e

electronics, electr-n-k-s

WRITING ASSIGNMENT

Write the following sentences in *Speedwriting*.

1. Insuring teenage drivers can be a great headache. Indeed, some parents have called it highway robbery. If you are paying too much to insure your teenage drivers, let GENERAL LIFE help. GENERAL LIFE can insure your teenager for 10 percent less than any large company in town.

2. Here is great news for the head of the family. Our health benefits now pay as much as 90 percent of the total hospital bill. When can we arrange to show you this policy?

3. Attention Policyholders: We are now offering the new dental coverage you have been asking for. You, as well as your family, will benefit greatly from this policy.

4. In response to the increased need, we are opening a central claims department to serve the entire company. Beginning January 2, all claims should be referred to the central claims department. This change will provide an efficient means of processing all claims.

5. My files show that it is now time to review your homeowner's insurance policy. May we get together soon? I will call this week for an appointment.

READING AND WRITING EXERCISES

1

Electric Lights

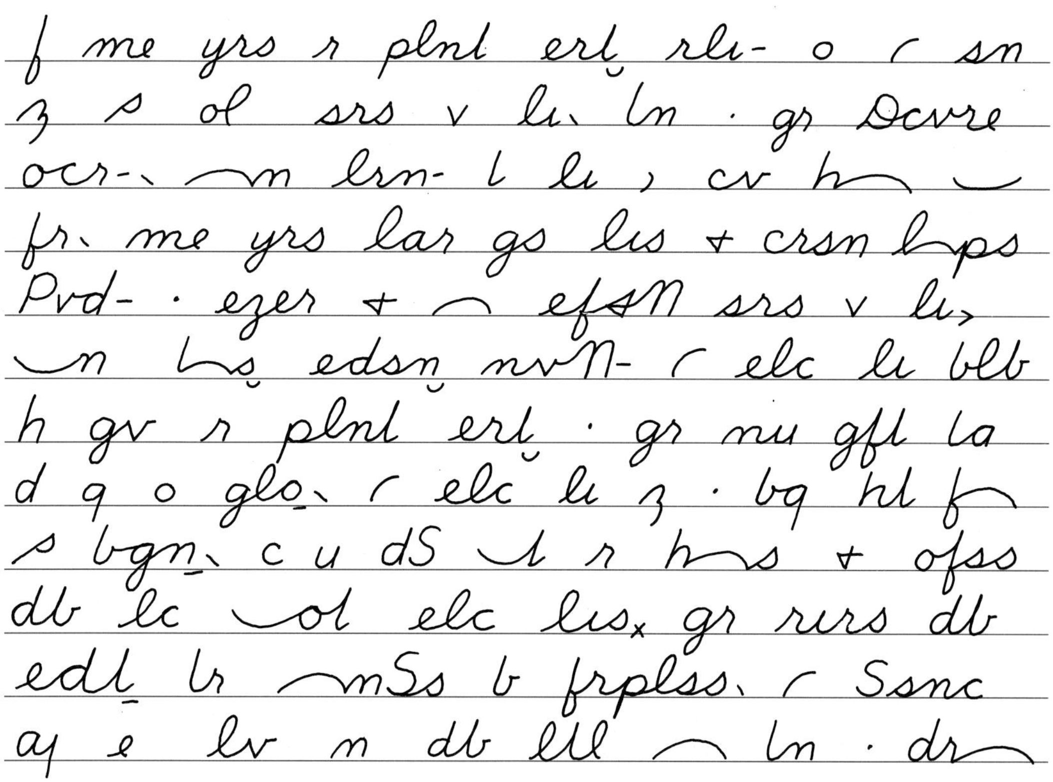

+ ls vgs̆ db . drc lll lon n c
dzrl,

2

d-rs bron r u lc̲
f . nu elnc lprir.
ev . nu -dl e cl c
Ssnc, s . nu lp v
elnc mre lprir
-C l Cry u ofs
rln, ls gr lll -sn
dz bq jbs, u m- /,
r -sn dz /, u +
u sec c op / ezl,
ho. b prs̲ . fu ces
uc Pds . L n secs
or . nlr rpl n mls,
ur c Svzr, c -sn
dz a c hrd jbs,
dS̲ ls unl z -rl .
ēlnc lprir db .
Mlc, s fr - ln
la, l so u -l e
-n er enc̲ . brsr
dS̲ ho r -sn ops,
er prod l sa la c
brsr z Pds-o ls
elnc unl, ll s
so u -, pa s .
vzl + lri c Ssnc,
e lq u'l lv /, s

3

ddr evns dr grn̆
Avz- -e la h l n
b lC̲ f s ls fl, z
uno dr grn̆ , .
elcl nynr + hd
v nynr̲ dpl hr, h
, lv̲ r scl l jyn
. lcl fr, z VPhl

Svz elnc Pq- f nlr corp, er hpe f dr grn b sre lse h q. h l n b eze l rpls b corps c pa elcl nynrs — ln

ec, dr grn, ofr l ri. a dS, jb. i sug la e pls / n / nynr jrnls + se — l hpns. ul

KEY

WRITING ASSIGNMENT

1. nsr lnaj drvrs c b . gr hdac. ndd s— prNs v cl- / hi a rbre. if ur pa l —C l nsr u lnaj drvrs ll jn lf hlp. jn lf c nsr u lnajr f 10% ls ln ne lry co n lon.
2. hr , gr nz f hd v fl. r hll bnfls no pa z —C z 90% v lol hsp bl. —n c e ar l so u ls plse.
3. all plsehldrs er no ofr / nu dNl cvrj uv b asc f. u z lz u fl l bnfl grl f ls plse.
4. n rsp l / ncrs- nd er opn . sNrl cls dpl l Sv / nlr co. bgn Ja 2 a

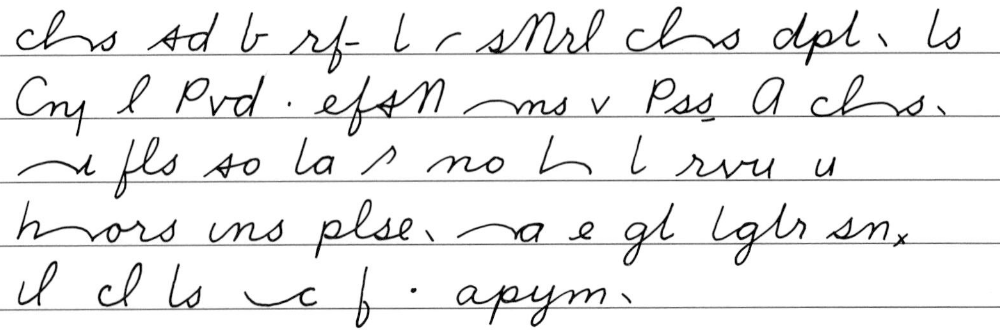

5.

READING AND WRITING EXERCISES

1

Electric Lights

For many years our planet Earth relied on the sun as its only source of light. Then a great discovery occurred.[1] Man learned to light his cave home with fire. Many years later gas lights and kerosene lamps provided an easier[2] and more efficient source of light.

When Thomas Edison invented the electric light bulb, he gave our planet[3] Earth a great new gift that would go on glowing. The electric light was a big hit from its beginning. Can you[4] describe what our homes and offices would be like without electric lights? Great writers would be editing their[5] manuscripts by fireplaces. The supersonic age we live in would be little more than a dream, and Las Vegas[6] would be a dark little town in the desert. (127)

2

Dear Mrs. Brown:

Are you looking for a new electronic typewriter? We have a new model we call the[1] SUPERSONIC. It is a new type of electronic memory typewriter which will change your office routine.[2] This great little machine does big jobs. You name it. Our machine does it.

You and your secretary can operate it[3] easily. How? By pressing a few keys, you can produce a letter in seconds or an entire report in minutes.[4] You are the supervisor. The machine does all the hard jobs. Describing this unit as merely an electronic[5] typewriter would be a mistake. It is far more than that.

To show you what we mean, we are enclosing a brochure[6] describing how our machine operates. We are proud to say that the brochure was produced on this electronic[7] unit.

Let us show you more. Pay us a visit and try the SUPERSONIC. We think you'll love it. Sincerely,[8] (160)

3

Dear Dr. Evans:

Dr. Green advised me that he will not be teaching for us this fall. As you know, Dr. Green[1] is an electrical engineer and head of the engineering department here. He is leaving our school to[2] join a local firm. As vice president, he will supervise electronic programming for the entire corporation.[3]

We are happy for Dr. Green, but sorry to see him go. He will not be easy to replace, but[4] corporations can pay electrical engineers more than we can.

Dr. Green is offering to write an ad[5] describing his job. I suggest that we place it in the engineering journals and see what happens. Yours truly,[6] (120)

UNIT 16 Summarizing and Synthesizing Your Notes

Summarizing and synthesizing involve reducing a large amount of material to its essential points and then combining these points into an integrated presentation. Making notes as you read requires careful reading of the material and eliminating all unnecessary words or unimportant information.

An editor goes through the copy in a newspaper, magazine, or book before it goes to press. Whatever is unimportant to the central thought is struck out by drawing a line through it. This practice is called *blue-penciling* or *editing* and is a useful skill for you to learn and practice.

You will have many occasions to express yourself briefly and succinctly. If you were preparing a speech, for instance, you would go through your first drafts and blue-pencil the speech into a clear and concise document. In school, you will apply the blue-penciling technique when taking notes, outlining, and writing reports. You may also find the skill useful when writing reviews of books, taking minutes of meetings, or completing other similar activities.

SPEEDWRITING PRINCIPLES

1. Write *w* for the word ending *ward.*

backward, b-k-ward	*bcw*	downward, d-ow-n-ward	*donw*
forward, for-ward	*fw*	toward, to-ward	*tw*
rewarding, re-ward-ing	*rw_*	awards, a-ward-s	*aws*

2. Write *h* for the word ending *hood.*

boyhood, b-oi-hood	byh	neighborhood, n-b-r-hood	nbrh
girlhood, guh-r-l-hood	grlh	likelihood, l-k-ly-hood	lclh
childhood, chay-l-d-hood	Cldh	parenthood, p-r-nt-hood	prNh

ABBREVIATIONS

avenue	ave	hour	hr
boulevard	blvd	record	rec
day	d	example, executive	ex
month	~o		

BRIEF FORMS

appreciate	ap	distribute	D
please, up	p	present	P
specific, specify	sp	correspond, correspondence	cor

BRIEF FORM AND ABBREVIATED WORD DEVELOPMENT

upon	po	pleasing	p_
today	td	specifically	spl
daily	dl	monthly	~ol

PHRASES

I would	id	you can be	ucb
I would appreciate	idap	you would like	udlc
I would be	idb	and the	+/
we should	e⁴d	at the	/
we will	el	that we	lae
we would appreciate	edap		

VOCABULARY STUDY

likelihood *lclh* — The probability that something will happen.

specify *sp* — To state explicitly.

company records *co recs* — Items kept on file (letters, reports, contracts, receipts, and so on).

SPELLING STUDY

Learn to Spell Correctly. Correct spelling is extremely important. To build spelling skills, learn to rely upon the dictionary. Look up any word you are not sure about. Read the definition and the correct spelling for that particular usage.

Some words are so commonly misspelled that it is difficult to detect an error in them. As your spelling skill grows, you will learn to identify these problem words. This text will highlight some of these problem words in special study sections.

COMMONLY MISSPELLED WORDS

The following words have similar sounds but totally different meanings, depending upon how they are spelled and used. Notice how their meanings differ in each of the sentences below.

their *lr* — Shows possessive for more than one:

□ Please tell the *Smiths* that *their* payment is overdue.

there *lr* — Used to designate a place:

□ We will be *there* on Friday.

there *lr* — Used in place of the subject:

□ *There* will be six vice presidents at the meeting.

PRINCIPLES SUMMARY

1. Write *w* for the word ending *ward*: backward, b-k-ward *bcw*.

2. Write *h* for the word ending *hood*: boyhood, b-oi-hood *byh*.

WORD DEVELOPMENT

Write the following related words in *Speedwriting* in your notebook.

present *p*	-ing	-ed	-s
award *aw*	-s	-ed	-ing
reward *rw*	-s	-ing	-ed
girl *grl*	-s	-ish	-hood
boy *by*	-s	-ish	-hood

WORD CONSTRUCTION

Practice writing these words in *Speedwriting* in your notebook.

upward, up-ward

inward, in-ward

forwarding, for-ward-ing

hours, h-r-s

hourly, h-r-ly

outward, ow-t-ward

awkward, aw-k-ward

sideward, s-d-ward

livelihood, l-v-ly-hood

brotherhood, b-r-ith-r-hood

WRITING ASSIGNMENT

Write the following sentences in *Speedwriting*.

1. The doctor gave him a good report and sent him home.
2. He wants to go away for a short time.
3. We had a delay in the direct flight from Denver to San Francisco.
4. I am planning to charge more than he charges.
5. He is now senior vice president of the bank.

READING AND WRITING EXERCISES

1

Westward Ho!

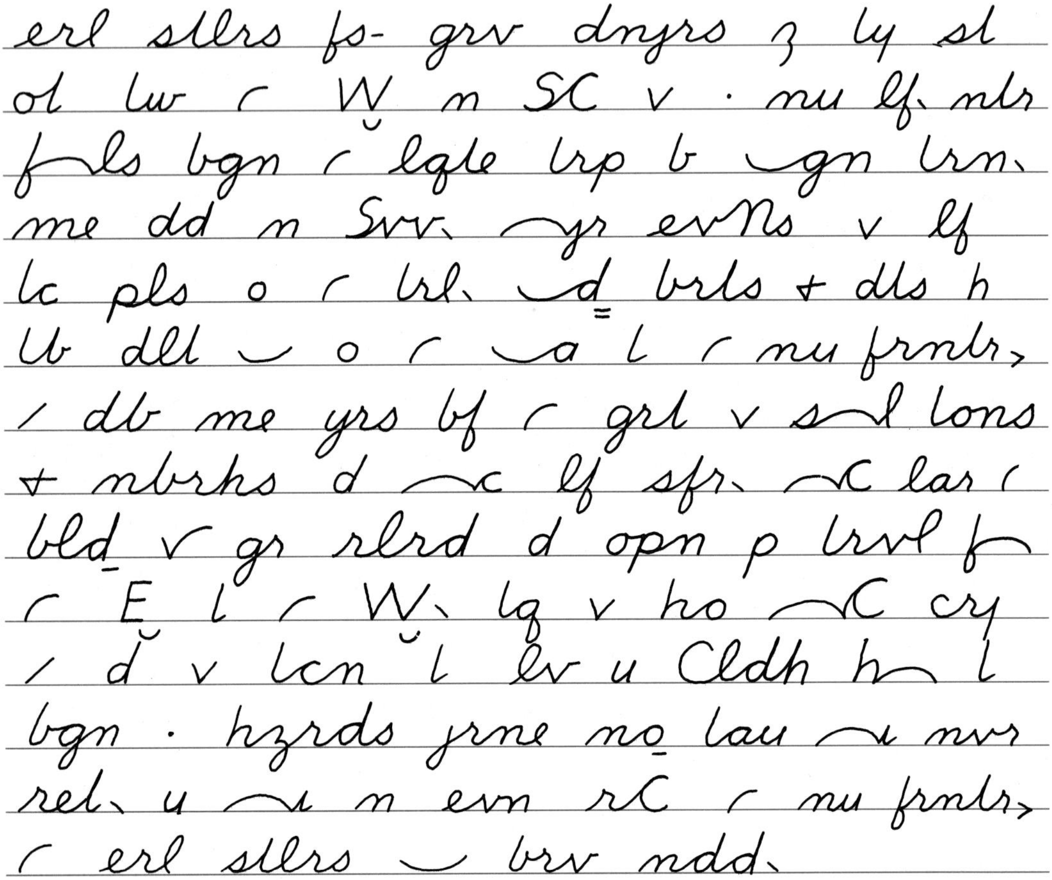

2

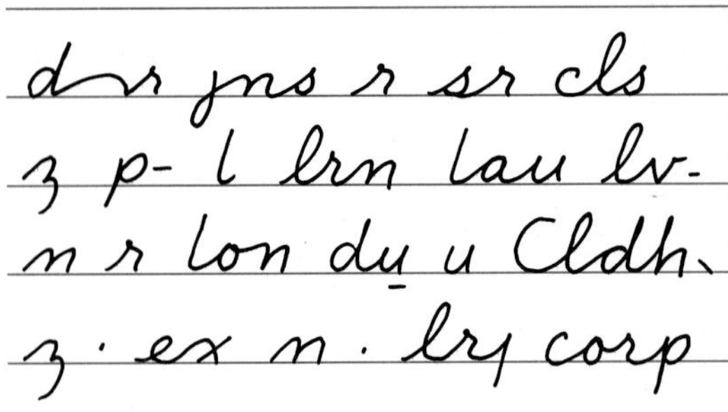

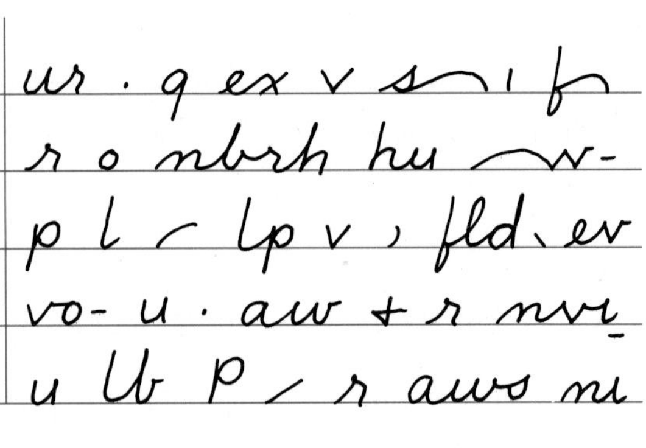

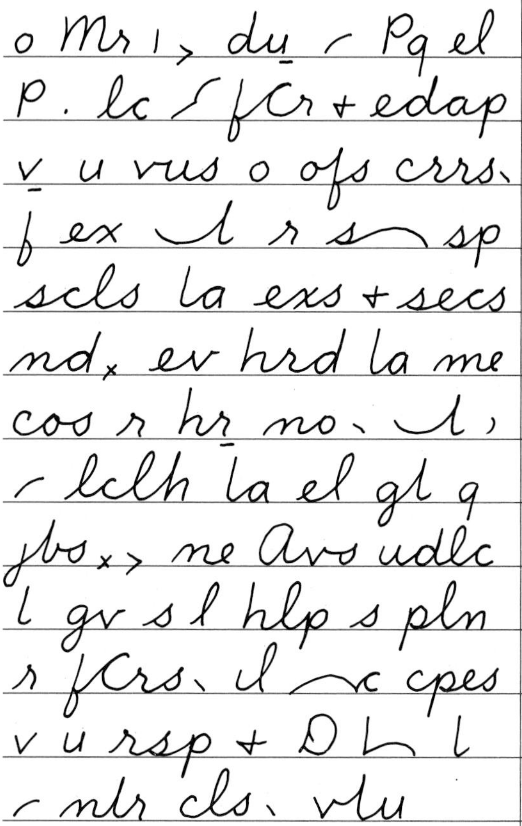

3

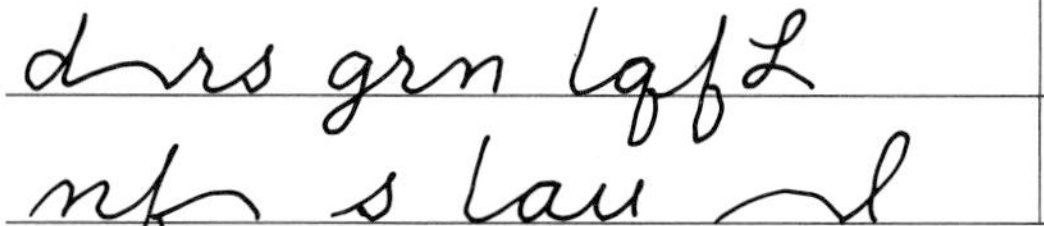

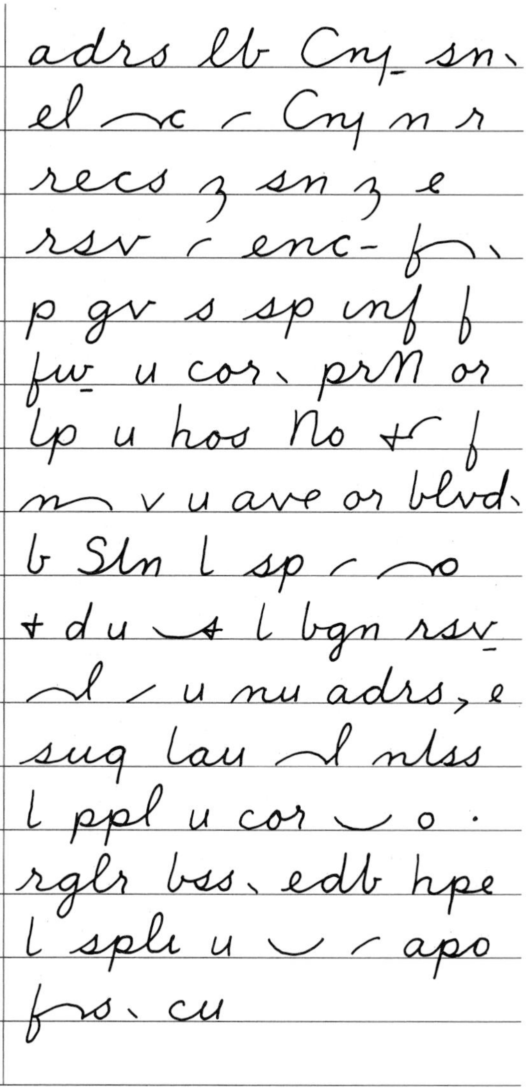

KEY

WRITING ASSIGNMENT

1. 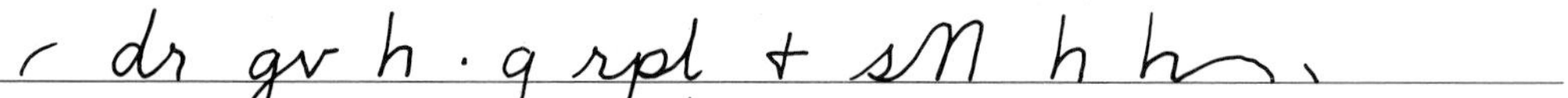

2. 

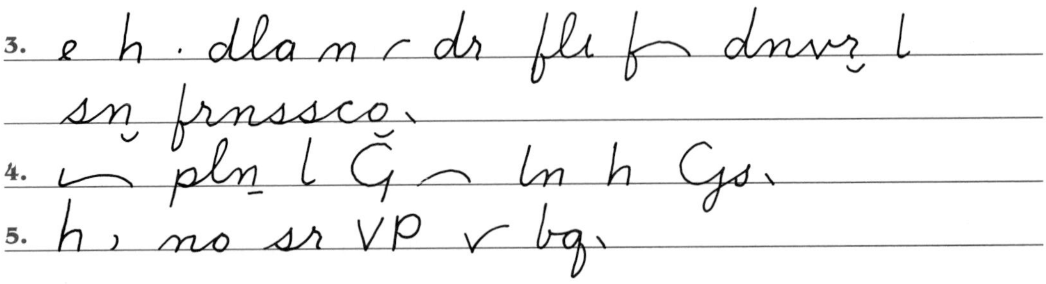

READING AND WRITING EXERCISES

1

Westward Ho!

Early settlers faced grave dangers as they set out toward the West in search of a new life. Entire families began[1] the lengthy trip by wagon train. Many did not survive. Major events of life took place on the trail. Weddings, births,[2] and deaths had to be dealt with on the way to the new frontier.

It would be many years before the growth of small towns[3] and neighborhoods would make life safer. Much later, the building of the great railroad would open up travel from the[4] East to the West. Think of how much courage it would have taken to leave your childhood home to begin a hazardous[5] journey knowing that you might never return. You might not even reach the new frontier.

The early settlers were brave[6] indeed. (121)

2

Dear Mr. Jones:

Our senior class was pleased to learn that you lived in our town during your childhood. As an executive[1] in a large corporation, you are a good example of someone from our own neighborhood who moved up to[2] the top of his field. We have voted you an award and are inviting you to be present at our awards night[3] on March 1.

During the program, we will present a look at the future, and we would appreciate having your[4] views on office careers. For example, what are some specific skills that executives and secretaries need?[5] We have heard that many companies are hiring now. What is the likelihood that we will get good jobs?

Any advice[6] you would like to give us will help us plan our futures. I will make copies of your response and distribute them[7] to the entire class. Very truly yours, (148)

3

Dear Mrs. Green:

Thank you for your letter informing us that your mailing address will be changing soon. We will make[1] the change in our records as soon as we receive the enclosed form. Please give us specific information for[2] forwarding your correspondence. Print or type your house number and the full name of your avenue or boulevard. Be[3] certain to specify the month and day you wish to begin receiving mail at your new address.

We suggest that[4] you mail notices to people you correspond with on a regular basis. We would be happy to supply[5] you with the appropriate forms. Cordially yours, (109)

UNIT 17

More Summarizing and Synthesizing

Imagine that you have spent Saturday afternoon at the library reading an outside assignment. You will need to summarize and synthesize the material as you take notes. After completing your notetaking activities, you can even further summarize the presentation of your notes by following these steps.

1. Give your presentation or report a title.
2. Skim and edit your notes.
3. Blue-pencil any unnecessary words or details.
4. Estimate the length of your synthesized report or presentation.
5. Use your judgment in deleting or expanding the contents, based upon the requirements of the assignment.
6. Make a rough draft of your edited notes.
7. Include a final section entitled "Summary" or "Conclusions," if appropriate.
8. Polish the rough draft of your presentation so that it reads easily and is technically correct.

Summaries of your notes are also useful when doing oral reports or making speeches. First read your finalized report or speech and then reduce the contents to a list of brief memory joggers written plainly on index cards.

Making summary notes while you are reviewing your notebook notes for a test will help reinforce the contents. Reviewing with a pen poised to write will help keep you actively involved in the review process. Summarizing and synthesizing your original notes will help both your understanding and recall for tests.

SPEEDWRITING PRINCIPLES

1. Write j for the word ending *tion* (pronounced *shun, zhun,* or *chun:* sion, cian, shion, cean, cion) or for a vowel + *tion* (a-tion, e-tion, i-tion or ish-un, o-tion, u-tion).

vacation, v-k-tion vcj
position, p-z-tion pzj
nation, n-tion nj
supervision, super-v-sion Svj
physician, f-z-cian fzj
ocean, o-cean oj
fashion, f-shion fj
session, s-sion sj

These additional constructed words and brief form derivatives will appear in future Reading and Writing Exercises.

application, a-p-l-k-tion aplcj
addition, a-d-tion adj
decision, d-s-sion dsj
solution, s-l-tion slj
national, n-tion-l njl
situation, situate-tion sitj
operation, operate-tion opj
suggestion, suggest-tion sugj
distribution, distribute-tion Dj

PHRASES

I believe iblv
you do udu
you should usd
to keep lcp
could be cdb
for you fu
for your fu
in the n
of you vu
of your vu
will you lu
will your lu

COMMONLY MISSPELLED WORDS

here  To designate a place:

□ Someone will be *here* at noon.

hear  To perceive a sound:

□ If you *hear* the telephone, please answer it.

VOCABULARY STUDY

marketing division 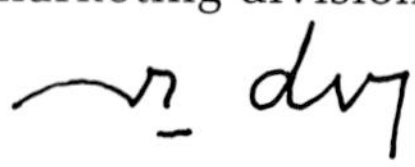 Those departments of a business concerned with the sales, promotion, and distribution of a product.

PRINCIPLES SUMMARY

1. Write  for the word ending *tion* or for a vowel + *tion*: vacation, v-k-tion 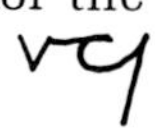 .

WORD DEVELOPMENT

Write the following related words in *Speedwriting* in your notebook.

mention 	-ed	-s	-ing
portion 	-s	-ed	pro-
position 	-ed	-s	-ing
fashion 	-s	-ed	-ing
division 	-s	-al	

WORD CONSTRUCTION

Practice writing these words in *Speedwriting* in your notebook.

locations, l-k-tion-s

protection, pro-t-k-tion

description, d-scrip-tion

production, pro-d-k-tion

selection, s-l-k-tion

option, o-p-tion

provisions, pro-v-sion-s

edition, e-d-tion

recommendations, r-k-mend-tion-s

professional, pro-f-sion-l

WRITING ASSIGNMENT

Write the following sentences in *Speedwriting.*

1. Attached is a letter from Bill Smith asking to reapply for a loan. Can we reassess his credit and arrange a loan for the full amount?
2. This letter is to inform you that your payment was due on the 30th. If there is some reason why you cannot pay the total amount, let us know. We will determine a new minimum payment based on the amount you can pay.
3. We generally mail our billings on the 15th. If you return your payment within one week, you will be credited with a savings. Your savings will amount to 2 percent of the total bill.
4. Our bank will grant the second mortgage that you applied for. We will certainly try to finalize the loan and have the money ready for you between the dates of August 30 and September 6. In the meantime, someone from our firm will visit the property to make an assessment of the current value.
5. From this point on, your charges will be processed by a new manager assigned to give you the personal attention that you need. If you wish to discuss a billing procedure, you may call that person directly. He or she will respond without delay.

READING AND WRITING EXERCISES

1

Anticipating Change

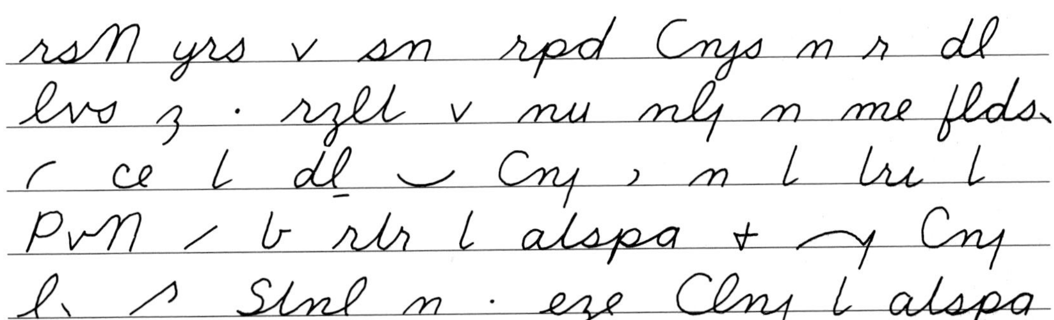

Cnj b / dz sn lb · njr lsc f
r jnrj + l la cn b ignr-, no
la Pgrs, b̲ nd o me frNs r
cNre sns lc · snlr pls n uC
l lv. ec evn se r lcl sujs n rlj
l c lol Cn v evNs hpn̲ lruol
r cNre. c snl Psn l lc S
brdr cAus bf nc̲ dsjs la nu b
srlsi-, ne slj, ol z 9 z c rzlls
/ aCvs.

2

ds sl lgfL v
aplcj. S P L ev
no opn̲ w dpl v
bj dzn. n fw̲ u
L l r nr̲ dvj uc
sugj la c njr cor
drl u u, er Pds̲.
nu fj ln uC lb
rde f Dj bln Jl 15
+ Jl 30. e na dsd

l nr lz ls o.
nyl bss. if so / lb
nes l A n Psnl.
u ejcj + lrn̲ d s
lb apo f sC. pzj>
if udu n hr f c
njr un. fu ds
Ph usd gv h. cl.
w nnl llb hpe
lcp. cpe vu L n r
recs. if r suj dz

Cny el ll uno. cu

3

dr + mrs gra
rmbr mn (2
vu hp-l nyy (vc
vu drs abrd.
oj lnr. ys af ys u
M- lq b ddN. cd
(Pbl v b me.x>
if u asr, ys ev.
slj fu. r s l sl o
(rn v Ma 10 l
7 dfrN pls o (
allNc oj. l.
vc la lb! if uv h
.rlys r bq f 3
yrs or ul rsv.
rds- ra. n adj
sr slzns a pp
n. cr pln lo
ol pams, ec
ac aplcys no lar
ln Ap, so p dN
dla. 's. bo u cN
afd l M. cu

KEY

WRITING ASSIGNMENT

1. alC-, . L f bl s l asc l rapl
f. ln. c e rass, cr + ar. ln f
f al.x
2. ls L, l nf u lau pam z du o (
30l. if lr, s rzn y u cn pa (
lol al ll s no. el dl. nu mm

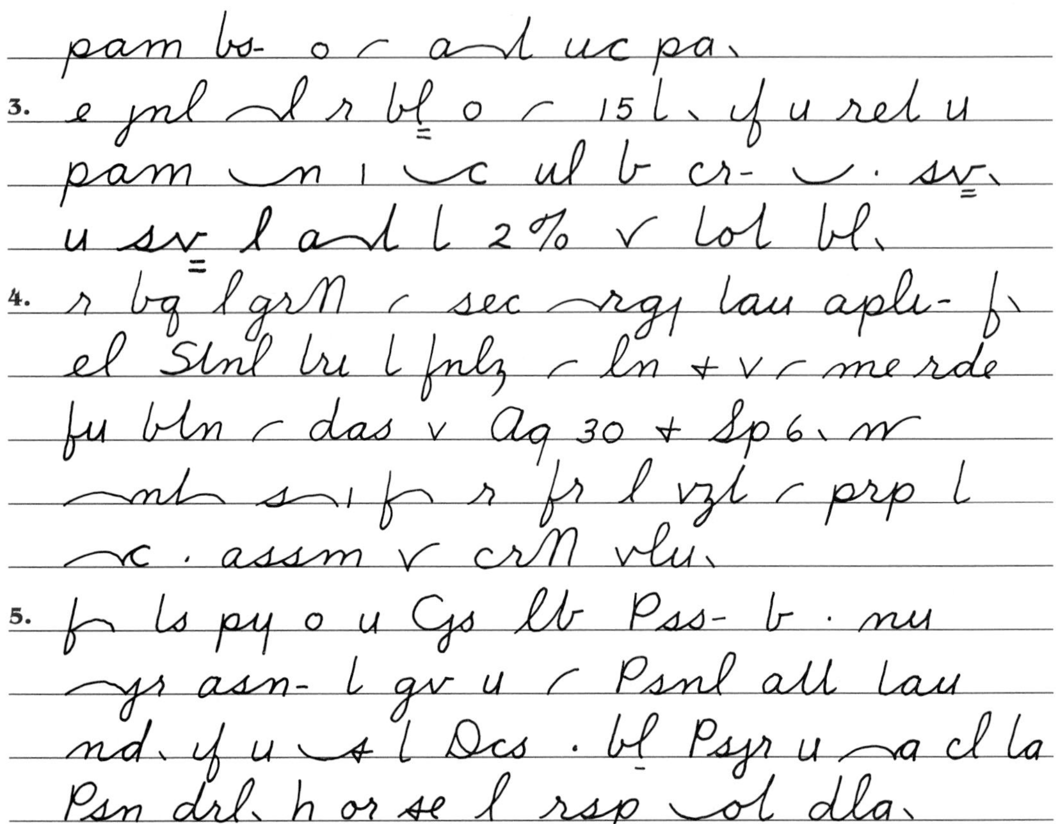

READING AND WRITING EXERCISES

1

Anticipating Change

Recent years have seen rapid changes in our daily lives as a result of new knowledge in many fields. The key[1] to dealing with change is not to try to prevent it but rather to anticipate and manage change well. It is[2] certainly not an easy challenge to anticipate change, but it does seem to be a major task for our[3] generation and one that cannot be ignored.

Now that progress is being made on many fronts, our country seems like[4] a smaller place in which to live. We can even see our local situations in relation to the total[5] chain of events happening throughout our country. The smart person will look at the broader issues before making[6] decisions that might be shortsighted. Any solution is only as good as the results it achieves.[7] (140)

2

Dear Ms. Smith:

Thank you for your letter of application. At the present time we have no openings in the[1] department of fashion design. I am forwarding your letter to our marketing division with the suggestion[2] that the manager correspond directly with you.

We are producing a new fashion line which will be ready[3] for distribution between July 15 and July 30. We may decide to market these items on a[4] national basis. If so, it will be necessary to add more personnel. Your education and training[5] would seem to be appropriate for such a position.

If you do not hear from the manager within a few[6] days, perhaps you should give him a call. In the meantime, I will be happy to keep a copy of your letter[7] in our records. If our situation does change, we will let you know. Cordially yours, (155)

3

Dear Mr. and Mrs. Gray:

Remember when the two of you hoped to enjoy the vacation of your dreams aboard[1] an ocean liner? Year after year you wanted to go, but didn't. Could the problem have been money?

If your[2] answer is yes, we have a solution for you. Our ship will sail on the morning of May 10 to seven different[3] ports on the Atlantic Ocean. What a vacation that will be! If you have had a relationship with our bank[4] for three years or more, you will receive a reduced rate. In addition, senior citizens may participate in[5] a credit plan with low monthly payments.

We can accept applications no later than April 1, so please don't[6] delay. It's a boat you can't afford to miss. Cordially yours, (131)

UNIT 18

Proper Names and Abbreviations

It is possible to apply *Speedwriting* principles to the writing of names. If the name is easy to write in *Speedwriting* and will stand out in your notes, by all means use *Speedwriting* shortcuts. However, if a name or term is unusual because of its unique spelling, foreign derivation, etc., write it in full. For instance, an unusual word or technical term that might be a puzzle later on should be verified for correct spelling and then written out in full, such as the *Cheniere-Smythe* case. Specialized fields such as law and medicine use unusual words, names, or technical terms that should be written in full if there is any doubt about the spelling.

There will be occasions in notetaking when a name or expression occurs again and again. Then it is helpful to use commonly accepted abbreviations or to devise special abbreviations using longhand initials or a combination of *Speedwriting* and longhand initials. Here are just a few examples:

JFK = John Fitzgerald Kennedy
USAF = United States Air Force
GNP = gross national product
CPU = central processing unit

You may want to create your own appropriate abbreviations. It is a good idea to make a key for your abbreviations to avoid possible confusion. Some shortcuts of this type will be put only into your short-term memory, used as long as needed, and then discarded. Other shortcuts you will use repeatedly. For instance, in a later lesson you will learn how to use the two-letter state abbreviations to write the names of all the states.

SPEEDWRITING PRINCIPLES

1. Write amounts of money in the following way:

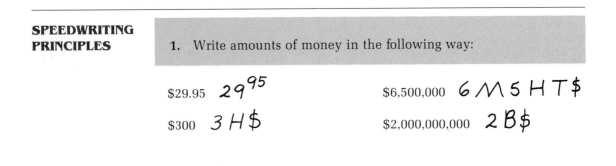

\$29.95	29^{95}	\$6,500,000	6M5HT\$
\$300	3H\$	\$2,000,000,000	2B\$

ABBREVIATIONS

cent, cents	¢	hundred	H
dollar, dollars	$	thousand	T
pound	lb	million	M
inch	in	billion	B
ounce	oz		

BRIEF FORMS

about	ab	over	O
has	hs	under	U
order	od	customer	K
include	I		

BRIEF FORM AND ABBREVIATED WORD DEVELOPMENT

customers	Ks	orders	ods
overall	Oa	holidays	hlds
included	I-	inclusion	Ij

PHRASES

we do	edu	have been	vb
we feel	efl	of our	vr
you need	und	to you	lu
to make	Lmc	to your	lu

COMMONLY MISSPELLED WORDS

cancellation	cslj
recommend	rcm

VOCABULARY STUDY

word processing unit
wd Pss unl

Computerized typewriting equipment having many automatic features, including text editing and high-speed printing.

PRINCIPLES SUMMARY

1. Amounts of money.

WORD DEVELOPMENT

Write the following related words in *Speedwriting* in your notebook.

over O	-all	more-	-ly
inch in	-es	-ing	-ed
order od	-ly	-ing	re-
day d	-s	to-	holi-
include 	-s	-ing	-d

---

WORD CONSTRUCTION

Practice writing these words in *Speedwriting* in your notebook.

reordering, re-order-ing

overdue, over-d-u

overlooked, over-l-k-duh

overhead, over-h-d

overtime, over-t-m

hasn't, has-nt

undertake, under-t-k

underwrite, under-r-ite

underscore, under-s-k-r

underline, under-l-n

WRITING ASSIGNMENT

Write the following sentences in *Speedwriting*.

1. I would appreciate it if you would specify the items you wish to see.
2. Please let me know if you can be present at the meeting.
3. We plan to distribute those machines to specific dealers in this town.
4. Let me know when my time is up.
5. Who will present the program for us?

READING AND WRITING EXERCISES

1

Personal Savings

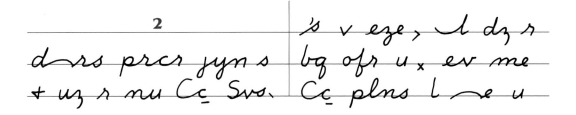

sv̲ me ⁀a n b eze b lr r ‿as f evn . s‿l sv̳ pln l gro. evn ⁀drl plns rlnl yld . ra v 6% or ⁀. lz plns r nyll nsr- + O · fu yrs (ern̳ c a‿l l Ts v $, ‿ . pln la pas 7% . sv̳ v 5T$ d gro l ⁀ ln 7T$ n 5 yrs. Psnl sv̳ v . lry br̲ o (spli v me nyll. sv̳ r uz- b bqs z . rsrs f lns. / ⁀a b hrd l blv lau 5T$ hs ne̲ l du ‿ (nyl dl + pr⁀ ra b (ac‿ly v me n sv̳ plns , . ‿lr U Dq b nyl ldrs n alz̲ crN nyl ‿rl + mlre plses.

2

drs prcr jyns s + uz r nu Cç Svs. 's v eze, ‿l dz r bq ofr u. ev me Cç plns l‿e u

nds. f ex if u cp
. mm v 2H$ w
bq lr lb no Svs
G. if u dN ⌣
lcp . mm a–l uc
pa . –ol fe v 4^{50}.
u –a Pfr lpa f eC
Cc u ri / 10¢ P Cc,
lr , no h–l o /
No v Ccs u –a
ri. if u od no ul
rsv 2 H Ccs fre
v G. drp b u lcl
brnC ofs o srln
ave + ll s ll u –
ab r Cc + sv plns.
r bq Svss r dzn-
hc efsN me –ym
eze f r Ks. cu

3

d–rs crlsn e rgrl
l nf– u la / blu
fbrc u od- , n –d
n . 54= in ⌣dl. cd
u uz / n . 45= in
⌣dl. Alo edu n
crNl v / 45= in fbrc
n r sp edb hpe l
od / fu. sC ods
lc ab 2 l 3 ⌣cs l
arv, / r–m ch–s
u sp- ⌣ s- ld. /
lol a–l vu od ,
79^{96}. v crs la a–l
dz n –l / prs √ blu
fbrc or s s Gs. /
s ⌣a √ 45= in
fbrc , 7 lbs 6 ozs,
e lc fw l Sv u w
fCr. ul

KEY

WRITING ASSIGNMENT

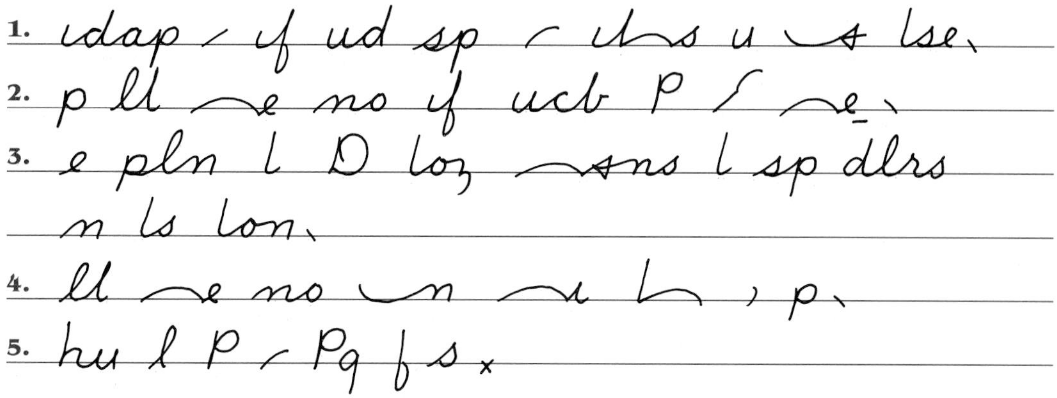

READING AND WRITING EXERCISES

1

Personal Savings

Saving money may not be easy, but there are ways for even a small savings plan to grow. Even moderate[1] plans routinely yield a rate of 6 percent or more. These plans are nationally insured, and over a few years[2] the earnings can amount to thousands of dollars.

With a plan that pays 7 percent, a savings of $5,000[3] would grow to more than $7,000 in five years. Personal savings have a large bearing on the supply[4] of money nationally. Savings are used by banks as a resource for loans. It may be hard to believe that[5] your $5,000 has anything to do with the national debt and the prime rate, but the accumulation[6] of money in savings plans is a matter under discussion by national leaders in analyzing[7] current national worth and monetary policies. (151)

2

Dear Mrs. Parker:

Join us and use our new checking service. It's very easy.

What does our bank offer you? We[1] have many checking plans to meet your needs. For example, if you keep a minimum of $200 in[2] the bank, there will be no service charge. If you don't wish to keep a minimum amount, you can pay a monthly fee[3] of $4.50. You may prefer to pay for each check you write at 10¢ per check.

There is no limit[4] on the number of checks you may write. If you order now, you will receive 200 checks free of charge. Drop by[5] your local branch office on Shoreline Avenue and let us tell you more about our checking and savings plans. Our[6] banking services are designed to make efficient money management easy for our customers. Cordially[7] yours, (141)

3

Dear Mrs. Carlson:

We regret to inform you that the blue fabric you ordered is not made in a 54-inch[1] width. Could you use it in a 45-inch width? Although we do not currently have the 45-inch fabric[2] in our shop, we would be happy to order it for you. Such orders take about two to three weeks to arrive.[3]

The remaining items you specified were shipped today. The total amount of your order is[4] $79.96. Of course, that amount does not include the price of the blue fabric or its shipping[5] charges. The shipping weight of the 45-inch fabric is 7 pounds 6 ounces.

We look forward to serving[6] you in the future. Yours truly, (125)

UNIT

19

Memory

Memory is extremely important. Without it, you would have to relearn everything every day. There are two types of memory—*short-term* and *long-term*. Short-term memory is used when you need to remember something for only a short time, like an item you need to buy; however, there is usually no need to store this information for future recall after the purchase has been made.

Long-term memory is used when you need to remember information for a longer period of time, such as your telephone number or social security number. Information of this type must be repeated and reviewed until it is stored in your long-term memory bank.

Good memory skills can be very important to you throughout life—remembering directions, people's names when you are introduced, and important numbers and dates. In school, developing good memory skills is essential for remembering such things as facts in social studies courses, correct spellings of words, mathematical equations, genders in foreign languages, science formulas, or lines of poetry.

To develop better memory skills, it is important to:

1. Exercise your memory; the more you memorize, the easier the process becomes.

2. Work on memorization only when you are alert and well rested.

3. Understand what you are memorizing. Read material carefully and take notes on important points and on anything you do not understand. Find the answers to your questions and summarize the data in your notes. Work at memorizing when you study your notes later, not while you are taking them.

SPEEDWRITING PRINCIPLES

1. Write *a* for the initial and final sound of *aw*.

law, l-aw *la* saw, s-aw *sa*

audit, aw-d-t adl	authorized, aw-ith-r-z-duh alrz-
auto, aw-t-o alo	drawings, d-r-aw-ings dra=

2. Write q for the sound of *kw* (qu).

quite, q-ite qi	equipment, e-q-p-ment eqpm
quickly, q-k-ly qcl	adequate, ad-q-t aql
quote, q-ote qo	frequent, f-r-q-nt frqN

PHRASES

we appreciate eap	to use luz
we had eh	have had vh
we were e	on the o
you were u	

COMMONLY MISSPELLED WORDS

personnel Psnl Employees:

□ We will employ more *personnel* in the new office.

personal Psnl Private:

□ Jane is away on *personal* business today.

VOCABULARY STUDY

resumé rzma A document summarizing a job applicant's education, skills, and employment history.

authorized alrz- Having the right to make decisions and take specific action.

PRINCIPLES SUMMARY

1. Write *a* for the sound of *aw*: saw, s-aw *sa*.
2. Write *q* for the sound of *kw*: quite, q-ite *qi*.

WORD DEVELOPMENT

Write the following related words in *Speedwriting* in your notebook.

equal *eql*	-ly	-s	-ing
equip *eqp*	-ped	-s	-ment
authorize *alrz*	-d	-s	-ing
draw *dra*	-s	-ing	with-
acquaint *aqN*	-s	-ed	-ing

WORD CONSTRUCTION

Practice writing these words in *Speedwriting* in your notebook.

auditing, aw-d-t-ing

quicker, q-k-r

automatic, aw-t-m-t-k

auditor, aw-d-t-r

authors, aw-ith-r-s

authorization, aw-ith-r-z-tion

quit, q-t

quoted, q-ote-ed

adequately, ad-q-t-ly

frequently, f-r-q-nt-ly

WRITING ASSIGNMENT

Write the following sentences in *Speedwriting*.

1. Please give me the name of your avenue or boulevard for our records.
2. During this month, we are asking each person to record the hour that he or she arrives each day.
3. Mr. Snow is an executive with our firm.
4. I will show you an example of the correspondence we are looking for.
5. How often do you correspond with him?

READING AND WRITING EXERCISES

1

The Oval Office

z (Cf ofsr v · ld Spor (P
v US , C- ⌣ · hve brdn v
ldr4. (P apys cbnt mbrs hu
Pvd avs re (fly v plses f
nyl + fn afrs. lz plses rny f
prpry v byl l nfsm v las.
ld r las l-d ne P l 2 f lrs
n ofs. (ol P l Sv 3 f lrs
z frgln rzvlt hu di- (bgn v
; 4l lr. alo ev nvr h · m
Sv n ovl ofs me pltcl obzrvrs
fl la sC · evN , n fr a-a. rsN
yrs v sn ⌢ m apy- l hi ofss
n cbnt pzys + spr crt.

2

dr lsn r ofs
bld , qi old. rsNl
e lld la r li ,
n aql l e crN
las. er fs- ⌣ · dsp.
c e slv (Pbl b
eqp a dscs ⌣ elc

lrps or sd e cl n
. co sC z us l rpls
r Ohd lis ⌣ nu
unls x, r elcl nynr
hs sd la nu Ohd
lis d Pvd blr l̲, h
Aso A- la c lol a⌒l
f sC . PCs cd rn ab
2T$ or ⌒, er hzlN
l alo c prs lq O
2T$ bcz me vr ppl
v suq- la ly db eqll
hpe ⌣ elc lrps, d
u b l̲ l gv s u suggs
o ho l slv r Pblms x
idap u rsp z qcl z
uc gv / l s, cu

3

dK cd u fnl uz .
sec cr x if so ev c
alo fu, ls ⌒dl ,
gr f frqN lrps ab
lon b 's eqll q f
h⌒a drv̲, elr ⌣a
u pln luz / ls alo
l sv me o gsln, /
gls blr ⌒ly ln ne
nu ⌒dl crNl σ
⌒r, du̲ c ⌒o v
Fb er alrz-l sl ls
cr / . v lo prs, blv
/ or n la prs l cl
u Cys v eqpm, ⌒N
u drv b r sor⌒ +
se ls gr vlu x, l ur
hr sn p f r fre drq̲,
. lvl nu cr lb aw-
l . lce rzdN vr
sle, la ⌣nr cdb
u, ul

KEY

WRITING ASSIGNMENT

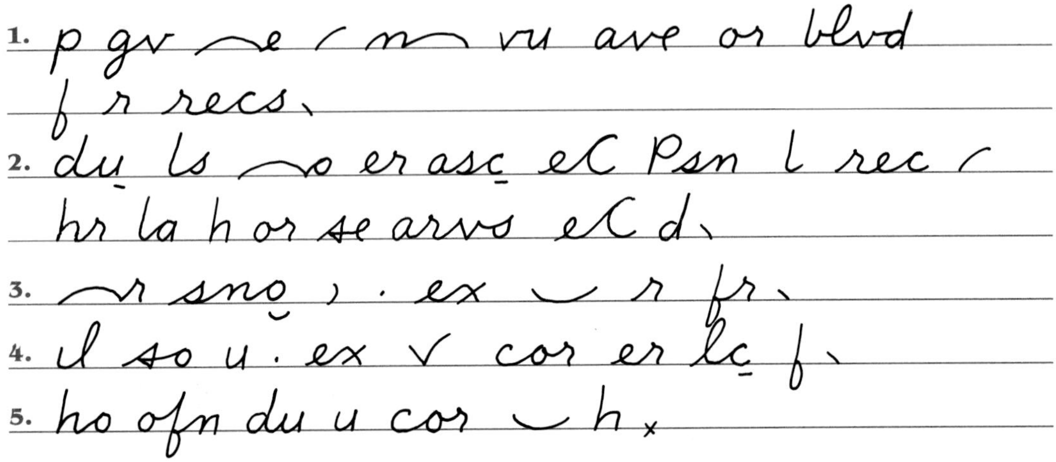

READING AND WRITING EXERCISES

1

The Oval Office

As the chief officer of a leading superpower, the President of the U.S. is charged with a heavy[1] burden of leadership. The President appoints Cabinet members who provide advice regarding the[2] formulation of policies for national and foreign affairs. These policies range from preparation of the[3] budget to enforcement of laws.

Today our laws limit any President to two full terms in office. The only[4] President to serve three full terms was Franklin Roosevelt, who died at the beginning of his fourth term. Although we have[5] never had a woman serve in the Oval Office, many political observers feel that such an event[6] is not far away. Recent years have seen more women appointed to high offices in Cabinet positions[7] and the Supreme Court. (144)

2

Dear Mr. Wilson:

Our office building is quite old. Recently we were told that our lighting is not adequate[1] to meet current laws. We are faced with a decision. Can we solve the problem by equipping all desks with electric[2] lamps, or should we call in a company such as yours to replace our overhead lights with new units?

Our[3] electrical engineer has said that new overhead lights would provide better lighting. He also added that the[4] total amount for such a purchase could run about $2,000 or more. We are hesitant to allow[5] the price to go over $2,000 because many of our people have suggested that they would be[6] equally happy with electric lamps.

Would you be willing to give us your suggestions on how to solve our problems?[7] I would appreciate your response as quickly as you can give it to us. Cordially yours, (156)

3

Dear Customer:

Could your family use a second car? If so, we have the auto for you. This model is great[1] for frequent trips about town, but it's equally good for highway driving. Either way you plan to use it, this auto[2] will save money on gasoline. It gets better mileage than any new model currently on the market.[3]

During the month of February, we are authorized to sell this car at a very low price. Believe it or[4] not, that price will include your choice of equipment. Won't you drive by our showroom and see this great value?

While you're here,[5] sign up for our free drawing. A lovely new car will be awarded to a lucky resident of our city.[6] That winner could be you. Yours truly, (126)

UNIT 20 Memory Stretching for Notetaking

Some specific suggestions to help improve your memory are presented below.

1. Write down what you are learning. Rewriting it a few times should fix it in your memory.

2. Use an index card to cover material. Move the card up and down a line at a time as you memorize.

3. Repeat a passage aloud, glancing back at it only when necessary. This procedure works particularly well if your mind has a tendency to wander as you study.

4. Try the association method for facts, names, and dates that are difficult for you to remember. Work out some device—the sillier the better—to help you remember.

5. For troublesome spelling words, develop a memory device. As an example, for a difficult word like *thorough*, think of it as tho-**rough,** a *rough* word to spell; and to avoid confusing *thorough* with *through*, remember that *thorough* has two *o's* and two syllables.

6. Try seeing a mental picture or image in your mind's eye as a way of remembering. This process is called *visualizing*. Close your eyes and form a mental picture for each idea you want to remember. If you took some notes in a diagram or chart format, for example, you could practice forming a mental picture of your notes.

7. Remembering numbers requires special attention. Are you able to remember someone's telephone number when taking a message without asking to have it repeated? Although repeating a number is good reinforcement and should be used for verification, concentration and practice are required for remembering numbers. Use number patterns, sequences, or repetition to assist you.

SPEEDWRITING PRINCIPLES

1. Write a capital N for the sound of *end, nd* (pronounced *end*).

friend, f-r-nd	frN	indicate, nd-k-ate	Nca
sending, s-nd-ing	sN̲	found, f-ow-nd	foN
handling, h-nd-l-ing	hNl̲	foundation, f-ow-nd-tion	foNy

ABBREVIATIONS

feet	ft	agriculture	agr
square	sq	economic, economy	eco
yard	yd		

BRIEF FORMS

advantage	avj	business	bs
again, against	ag	several	sv

Write the following additional words.

land, l-nd	lN	find, f-nd	fN
fund, f-nd	fN	window, w-nd-o	⁀No
bonds, b-nd-s	bNs	ground, guh-r-ow-nd	groN
dividends, d-v-d-nd-s	dvdNs	economical, economic-l	ecol

PHRASES

I know	ino	to get	tgt
we are not	ern	to hear	thr
we will be	elb	to send	tsN
you will be	ulb	can be	cb

COMMONLY MISSPELLED WORDS

customer K

occurred ocr-

VOCABULARY STUDY

dividends dvdNs — Profits received from shares of ownership in a corporation.

purchasing department PCs dpl — That department responsible for buying equipment and supplies for the entire company.

PRINCIPLES SUMMARY

1. Write a capital N for the sound of *end, nd*: friend, f-r-nd frN.

WORD DEVELOPMENT

Write the following related words in *Speedwriting* in your notebook.

attend aN	-ed	-s	-ing
indicate Nca	-ing	-s	-d
intend nN	-ed	-ing	-s
sound soN	-ed	-s	-ing
refund rfN	-s	-ed	-ing

WORD CONSTRUCTION

Practice writing these words in *Speedwriting* in your notebook.

kind, k-nd	behind, b-h-nd
depend, d-p-nd	spending, s-p-nd-ing
bound, b-ow-nd	around, a-r-ow-nd
hands, h-nd-s	calendar, k-l-nd-r
friendship, f-r-nd-ship	background, b-k-guh-r-ow-nd

WRITING ASSIGNMENT

Write the following sentences in *Speedwriting*.

1. The enclosed catalog includes over 200 items that your customers may order directly from our national sales office.
2. Please remind customers to write the price of each item under the appropriate order number.
3. We feel that a second report is in order before making further plans for a supermarket for $1,200,000.
4. You may purchase the 20-pound paper for $60.24, and the price includes shipping charges under this agreement.
5. The invoice shows that your price of $4,230.54 includes charges for any shipment over the weight of 2,000 pounds.

READING AND WRITING EXERCISES

1

Friends

. frN n nd , . frN ndd. / ~a b
. old sa_ b / r~ns tru td. frNs
r ppl hu fN c h l hlp u evn
~n c h , hrd l fN. frNs r n
qc l jj. ly r lyl + du n trn
aq u ~n ly no und tr hlp, lq
√ ppl n u lf o h~ uc dpN.
tw 1 q frN , . bls. tw sv sC
frNs , . ~ll la cn b ~C- b
me or gld. . q frN , . rr Psn
tb ap- + nvr tb tcn f grN-. tcp

. frN b . frN. ⌒c . py l eN
. hN ⌣n . frN nds u.

2

d hord ulb p- lhr
la ⌒ ⌒c Pgrs 6
Pfl + ls rpl u ⌣N-.
usd v / b ⌐ ⌐ u
grp ⌒es aq, l qi
agre la esd ⌒c
s⌒ Cnys n r ⌒ym
v cpll. ⌐c loz
dsys esd lc . q lc
f nyl eco. w rd
sv artcls sug la
ls , n . apo ⌐ l
b or sl bNs so lr
db lll Avq l c+
n r dvdNs no,
n jn cd Aso rcm
aq b eN f 2 rzns=
prp vlus r hi +
⌒rgy me , hrd l
obln. cblv esd lc
nl b fr⌒ eN. ⌐
sec v agr hs Ppz-
lgslj ⌣C d P⌐l nu
fr⌒ ors lgl lns /
. %q ra l U ⌐ P
⌒r ra. uvl

3

d frN l so u ho
⌣C eap u bs er
pln . sls evN. du
⌐ ⌒o v Ap el ⌒rc
20% of A crpl. z
r cr crd K ulb
nvr- l Gz ne cN
v crpl u ⌣A. f ex
loz rglrl prs- /

1499 P sq yd lb
ofr- / 1196 P sq
yd. ~l . ecol ~a l
A nu lf lu h~!,
ehp ul lc Avj v
ls gr ofr. elb

hpe lpa u . Psnl
vzl l dl / No v
sq yds ul nd. ls
, r ~a v sa lqf
bo. su

KEY

WRITING ASSIGNMENT

1. / enc- cal ls O 2H ~ lau Ks
~a od drl f~ r nyl sls ofs.
2. p rm Ks l ru / prs v eC ~
U / apo od No.
3. efl la . sec rpl , n od bf
~c frlr plns f . S~r f 1M2HT$.
4. u ~a PCs / 20= lb ppr f 60^{24}
+ / prs ls 4 Gs U ls agrem.
5. / inv sos lau prs v 4230^{54} ls Gs
f ne Am O / ~a v 2T lbs.

READING AND WRITING EXERCISES

1

Friends

A friend in need is a friend indeed. It may be an old saying, but it remains true today. Friends are people who[1] find the time to help you even when the time is hard to find. Friends are not quick to judge. They are loyal and do not[2] turn against you when they know you need their help.

Think of the people in your life on whom you can depend. To have one[3] good friend is a blessing. To have several such friends is a wealth that cannot be matched by money or gold. A good[4] friend is a rare person to be appreciated and never to be taken for granted. To keep a friend, be[5] a friend. Make a point to lend a hand when a friend needs you. (110)

2

Dear Howard:

You will be pleased to hear that I am making progress on the profit and loss report you wanted. You[1] should have it by the time your group meets again.

I quite agree that we should make some changes in our management of[2] capital. To make those decisions, we should take a good look at the national economy. I have read[3] several articles suggesting that this is not an appropriate time to buy or sell bonds, so there would be little[4] advantage to cashing in our dividends now.

In general, I would also recommend against buying land[5] for two reasons—property values are high and mortgage money is hard to obtain. I believe we should look into[6] buying farm land. The Secretary of Agriculture has proposed legislation which would permit new farm[7] owners to get loans at a percentage rate well under the present market rate. Yours very truly, (158)

3

Dear Friend:

To show you how much we appreciate your business, we are planning a sales event. During the month of[1] April, we will mark 20 percent off all carpeting. As our credit card customer, you will be invited[2] to choose any kind of carpet you wish. For example, those regularly priced at $14.99[3] per square yard will be offered at $11.96 per square yard. What an economical way[4] to add new life to your home!

We hope you will take advantage of this great offer. We will be happy to pay you[5] a personal visit to determine the number of square yards you will need. This is our way of saying thank you[6] for your business. Sincerely yours, (126)

UNIT 21

Review and Reinforcement

1. The following word beginnings were presented in Units 15–20:

super S	electr el

2. These word endings were presented:

ward w	hood h
tion ɥ	scribe, script S

3. The following *Speedwriting* words represent all of the principles you studied in Units 15–20:

manuscripts, m-n-script-s ⌒mSs	prescribe, pre-scribe PS
vacation, v-k-tion vcɥ	supermarket, super-market S⌒r
auto, aw-t-o ato	backward, b-k-ward bcw
electrical, electr-k-l elcl	quite, q-ite qi
childhood, chay-l-d-hood Cldh	friend, f-r-nd frN
neighborhood, n-b-r-hood nbrh	electrician, electr-cian elɥ
toward, to-ward tw	law, l-aw la

4. You learned to write money amounts this way:

\$29.95 29^{95}	\$2,000,000 2M\$

$300,000 3HT$

5. What words do these abbreviations represent?

ave	lb	d
B	in	rec
sq	H	agr
⌒o	blvd	T
hr	oz	ft
M	$	eco
ex	¢	yd

6. Write these brief forms in *Speedwriting* in your notebook.

appreciate	present	about
over	advantage	under
correspondence	distribute	please
specify	has	again
order	against	specific
several	up	business
customer	correspond	include

READING AND WRITING EXERCISES

1

The Daily Grind

eC d Ms v ppl aroN (glb
bgn (⌒rn̲ + ofn fnS (evn̲
⌣ . cp v hl cfe, I cb so apl̲
ab . drq Sv- m . hve ⌒q l bgn

(d or Sv- n . dlcl Cna cp af
dnrx> cfe cb lrs- l afrca z erl
z (1300s ⌣r / z uz- z . fd
+ lar ⌒d nl ⌣n. (⌣rd "cfe"
, drv- f⌒ (arbc ⌣rd f ⌣n,
cfe gs lru sv fzs bf / rCs u
lcl S⌒r. ⌒C UN lcs pls bln (
b⌒ cfe , plN- + ⌣n s bru-n
u elc pl. (cfe plN lcs 7 yrs l
⌒lr + gros l ab 6 fl h. (bns
r pc- ⌣n ly r rd + rp. lz bns
r ln Pss- + blN- bf ly r rde
f Dj, cfe , (pr⌒re agrl crp v
sv cNres. (ecos v lz cNres
dpN lryl po r dl cp v cfe. ls
pl vr dl grN cb gi rfrt.

2

drr ⌣lsn enc- , (
bl f rpr u Ulvj sl.
z uc se (Gs lol
59 95. ls prs ls .

30 = d grnle o pls +
Svs. f uv ⌒ Pbls
b Sln l cl r K Svs
dpl ⌣l (rprs r
U ⌣rNe. el vzl u

hm + mc c rprs
/ no adjl G lu,
u sl , n q sp jnl
+ sd Pvd u me
yrs v q Svs b y n
lq ab A . sec sl
lu hm, ev sv
mdls C u cd
ezl mv f m l
m . f u b no el
l . fn rl crl fre
v G u PCs.
ehp ul lc Avj vr
ofr. su

3

d jsn z i z Ppr c
Pq f r me i Dcvr-
la ev sv ls v
nu bs l cvr. no
m afrd la r me
l rn O c h ev
alo-. c u me
me n od lq O
sm v lz ls, Ph
sm v h cb hNl-
/ . fCr me, aso
du u pln l P u fN
o mr Sva, f so p
ll me no ho mC
h ul nd. r bld
jr hs lcn . pzl
aq PCs Sln cNs v
elcl eqpm. h
alspas lc ab 10
mls l Dcs sp
exs, w asc- eC
dpl jr lb P f ls
me. so fr w rsv-
i csl. ms lsn
cl- l sa la se lb
o vq la c + hs
asc- dr evns l lc
hr pls. ul

KEY

ABBREVIATIONS

avenue	pound	day
billion	inch	record
square	hundred	agriculture
month	boulevard	thousand
hour	ounce	feet
million	dollar, dollars	economic, economy
example, executive	cent, cents	yard

BRIEF FORMS

ap	p	ab
O	avj	U
cor	D	p
sp	hs	aq
od	aq	sp
sv	p	bs
K	cor	I

READING AND WRITING EXERCISES

1

The Daily Grind

Each day millions of people around the globe begin the morning and often finish the evening with a cup of[1] hot coffee. What can be so appealing about a drink served in a heavy mug to begin the day or served in a delicate china cup after[2] dinner?

Coffee can be traced to Africa as early as the 1300s where it was used as a food and[3] later made into wine. The word "coffee" is derived from the Arabic word for wine.

Coffee goes through[4] several phases before it reaches your local supermarket. Much tending takes place between the time coffee is[5] planted and when it is brewed in your electric pot. The coffee plant takes seven years to mature and grows to about[6] six feet high. The beans are picked when they are red and ripe. These beans are then processed and blended before they are ready[7] for distribution.

Coffee is the primary agricultural crop of several countries. The economies[8] of these countries depend largely upon our daily cup of coffee. This part of our daily grind can be quite[9] refreshing. (182)

2

Dear Mr. Wilson:

Enclosed is the bill for repairing your television set. As you can see, the charges total[1] $59.95. This price includes a 30-day guarantee on parts and service. If you[2] have more problems, be certain to call our customer service department while the repairs are under warranty.[3] We will visit your home and make the repairs at no additional charge to you.

Your set is in good shape generally[4] and should provide you with many years of good service, but why not think about adding a second set to your[5] home? We have several models which you could easily move from room to room. If you buy now, we will include[6] a fine rolling cart free of charge with your purchase. We hope you'll take advantage of our offer. Sincerely yours,[7] (140)

3

Dear Jason:

As I was preparing the program for our meeting, I discovered that we have several items[1] of new business to cover. Now I am afraid that our meeting will run over the time we have allowed. Can you[2] meet with me in order to go over some of these items? Perhaps some of them can be handled at a future[3] meeting.

Also, do you plan to present your findings on the marketing survey? If so, please let me know how much[4] time you will need. Our building manager has taken a position against purchasing certain kinds of electrical[5] equipment. He anticipates taking about ten minutes to discuss specific examples.

I have asked[6] each department manager to be present for this meeting. So far I have received one cancellation. Ms.[7] Wilson called to say that she will be on vacation that week and has asked Dr. Evans to take her place. Yours[8] truly, (161)

PART FOUR

Developing Your *Speedwriting* and Notetaking Skills

Congratulations! You have learned over half of the *Speedwriting* principles and made hundreds of words part of your *Speedwriting* vocabulary. Best of all, you have begun to develop a skill that you can be proud of and that will serve you well throughout your career.

Learning *Speedwriting* is similar to learning other skills, both in the classroom and on the job. Each new principle that you learn builds upon the ones you have learned previously, and it is easy to see the rapid progress that you are making. As you study and use *Speedwriting*, your *Speedwriting* and notetaking skills will improve. You will experience the satisfaction of learning and implementing new skills and knowledge.

Learning *Speedwriting* and taking good notes are skills that come with study and practice. As you progress through this book, your writing speed, notetaking efficiency, and confidence will continue to increase. Later, when you are on the job or are furthering your education and recording notes regularly, your writing and notetaking efficiency will increase even more. You will become familiar with the words used most often in your particular situation and will learn to write and apply common phrases and terms for notetaking purposes as quickly as you hear them.

Language Arts Applications. Because language arts usage is an integral part of the notetaking process, special emphasis is devoted in this textbook to the development of language arts skills. Beginning with Unit 16, spelling words were highlighted. Those selected for practice are among the most commonly misspelled words. In addition, the appendix of this textbook contains a list of 600 commonly misspelled words. This list is an excellent source for review.

Beginning in Unit 22, basic rules for punctuation will be presented. The rules are simple, but very important. They are the most commonly used punctuation rules in written communication.

If spelling and punctuation are not among your favorite subjects, don't despair. You are not alone! You will, however, need these skills to be successful as an effective communicator. The language arts applications in this text will help you master these skills.

UNIT

Systematic Reviewing of Notes

22

You have been learning how to transfer material from books and lectures into your notes and, eventually, into your memory. An important step in committing material to memory is frequent and thorough reviewing.

Before reviewing or engaging in any study activity, avoid distracting pre-study rituals such as making phone calls, preparing snack food, visiting with friends, or staring into space. Eliminating these activities will make your studying and reviewing easier and will put you in control of your study habits. Use such activities as these as rewards *after* you have completed your study session.

Studying is different from *reviewing*. You study to learn new material; you review to reinforce material previously learned. You may, through reviewing, learn things that were not learned the first time. The repetition of frequent reviewing sets the material in your memory.

You must be actively involved in the review process to derive the most from it. You need to give yourself feedback from your notes by asking yourself questions and answering them either orally or in writing. Writing provides the more beneficial form of feedback because it more actively involves you in the review process.

A systematic review produces the best results and should follow a schedule similar to this one.

1. Set aside 15 to 20 minutes after each class to copy or type your notes, if necessary. Omit any material you now feel is irrelevant. Fill in important information your memory provides that you may have omitted or only partially noted. Prompt review will help you remember the material and determine if additional reading or studying is necessary at this time.

2. Review your notes briefly prior to the next study session and before beginning new material.

3. At least once a week, review your notes from the beginning to the present, making sure you are actively involved in the review process and are not just a passive reader.

4. Review your notes before an exam. A systematic practice of

reviewing immediately after notes are taken and once a week or so thereafter should make reviewing for exams an easy process. You want to avoid last-minute cramming and anxiety. Review your material once or twice and then get a good night's sleep.

SPEEDWRITING PRINCIPLES

1. Write ⌒ for the initial sound of *em* or *im* (pronounced *m*).

emphasize, em-f-s-z

embarrass, em-b-r-s

image, im-j

impress, im-p-r-s

impatient, im-p-ish-nt

impose, im-p-z

2. Omit *p* in the sound of *mpt*.

attempt, a-t-m-t

temptation, t-m-t-tion

prompt, prah-m-t

promptly, prah-m-t-ly

ABBREVIATIONS

merchandise

question q

quart qt

especially esp

et cetera etc

university U

BRIEF FORMS

ever, every E

other ot

satisfy, satisfactory sat

character, characteristic crc

industry N

BRIEF FORM AND ABBREVIATED WORD DEVELOPMENT

however hoE

satisfaction

questionnaire

whatever

another aot

quarterly qtrl

everyone  industries 

PHRASES

I have been  we believe 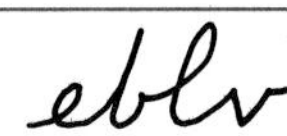

I should  we know 

I was  as well as 

PUNCTUATION STUDY

Learn to Punctuate Correctly. Writing is punctuated for one reason—to add clarity. When you speak, you use voice tones and pauses to punctuate. You use an uplifted tone to ask a question. You pause between words and phrases to give order and meaning to the thought you are expressing. Without changes in voice tone and natural pauses, words would run together and much of the meaning would be lost.

On the printed page, however, you do not have the benefit of voice tones or natural pauses. You use punctuation marks instead.

The comma is an important mark of punctuation. It forces you to pause as you read. To help you understand when and where to use commas, examples will be presented in future lessons.

USE COMMAS BETWEEN THREE OR MORE WORDS IN A SERIES.

The last word in a series will be preceded by either of these two words: *and, or.* In this text, a comma is always placed before *and* and *or* in a series. Some organizations, however, may prefer that this comma be omitted. Use the style preferred in your organization.

- □ Letters arrived for Mary, Todd, Steven, and James.
- □ Please ask someone to answer the phone, sort the mail, and file all correspondence.
- □ There are three subjects I especially enjoy—accounting, typewriting, and history.

In the Reading and Writing Exercises, commas in a series will be circled. The word **Series** will be highlighted.

VOCABULARY STUDY

merchandising 

The planning of sales programs directed toward creating a market demand for a product.

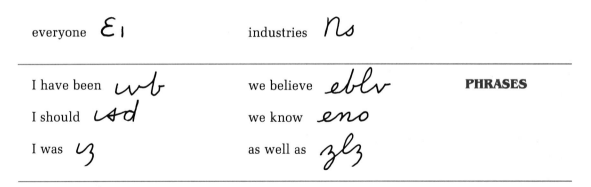

market analysis 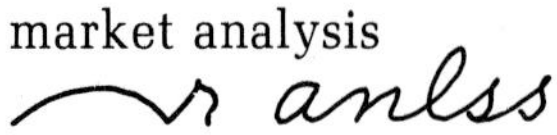 — Research concerned with all factors that affect the sales of goods and services.

PRINCIPLES SUMMARY

1. Write  for the initial sound of *em* or *im*: emphasize, em-f-s-z .
2. Omit *p* in the sound of *mpt*: prompt, prah-m-t .

WORD DEVELOPMENT

Write the following related words in *Speedwriting* in your notebook.

quart 	-s	-er	-ers
tempt 	-s	-ing	-ation
empty 	-ies	-ied	-ing
ever 	for-	when-	where-
implement 	-ed	-ing	-ation

---

WORD CONSTRUCTION

Practice writing these words in *Speedwriting* in your notebook.

whichever, w-chay-ever

imports, im-port-s

otherwise, other-w-z

impression, im-p-r-sion

everything, every-thing

imposition, im-p-z-tion

attempted, a-t-m-t-ed

emblem, em-b-l-m

prompted, prah-m-t-ed

embassy, em-b-s-e

WRITING ASSIGNMENT

Write the following sentences in *Speedwriting*.

1. I have been authorized to quote a new price for your paper based on an order of 2,500 pounds.

2. We were very pleased to see that hospital and dental charges will be adequately covered under this new benefit plan.
3. We can process orders much more quickly now that we know how to use the automated equipment.
4. We would have to pay a monthly service charge of $79 for the equipment purchased under the terms of this agreement.
5. You can be certain that 18 yards of the 54-inch fabric will adequately cover the chairs you have described.

READING AND WRITING EXERCISES

1

The Industrial Revolution

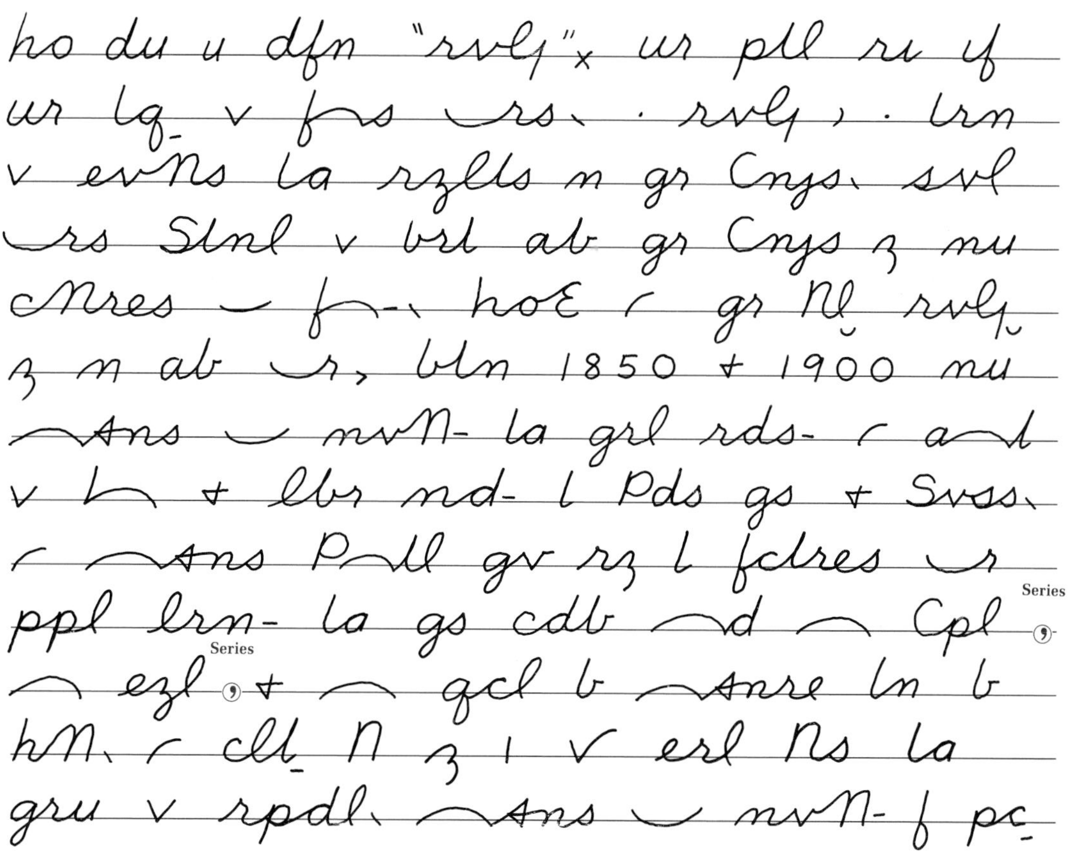

cln, v cll, + so fbrcs, ol ...ns
brt ab nu ...lds f fr..., ...br, +
bld. sn r fclres ... trn ol ...dse
/ ...prsv lvls la d fE Cny r ...a
e lv. r Nl rvlj ...d r ny . ld eco
por.

2

ddr dvdsn rsNl
iz . psN U r cr vu
efsN Psnl. i esp
ap- r efls vu nrs
eln jfres. s n eze
l fN ppl hu Pf... O
+ abv r cl v dle b
...s jfres, l v loz
rr Psns. iz ...prs-
b hr cN ...nr, hr
ddcj, + P...l all
se gv l E psN U
hr cr, se z nvr l
bze l lsn l r Pbl...s
+ ofn dd so o hr o
...l. blv hr crc
z ncry l r ol Psnl
zlz l r psNs, / z
v sal lse r hi lvl
v Pfjl cr truol u
hsp. i ...N- u lno
Psnll la / ol psNs
+ i ap- / . su

3

dS iv sv qs ab u
U. d u p sN ...e .
cpe vu cal, . aplc
f, + ol jn infre

nrlm plses, n
enc cpes v i
acdc recs C
ihp ul fN sal. r
lr ol crss isd lc
l nsr la i aplc
lb ac-x, id aso lc
sp dlls ab u scl v
bs. crNl n lq v
yr n r .
fss n dse +
r anlss. ihp uc

avz e o ol flds
Series
sC z Psnl ym,
Series Series
sls ym, ecos, etc,
wb lld lau pls srs
n jbs rla- l lr Czn
flds f i f qlr du r
fnl yr. , ls r cs f
E sr x id aso ap
rsv ME inf uv
ab jb rs n bs +
N. uvl

KEY

WRITING ASSIGNMENT

1. wb alrz- l go . nu prs fu ppr bs- o . od v 2T5H lbs.
2. e v p- lse la hsp + dNl Cgs lb aqll cvr- U ls nu bnfl pln.
3. ec Pss ods C qcl no la eno ho luz r ala- eqpm.
4. ed v lpa . ol Svs G v 79$ f

eqpm PCs- U r trms v ls
agrem.

5. ucb Sln la 18 yds v 54 = in fbrc l
aqll cvr r Crs uv dS-.

READING AND WRITING EXERCISES

1

The Industrial Revolution

How do you define "revolution"? You are partly right if you are thinking of famous wars. A revolution[1] is a turn of events that results in great changes. Civil wars certainly have brought about great changes as[2] new countries were formed. However, the great Industrial Revolution was not about war.

Between 1850[3] and 1900 new machines were invented that greatly reduced the amount of time and labor needed[4] to produce goods and services. The machines promptly gave rise to factories where people learned that goods could be[5] made more cheaply, more easily, and more quickly by machinery than by hand. The clothing industry was one[6] of the early industries that grew very rapidly. Machines were invented for picking cotton, weaving cloth,[7] and sewing fabrics.

Other machines brought about new methods for farming, lumbering, and building. Soon our factories[8] were turning out merchandise at impressive levels that would forever change the way we live. The Industrial[9] Revolution made our nation a leading economic power. (193)

2

Dear Dr. Davidson:

Recently, I was a patient under the care of your efficient personnel. I[1] especially appreciated the efforts of your nurse, Ellen Jeffries. It is not easy to find people who[2] perform over and above the call of duty, but Ms. Jeffries is one of those rare persons. I was impressed by[3] her kind manner, her dedication, and the prompt attention she gave to every patient under her care.

She was[4] never too busy to listen to our problems and often did so on her own time. I believe her character[5] was encouraging to the other personnel as well as to the patients.

It was very satisfying to[6] see the high level of professional care throughout your hospital. I wanted you to know personally that[7] the other patients and I appreciated it. Sincerely yours, (152)

3

Dear Sir:

I have several questions about your university. Would you please send me a copy of your[1] catalog, an application form, and other general information regarding enrollment policies? I[2] am enclosing copies of my academic records, which I hope you will find satisfactory. Are there other[3] courses I should take to ensure that my application will be accepted?

I would also like specific[4] details about your School of Business. Currently I am thinking of majoring in marketing, with an emphasis[5] in merchandising and marketing analysis. I hope you can advise me on other fields such as[6] personnel management, sales management, economics, etc.

I have been told that you place seniors in jobs[7] related to their chosen fields for one full quarter during the final year. Is this the case for every senior?[8] I would also appreciate receiving whatever information you have about job markets in business[9] and industry. Yours very truly, (186)

UNIT 23

Preparing for Objective Tests

In many of your courses, your knowledge will be tested by an objective exam. To prepare for this type of test, concentrate on all details and memorize information. Review class, textbook, and lab notes and formulate possible questions and answers. Use the index of your text covering the chapters on which you will be tested. Read each entry one by one and check yourself on terminology, people, ideas, and other pertinent details. Look up what you don't know and make notes on these points. Read chapter summaries and answer any end-of-chapter questions.

Continual, systematic study and review from the first week of school is the best way to achieve good test results. Day-by-day activities should include:

1. Reviewing notes after class sessions and periodically throughout the term
2. Reading as much background material as possible
3. Finding answers to questions or concepts you don't understand
4. Engaging in mental or written feedback from notes.

There are also other ways to help ensure that you are well prepared for objective tests. Obtain a review book, if possible, containing past objective exams and test yourself by simulating exam conditions. Join or form a study group comprised of conscientious students of approximately your ability level. Working with a group can be helpful after you have studied by yourself and have a good grasp of the topics. Make up flash cards of possible test questions on one side and answers on the other for a quick review just prior to an exam. Experiment with various methods or techniques in studying for an exam and then determine which pre-test study habits work best for you. Strive to achieve maximum results from the amount of time you spend studying.

SPEEDWRITING PRINCIPLES

1. Write k for the sounds of *com, con, coun* (ow), *count.*

compare, com-p-r *kpr*	condition, con-d-tion *kdj*
accommodate, a-com-d-ate *akda*	council, coun-s-l *ksl*
convey, con-v-a *kva*	account, a-count *ak*
concern, con-s-r-n *ksrn*	county, count-e *ke*

2. Write *S* for the sound of *st* (pronounced *est*).

still, st-l *Sl*	trust, t-r-st *trS*
state, st-ate *Sa*	most, m-st *—S*
instead, in-st-d *nSd*	fastest, f-st-st *fSS*

Write these additional words:

discount, dis-count *Dk*	constant, con-st-nt *kSN*
commission, com-sion *kj*	cost, k-st *cS*
postage, p-st-j *pSj*	finest, f-n-st *fnS*
confirm, con-firm *kfr*	storage, st-r-j *Srj*
common, com-n *kn*	concerning, con-s-r-n-ing *ksrn_*

PHRASES

I would like *idlc*	you could *ucd*
we are pleased *erp-*	to receive *trsv*
you cannot *ucn*	to say *tsa*

COMMONLY MISSPELLED WORDS

accommodate *akda*

almost *a—S*

VOCABULARY STUDY

real estate rl eSa — A term that refers to land and the buildings or permanent structures on the land.

commerce krs — The buying and selling of goods and services; usually on a widespread basis, such as national commerce.

PRINCIPLES SUMMARY

1. Write k for the sounds of *com, con, coun* (ow), *count:* county, count-e ke
2. Write S for the sound of *st:* still, st-l Sl

WORD DEVELOPMENT

Write the following related words in *Speedwriting* in your notebook.

account ak	-s	-ing	-ant
adjust ajS	-ed	-ing	-ment
assist asS	-ed	-ing	-ant
cost cS	-s	-ing	-ly
condition kdj	-s	-ed	-ing

WORD CONSTRUCTION

Practice writing these words in *Speedwriting* in your notebook.

computer, com-p-ute-r	request, re-q-st
administer, ad-min-st-r	best, b-st
almost, al-m-st	comments, com-nt-s
construction, con-st-r-k-tion	stock, st-k
communication, com-n-k-tion	students, st-d-nt-s

WRITING ASSIGNMENT

Write the following sentences in *Speedwriting*.

1. You will be pleased to know that we are planning several meetings to talk about current trends in the economy.
2. Will you attend the meetings to discuss the role that agriculture plays in our local and national economies?
3. We are enclosing a copy of your order for 1800 square yards of carpeting that we processed today.
4. Please indicate in the space under the item's description the number of business cards that you wish to order.
5. We are not certain if 880 square yards of carpeting will be adequate to cover 8,000 square feet of floor space as shown in your plans.

READING AND WRITING EXERCISES

1

The New Age of Education

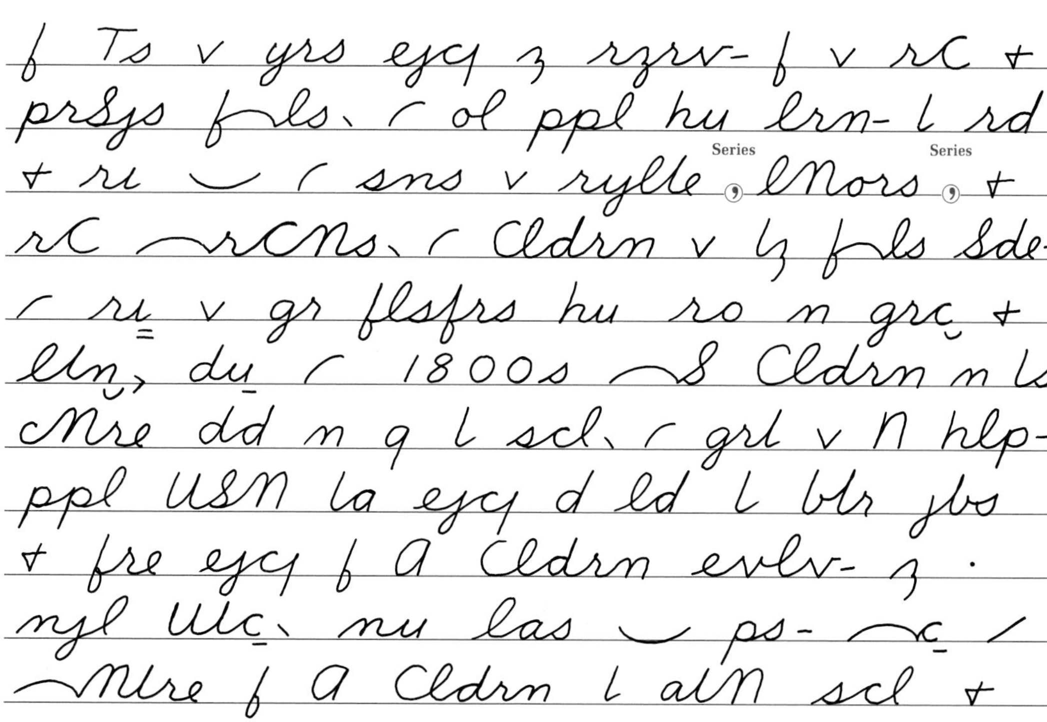

gr—r scls — gcl bll — Sa +
ke fNs. lz s—l scls — r bgn_
v ejcyl Pgs ev ld, r gl v ofr_ fre
+ lo=cS ejcj, hil vlu- n r nj.
la, y — ppl alN clj ld ln E bf.

2

1 / z —S sal_ l
rd u arlcl ksrn_
ar lrfc. —n r arpl
z bll r rn—a sz z
— ln Agl. du_ r lS
sv yrs kdjs v grl
Cnj-. e no v . —C
lrjr No v arcrfl uz_
r arpl o . dl bss, i
agre la r cS v ncrs-
Svss sd n b pd b r
sle aln. / db —
ecol f E, if r ke —
lpa . grr sr v cSs.

Psnll idlc lse .
Ppzl pls- bf r ke ksl
asc_ f . ncrs n fN_,
du uno if ne, hs
nvSga- uz_ ol rvnu?
idb l_ l hlp Srl .
fN drv n od l rz
me f— prvl srss
Series Series
sC z bs, N, +foNjs.
Ph ucd adrs ls lpc
n . frN=pj Sre, r
nd f ncrs- Svss, .
—yr isu ld. ihp ul
cp gv_ / r cvrj /
dzrvs. su

3

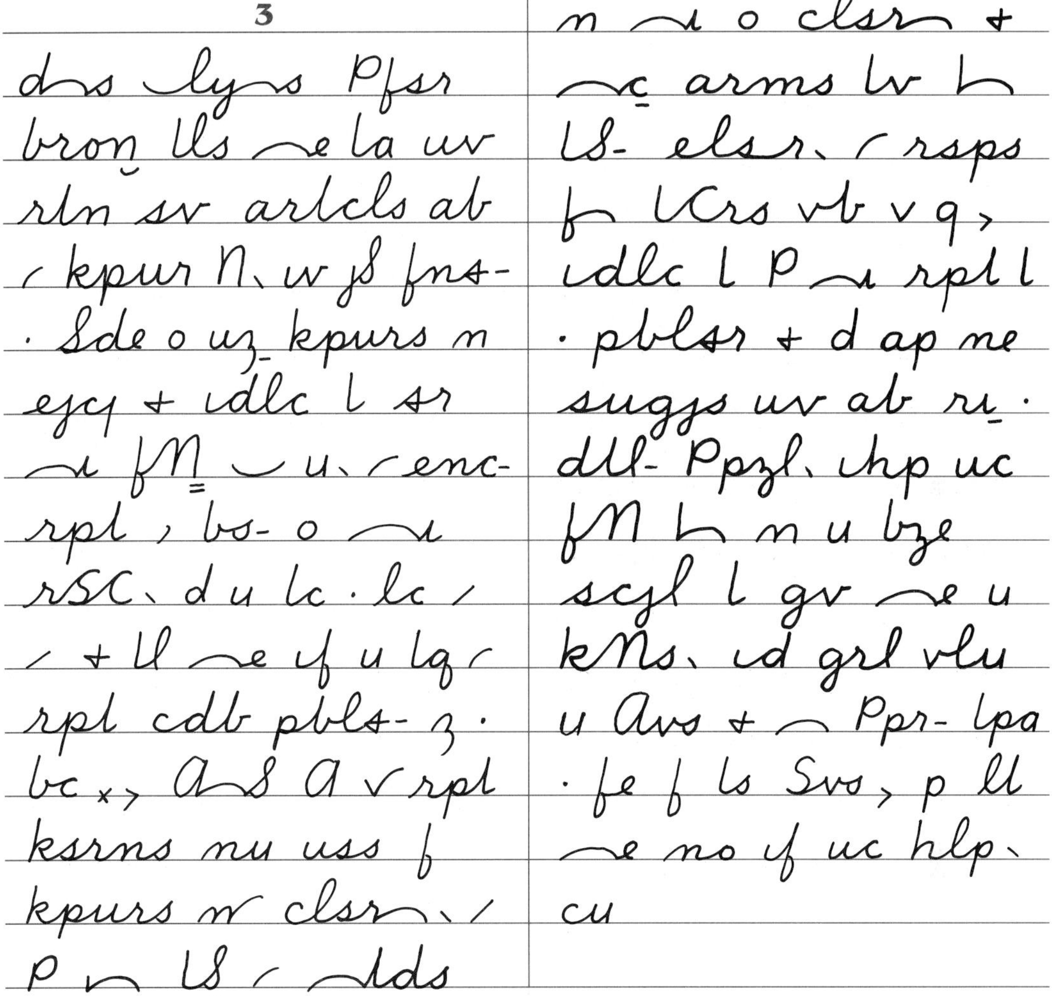

KEY

WRITING ASSIGNMENT

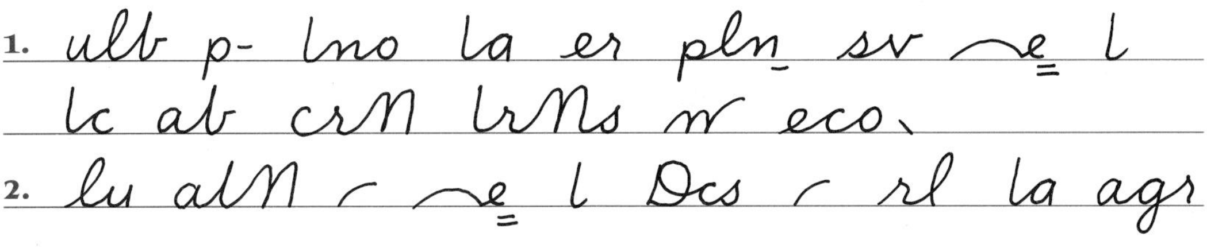

plas n r lcl + ntl ecos x

3. er enc . cpe vu od f 18H sq yds v crpt lae Pss-ld\

4. p Nca m sps U r uhs dSy r No v bs crds lau + l od\

5. ern Sln uf 880 sq yds v crpt lb Aql l cvr 8T sq ft v flr sps z sn n u plns\

READING AND WRITING EXERCISES

1

The New Age of Education

For thousands of years education was reserved for very rich and prestigious families. The only people[1] who learned to read and write were the sons of royalty, landowners, and rich merchants. The children of these families[2] studied the writings of great philosophers who wrote in Greek and Latin.

During the 1800s most children[3] in this country did not go to school. The growth of industry helped people understand that education would lead[4] to better jobs, and free education for all children evolved as a national undertaking. New laws were[5] passed making it mandatory for all children to attend school, and grammar schools were quickly built with state and county[6] funds. These small schools were the beginning of the educational programs we have today.

The goal of offering[7] free and low-cost education is highly valued in our nation. That is why more people attend college[8] today than ever before. (165)

2

Gentlemen:

It was most satisfying to read your article concerning air traffic. When the airport was built,[1] the runway size was more than adequate. During the last several years, conditions have greatly changed. We now have[2] a much larger number of aircraft using our airport on a daily basis.

I agree that the cost of[3] increased services should not be paid by the city alone. It would be more economical for everyone[4] if the county were to pay a greater share of the costs. Personally, I would like to see a proposal placed before[5] the county council asking for an increase in funding.

Do you know if anyone has investigated[6] using other revenue? I would be willing to help start a fund drive in order to raise money from private[7] sources such as business, industry, and foundations. Perhaps you could address this topic in a front-page story.[8]

The need for increased services is a major issue today. I hope you will keep giving it the coverage[9] it deserves. Sincerely yours, (185)

3

Dear Ms. Williams:

Professor Brown tells me that you have written several articles about the computer[1] industry. I have just finished a study on using computers in education, and I would like to share my[2] findings with you. The enclosed report is based on my research. Would you take a look at it and tell me if you think[3] the report could be published as a book?

Almost all of the report concerns new uses for computers in the[4] classroom. At present, I am testing the methods in my own classroom and making arrangements to have them tested[5] elsewhere. The responses from teachers have been very good.

I would like to present my report to a publisher[6] and would appreciate any suggestions you have about writing a detailed proposal. I hope you can find[7] time in your busy schedule to give me your comments. I would greatly value your advice and am prepared to pay[8] a fee for this service.

Please let me know if you can help. Cordially yours, (173)

UNIT

24 Taking Objective Tests

Objective tests are often easier than essay exams because the test material is presented to you and because many students find that recognition of concepts and details is easier than total recall. The answers are often either right or wrong in objective tests. Objective tests are also more frequently given, especially in large classes. There are five main types of objective tests.

True-False. For true-false tests, read each question carefully and look for clue words such as *never*, *seldom*, or *always*. If any part of a statement is false, the whole statement is false. True-false tests frequently contain statements that are almost true, but not quite true. Remember that for a question to be answered *True*, *all* of the question must be true. Watch for negative statements; these tend to be tricky. Some students feel that instructors follow a pattern for answering on true-false tests, such as T F T T F F or other configurations. There is absolutely no proof of this, so do not look for shortcuts or listen to rumors.

Multiple Choice. Multiple-choice tests are likely to be a frequently used form of testing. Read all choices carefully before answering a multiple-choice question. Avoid checking the first answer that seems correct to you. Eliminate the obviously incorrect answers and then select what you feel to be the correct answer. Test the answer by adding it to the question and reading the completed statement.

If you are dealing with problems and solutions in math or science, be aware of the time. If a math process requires more time than you have available in order to arrive at the correct answer, try to eliminate the obviously incorrect answers and take a guess from the remaining possibilities. Be sure to make a note on your scrap paper to go back to the question if time permits.

Do not skip questions; instead, take a guess if there is no penalty for guessing and make a note to go back later. This practice will prevent filling in a wrong answer space on a scanner sheet and leaving questions unanswered.

Matching Questions. Matching questions usually consist of two columns in which you match a term in one column with a term or statement in another column. Read through all the possibilities before answering. You are looking for the most appropriate answer. Unless otherwise noted, an answer may be used more than once. Match the items you are sure about first and then proceed to eliminate the choices for the rest.

Completion Questions. The fill-in-the-blank type of questions require specific answers. Read each question carefully and write the best possible answer. Check your answer by reading the completed sentence to make sure your response makes sense.

Problem Tests. The problem test is commonly used in testing science and math proficiency. Such tests may ask for the answer or be part of a multiple-choice format. To prepare for problem tests, do sample problems over and over until you are sure of yourself. You must know formulas and equations. On a problem test, read problems through carefully and leave time to check your work, making sure there are no careless errors in calculation.

In checking objective tests of any type, look for omissions or obvious errors and work on questions you have noted for further attention. Check your responses carefully and do make changes when you feel sure you have made an incorrect response.

With the competition for grades, cheating has become a more frequent occurrence on objective tests. DON'T DO IT! In addition to the many obvious reasons not to do so, you should be aware that instructors frequently design tests so that the page arrangements are alternated or two versions of a test may be given at the same time.

Also of major importance is to remember that the first activity to engage in before answering any examination question is to read the directions very carefully!

SPEEDWRITING PRINCIPLES

1. Write the days of the week as follows:

Sunday *Sn*
Monday *Mn*
Tuesday *Tu*
Wednesday *Wd*
Thursday *Th*
Friday *Fr*
Saturday *St*

ABBREVIATIONS

federal *fed*
government *gvt*
represent, representative *rep*
street *S*

okay ok	incorporate, incorporated inc

BRIEF FORMS

continue ku	accomplish ak
deliver dl	complete kp
opportunity opl	contribute kb
come, came, committee k	convenient, convenience kv

BRIEF FORM DEVELOPMENT

continued ku-	accomplishments akms
completed kp-	contributions kbjs
opportunities opls	income nk

PHRASES

I feel ifl	*as **soon** as zz
you would be udb	as we ze

*Omit the boldface word in the *Speedwriting* phrase.

PUNCTUATION STUDY

USE COMMAS AFTER INTRODUCTORY DEPENDENT CLAUSES.

An introductory dependent clause is a group of words containing a subject and a verb that occurs at the beginning of a sentence. However, this clause is not a complete thought and cannot stand alone. It requires a main (independent) clause to make the sentence complete.

Introductory dependent clauses usually begin with recognizable words. The most common words are *when*, *as*, and *if*. Other common examples are *although*, *though*, *unless*, *since*, *while*, *until*, *before*, *after*, *whether*, and *because*.

- □ *When* Dr. Ellis arrives, please have her call my office.
- □ *As* I may have mentioned earlier, that contract has already expired.
- □ *If* you prefer, we will have the order shipped directly to you.

Beginning with this unit, introductory dependent clauses that start with *when*, *as*, and *if* will be highlighted in your Reading and Writing Exercises with the abbreviation **Intro DC**.

VOCABULARY STUDY

capital investment
cpll nvsm

Funds spent for additions or improvements in plant, equipment, or personnel.

PRINCIPLES SUMMARY

1. Days of the week.

WORD DEVELOPMENT

Write the following related words in *Speedwriting* in your notebook.

continue ku	-s	-d	-ation
welcome lk	-s	-d	-ing
accomplish ak	-ed	-ing	-ment
complete kp	-s	-ing	-ly
represent rep	-s	-ed	-ing

WORD CONSTRUCTION

Practice writing these words in *Speedwriting* in your notebook.

just, j-st
convention, con-v-n-tion
statement, st-ate-ment
commerce, com-r-s
common, com-n
listing, l-st-ing
study, st-d-e
contained, con-t-n-duh
plastic, p-l-st-k
understanding, under-st-nd-ing

WRITING ASSIGNMENT

Write the following sentences in *Speedwriting*.

1. We would appreciate having a prompt distribution of the questionnaire as well as the other information.
2. We are attempting to meet increased enrollment in the university, especially in the Department of Business.

3. I would like to emphasize again how much we enjoyed taking a tour of your industry.

4. If you do not find this merchandise to be 100 percent satisfactory, your money will be returned to you without question.

5. It is characteristic of every branch office to provide prompt and friendly service to every customer.

READING AND WRITING EXERCISES

1

Roads to the Future

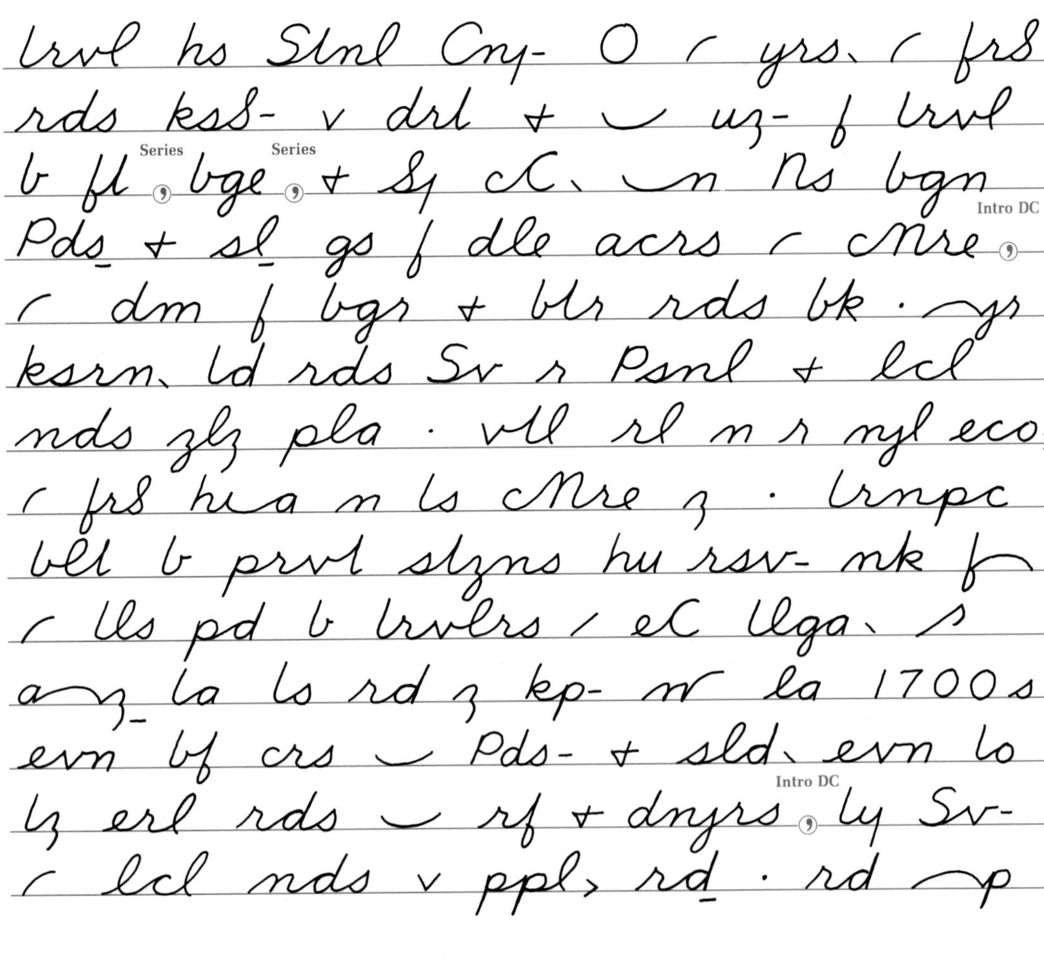

—S vb . ll s—plr bf (grl v
bs + N.

2

mo l A sls Psnl
usd b esp p- u u
akms ls yr. e n
ol —d r sls gls e
Sps- L, ls yrs rec
sls ofr . fn opl l
py ol (kbys —d b
sls reps. (grl vr
corp , drl rla- lu
olSN efls, ze lc
Intro DC
ahd l (k yr , ll's
sl r gls f ku- grl
n —rpls. ufl kfdN
la (nu yr l yld (
bS rzlts E. —n e
—e aq E rynl
Intro DC
kvnj, el Dcs ho l
aCv loz rzlts, p
ac (enc- bns Cc
— r kplms. / r
—a v so r apj f.
jb l dn.

3

mo l Pfsr edws
(P hs apy- . k l
rvu r plse o su
fed lns l SdNs.
d u b fre l rep (
scl v ejcj o la k.
(k l alz r crN
—lds v Pss aplcjs
+ nvSga nu —lds
la —l rzlt n . —
efsN sS. w .
fl kln bcgroN inf
—C l hlp u. / Ds

. cpe v gvl rglys
+. Sam v U plse.
ic Aso Pvd cpes
v f~s Ub kp-b
aplcNs, if s kv

Intro DC

fu,p pln l Sp b
~ ofs o Tu or
Wd. i lq u'l fN ls
asnm Ub v Clny-
+ rw.

KEY

WRITING ASSIGNMENT

1. edap v . P~l Dy v qr zlz ~
ol inf.
2. er at~l l ~e ncrs- nrlm n U
esp n dpl v bs.
3. idlc l ~fsz aq ho ~C e nyy-
lc . ls vu N.
4. if udu n fN ls ~dse Ub 1H%
sal u me lb rel- lu ~ol q.
5. s crc v E brnC ofs l Pvd P~l
+ frNl Svs l E K.

READING AND WRITING EXERCISES

1

Roads to the Future

Travel has certainly changed over the years. The first roads consisted of dirt and were used for travel by foot,[1] buggy, and stage coach. When industries began producing and selling goods for delivery across the country, the[2] demand for bigger and better roads became a major concern. Today, roads serve our personal and local needs[3] as well as play a vital role in our national economy.

The first highway in this country was a[4] turnpike built by private citizens who received income from the tolls paid by travelers at each tollgate. It is[5] amazing that this road was completed in the late 1700s even before cars were produced and sold.[6] Even though these early roads were rough and dangerous, they served the local needs of people.

Reading a road map must[7] have been a lot simpler before the growth of business and industry. (151)

2

MEMO TO: All Sales Personnel

You should be especially pleased with your accomplishments this year. We not only[1] met our sales goals, we surpassed them.

This year's record sales offer a fine opportunity to point out the[2] contributions made by sales representatives. The growth of our corporation is directly related to your[3] outstanding efforts.

As we look ahead to the coming year, let's set our goals for continued growth in the marketplace.[4] I feel confident that the new year will yield the best results ever. When we meet again at the regional[5] convention, we will discuss how to achieve those results.

Please accept the enclosed bonus check with our compliments.[6] It is our way of showing our appreciation for a job well done. (133)

3

MEMO TO: Professor Edwards

The president has appointed a committee to review our policy on[1] issuing federal loans to students. Would you be free to represent the School of Education on that[2] committee?

The committee will analyze our current methods of processing applications and investigate[3] new methods that might result in a more efficient system. I have a file containing background information[4] which will help you. It includes a copy of government regulations and a statement of university[5] policy. I can also provide copies of forms to be completed by applicants.

If it is convenient[6] for you, please plan to stop by my office on Tuesday or Wednesday. I think you'll find this assignment to be very[7] challenging and rewarding. (145)

UNIT 25

Preparing for and Taking Essay Tests

Frequent reviewing of your notes, as discussed in Unit 22, will prepare you well for a mid-term or final exam. List the topics you need to spend the most time in studying and check them off your list as you progress. Be sure to plan plenty of time to rest and eat balanced meals to maintain a good energy and alertness level.

Essay examinations determine your knowledge and understanding of the subject as well as your ability to formulate answers that are well organized and clearly expressed. Essay exams are less likely to be used in large classes because of the time required for grading them. Smaller classes are more likely to have essay tests.

Studying for an essay exam is somewhat different from studying for an objective test, although much of the test content and material remains the same. Sometimes you can study for both types of tests at the same time as long as you keep in mind that one type of essay exam question may cover a detailed listing or analysis of specific material while another type of question may concentrate on an overview of major events or issues.

Since the nature of an essay test limits the scope of the exam, make up possible essay questions and practice answering them. The type of course and the nature of the subject matter are major clues in anticipating the type and the scope of possible test questions.

Words frequently used to ask essay questions are *describe, explain, summarize, compare, contrast, evaluate, critique, justify, analyze,* and *discuss.* Read an essay question slowly and thoughtfully and then be sure to answer as requested. Take a piece of scrap paper and use your notetaking ability to write down the thoughts that will be racing through your mind. Jot down key points you want to include in your answer. Plan your response by outlining a beginning, a middle, and an end to the question and fill in with the ideas you jotted down while brainstorming.

Once you have an opening sentence for your answer, you can begin writing in the examination booklet. Write legibly. The opening may be an introductory statement to your answer. Sometimes you can restate the essay question and use that as part of your opening statement. Next, fill in the middle section with adequate support data. You must give facts and reasons why or how and use appropriate examples. Write your answers in clear, concise language. Limit your responses to answering the question.

Budget your time to provide adequate coverage for each question and allow extra time to proofread your responses. Leave some blank space at the end of each question for added thoughts that occur as you reread your answers. Conclude your essay answers with a summation of pertinent facts and thoughts.

Take-home exams require more research and time to complete than tests administered in class. They usually consist of two or three comprehensive questions.

Analyze the questions and obtain the necessary information to answer them. You can take more time to develop your answers and form conclusions, but more concerted effort is needed to succeed on a take-home exam. Take-home exams reduce the feeling of exam pressure, but they must be taken seriously and must be completed independently and on time.

SPEEDWRITING PRINCIPLES

1. Write q for the word ending *quire.*

require, re-quire	rq	requirements, re-quire-ment-s	rqms
inquire, in-quire	nq	inquiry, in-quire-e	nqe
acquire, a-quire	aq	required, re-quire-duh	rq-

2. Write z for the sound of *zh.*

pleasure, p-l-z-r	plzr	treasure, t-r-z-r	trzr
measure, m-z-r	mzr	leisure, l-z-r	lzr

WRITING STATE AND CITY NAMES

The United States Postal Service requests that two-letter state initials be used on all mail. To indicate states in your *Speedwriting* notes, write the same two-letter state initials that the Postal Service uses.

Alabama = AL	AL	California = CA	CA

City names are written according to rule. Listed below are examples of how to write city and state names. For a list of all the states, see the appendix at the back of this book.

Boston, MA	bSn MA	Columbus, OH	clbs OH
Tulsa, OK	Llsa OK	Las Vegas, NV	ls vgs NV
Madison, WI	mdsn WI	Buffalo, NY	bflo NY

The *Speedwriting* capitalization mark is used when writing the city name by itself, but not when both the city and the state are used. Note that the state is set off by commas in transcription.

Boston	bSn	Boston, MA	bSn MA

PHRASES

I look	ılc	to do	ldu
we could	ecd	to give	lgv
we have been	evb	to visit	lvzl
we would like	edlc		

COMMONLY MISSPELLED WORDS

representative rep
convenient kv

VOCABULARY STUDY

test market lS mr — A geographical area selected for sales of goods or services during a trial period to determine the marketability of a product.

PRINCIPLES SUMMARY

1. Write q for the word ending *quire*: require, re-quire rq
2. Write z for the sound of *zh*: pleasure, p-l-z-r plzr

WORD DEVELOPMENT

Write the following related words in *Speedwriting* in your notebook.

acquire 	-d	-s	-ing
require 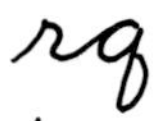	-s	-d	-ing
treasure 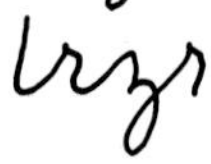	-d	-s	-ing
measure 	-d	-s	-ing
inquire 	-s	-d	-ing

---

WORD CONSTRUCTION

Practice writing these words in *Speedwriting* in your notebook.

composure, com-p-z-r	leisurely, l-z-r-ly
requirement, re-quire-ment	treasury, t-r-z-r-e
measurement, m-z-r-ment	disclosure, dis-k-l-z-r
inquiry, in-quire-e	inquiries, in-quire-e-s
displeasure, dis-p-l-z-r	treasurer, t-r-z-r-r

WRITING ASSIGNMENT

Write the following sentences in *Speedwriting*.

1. We are pleased to know that your county council has found the results of our study to be very satisfactory.
2. I would like to confirm that the study indicates that this city is the fastest growing city in the state.
3. Our accountant has suggested that we use a system in which funds would be distributed quarterly instead of monthly.
4. If you have other questions concerning our discount merchandise, we will be happy to send additional brochures, catalogs, etc.
5. I would like to receive your booklet showing how industries can reduce the cost of postage by using your system.

READING AND WRITING EXERCISES

1

Vacations

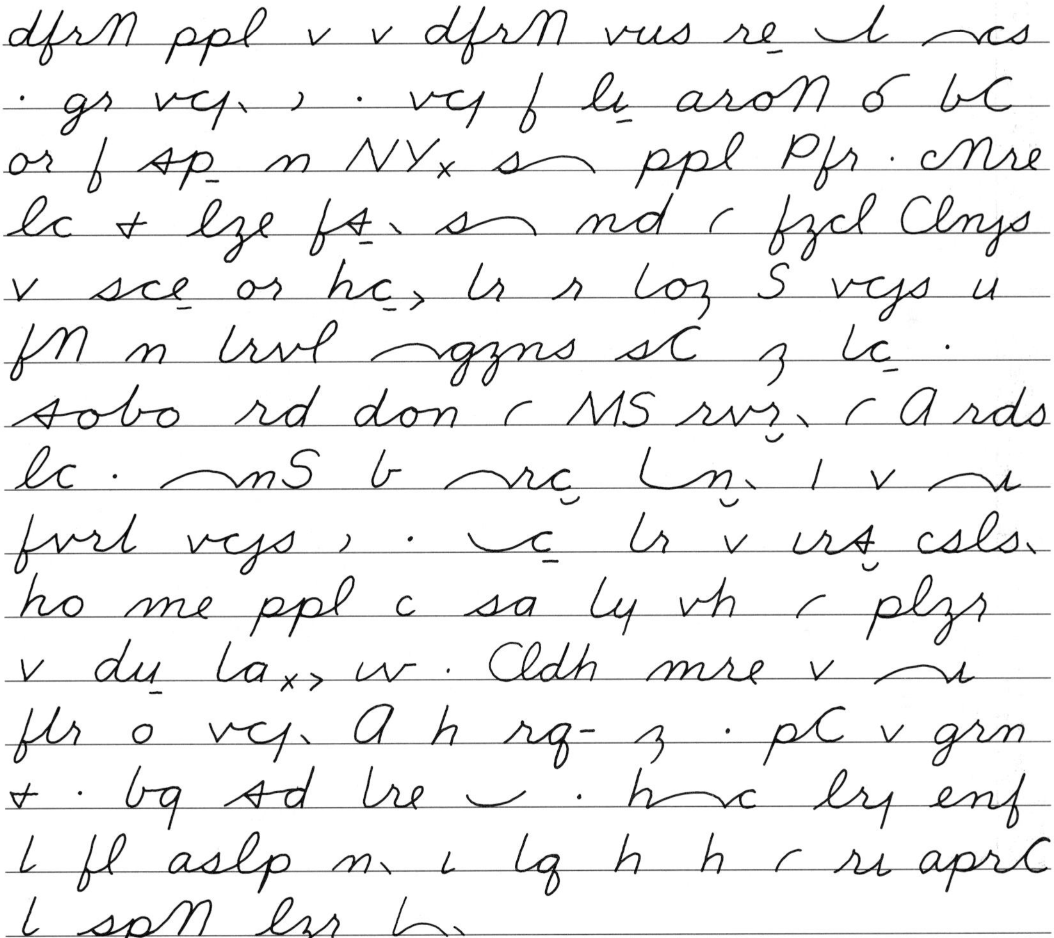

2

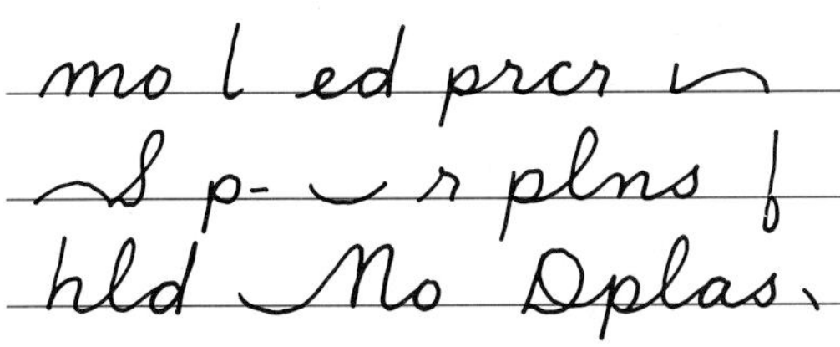

Intro DC

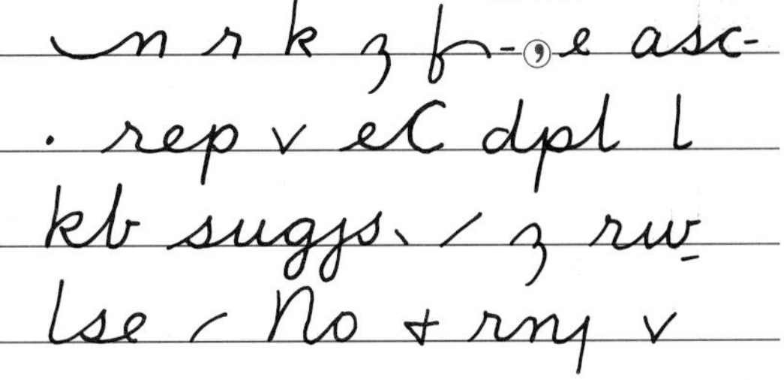

sugjs e rsv-, if
Intro DC
r plns r ok ⌣ u,
el inc nu lys ⌣
lrdyl ths v ps.
f ex e lca- s⌒ rr
alc lys l P aq .
bcgroN v ⌒drn
pN. edlc l aq .
sS⌒ v lis + soNs
lgv A- ⌒fss, ecd
Sl uz r pN-lNscps
if e gv L . nu lc.
e ⌒ lri az elnc
g⌒s + lys aq ⌒ old
bcgroN. zz uv ⌒
Intro DC
opl, ⌒N u ⌒e ⌣
⌒e l Dcs lz sugjs.

3

mo l ⌒yr v ⌒r +
sls ⌣n ⌒ brd v
Intro DC
drrs ⌒l ls Mn, ly
vo- l Srl . nu dvj l
Pds ppr gs. ls reps
. ⌒yr Cnj + ofrs
opls n . nu ⌒r,
el D ⌒ ppr gs lru
r fd dvj. ls sS⌒
aprs lb ⌒ ⌒S ecol
+ kv ⌒ld v hNl ⌒
nu ⌒dse, sls reps
hu cl o S⌒rs l
ncrs lr cls l ⌒l
Series Series
Dk Srs, drg Srs, +
ol rll ollls ⌣C
cre r gs, e alspa
uz dnvr CO z . lS
⌒r f nu ln. el
⌒zr ⌒ rzlls v . 6=
⌒o lS l f⌒ fCr
⌒r plns. if e ak
Intro DC
r gls w lS ⌒r, el
lrn r all l nyl sls.

KEY

WRITING ASSIGNMENT

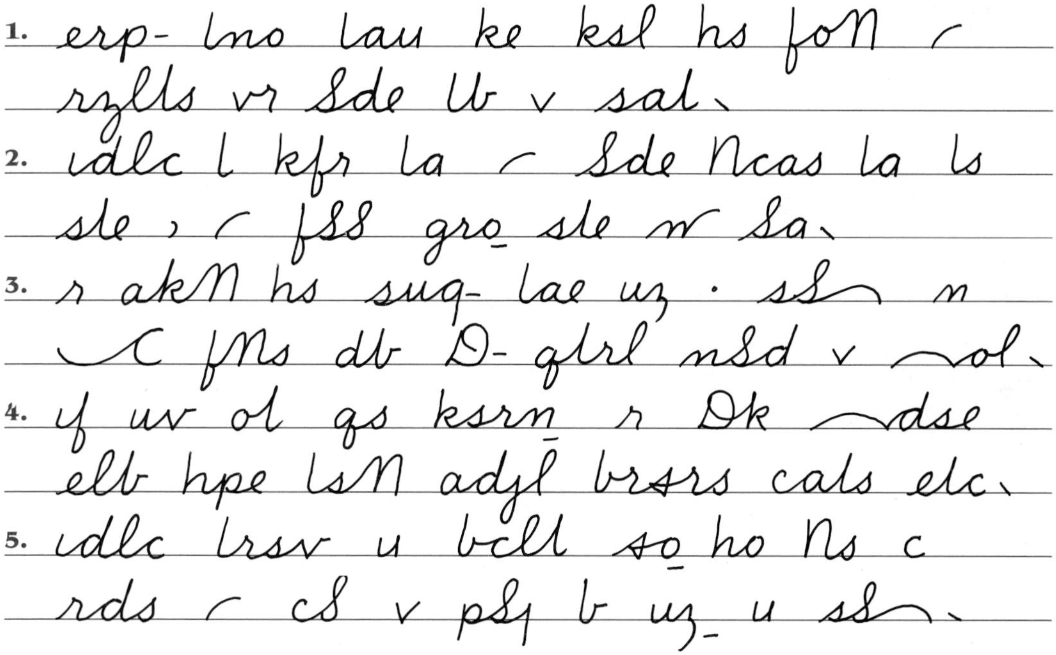

READING AND WRITING EXERCISES

1

Vacations

Different people have very different views regarding what makes a great vacation. Is a vacation for[1] lying around on the beach or for shopping in New York? Some people prefer a country lake and lazy fishing.[2] Some need the physical challenges of skiing or hiking.

There are those super vacations you find in travel[3] magazines such as taking a showboat ride down the Mississippi River. The ad reads like a manuscript by[4] Mark Twain. One of my favorite vacations is a walking tour of Irish castles. How many people can say[5] they have had the pleasure of doing that?

I have a childhood memory of my father on vacation. All he[6] required was a patch of green and a big shade tree with a hammock large enough to fall asleep in. I think he had[7] the right approach to spending leisure time. (147)

2

MEMO TO: Ed Parker

I am most pleased with our plans for holiday window displays. When our committee was formed,[1] we asked a representative of each department to contribute suggestions. It was rewarding to see the[2] number and range of suggestions we received.

If our plans are okay with you, we will incorporate new toys with[3] traditional items of the past. For example, we located some rare antique toys to present against a[4] background of modern paintings. We would like to acquire a system of lights and sounds to give added emphasis.

We[5] could still use our painted landscapes if we give them a new look. We might try arranging electronic games and toys[6] against the old background. As soon as you have the opportunity, won't you meet with me to discuss these suggestions?[7] (140)

3

MEMO TO: Manager of Marketing and Sales

When the Board of Directors met last Monday, they voted to start[1] a new division to produce paper goods. This represents a major change and offers opportunities in[2] a new market.

We will distribute the paper goods through our food division. This system appears to be the most[3] economical and convenient method of handling the new merchandise.

Sales representatives who call on[4] supermarkets will increase their calls to include discount stores, drug stores, and other retail outlets which carry our[5] goods.

We anticipate using Denver, Colorado, as a test market for the new line. We will measure the[6] results of a six-month test to form future marketing plans. If we accomplish our goals in the test market, we[7] will turn our attention to national sales. (148)

UNIT 26

Developing Better Library Skills

The library is one of the student's best resources. It is both a quiet place to study and a storehouse of the knowledge and thought of the human race.

Libraries have two very important helpers for the student—the librarian and the card catalog. Librarians devote their careers to helping people find the right books and information. The card catalog is a bibliography of all the books in the library. It is usually the starting point for most library research.

Many libraries have now computerized all card catalog information, making it easily accessible. Larger libraries often have computer software on how to use the library. Some time spent working through the questions and answers on these programs will be very helpful in improving your library skills. Learn all you can about your library and how to use it. You can count on the library being the most valuable building on campus.

Some basic information you will need about the library includes answers to the following questions.

1. What are the opening and closing times on weekdays, weekends, and holidays?
2. Are there study carrels?
3. Is there a photocopying service? How much does it cost?
4. How long may books be borrowed?
5. What is the fine for overdue books?
6. What microforms are available?
7. Is there a record, tape, compact disk, or video collection?
8. Are interlibrary loans available?
9. Are there clipping files? Picture files?

Next, you will need to know where to locate the following library tools and become familiar with them.

1. Card catalog or computerized catalog
2. *Readers' Guide to Periodical Literature*
3. Bound periodicals
4. Current magazines and newspapers
5. Reserve books
6. General and specialized reference books
7. Fiction
8. Non-fiction
9. Microforms (microfilm or microfiche readers and printers)
10. Government publications

Information for educational projects may be obtained from the following sources.

1. Books
2. Encyclopedias, handbooks
3. Yearbooks
4. Periodicals
5. Newspapers
6. Documents
7. Interviews with local or national experts

For some projects only one of the above sources needs to be used. For others, you must explore several sources. Books are one of the most important sources of information and are readily available in libraries or may be borrowed from other libraries. Books are usually the first source of information to be considered.

You may look through several books before deciding on the best ones for information for your project. Dust jackets on books sometimes contain information on the author's viewpoints. The preface or introduction should be read very carefully. It will typically explain the purpose and scope of the book. The publisher and copyright date are important information. Is the publisher one who specializes in the subject of the book? How up to date is the book? The table of contents and index can reveal the scope of the book by listing the topics discussed and the number of pages devoted to each topic.

Articles in encyclopedias, handbooks, and similar reference works are likely to be more up to date than many books, for these sources are constantly being revised. Periodicals and newspapers contain even more recent information.

SPEEDWRITING PRINCIPLES

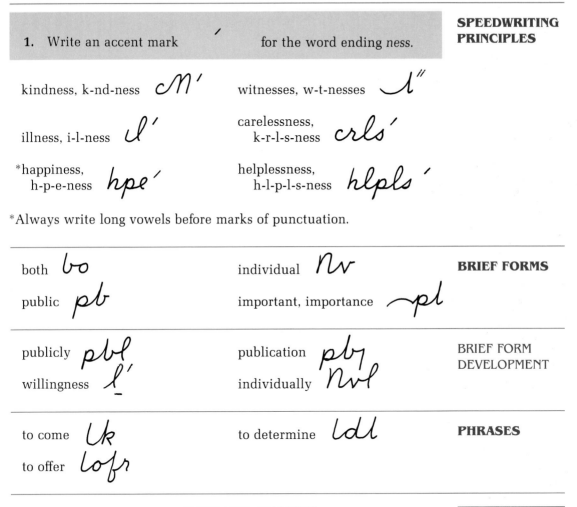

1. Write an accent mark ' for the word ending *ness.*

kindness, k-nd-ness cN'
illness, i-l-ness il'
*happiness, h-p-e-ness hpe'
witnesses, w-t-nesses wt''
carelessness, k-r-l-s-ness crls'
helplessness, h-l-p-l-s-ness hlpls'

*Always write long vowels before marks of punctuation.

BRIEF FORMS

both bo
public pb
individual Nv
important, importance -pl

BRIEF FORM DEVELOPMENT

publicly pbl
willingness l'
publication pbj
individually Nvl

PHRASES

to come tk
to offer tofr
to determine tdl

PUNCTUATION STUDY

MORE INTRODUCTORY DEPENDENT CLAUSES

In addition to *when, as,* and *if,* introductory dependent clauses beginning with such words as *although, before,* and *because* will be highlighted.

□ *Although* two months have passed, we still have not heard from you.
□ *Before* you order supplies, please contact our purchasing department.
□ *Because* you are a valued customer, you will receive a discount.

VOCABULARY STUDY

homeowner's policy
h-ors plse
An insurance policy covering the cost of the policyholder's home and personal belongings in case of damage or loss.

suggested retail price
sug-rtl prs
The ultimate sale price (sometimes referred to as *list price*) recommended by the manufacturer.

PRINCIPLES SUMMARY

1. Write ´ for the word ending *ness*: kindness, k-nd-ness kn´

WORD DEVELOPMENT

Write the following related words in *Speedwriting* in your notebook.

wit wt	-s	-ness	-nesses
will l	-ed	-ing	-ingness
kind kn	-s	-ness	-est
individual nv	-s	-ly	-ized
ill il	-ness	-nesses	

WORD CONSTRUCTION

Practice writing these words in *Speedwriting* in your notebook.

importantly, important-ly

weakness, w-k-ness

publications, public-tion-s

fairness, f-r-ness

eagerness, e-guh-r-ness

fitness, f-t-ness

loneliness, l-n-ly-ness

hardness, h-r-d-ness

emptiness, em-t-e-ness

weaknesses, w-k-nesses

WRITING ASSIGNMENT

Write the following sentences in *Speedwriting*.

1. Did you know that the committee hopes to complete its review in time for the council meeting on Wednesday?
2. I feel that you would be the best person to talk about the accomplishments of our committee at the meeting on Monday.
3. If Thursday is okay with you, we will use this opportunity to update our schedules and incorporate the latest changes.
4. The committee is preparing a budget to reduce the federal deficit by several billions of dollars each year.
5. We are continuing to make deliveries on time because of the prompt and efficient service that is representative of our staff.

READING AND WRITING EXERCISES

1

Wheels and Good Deals

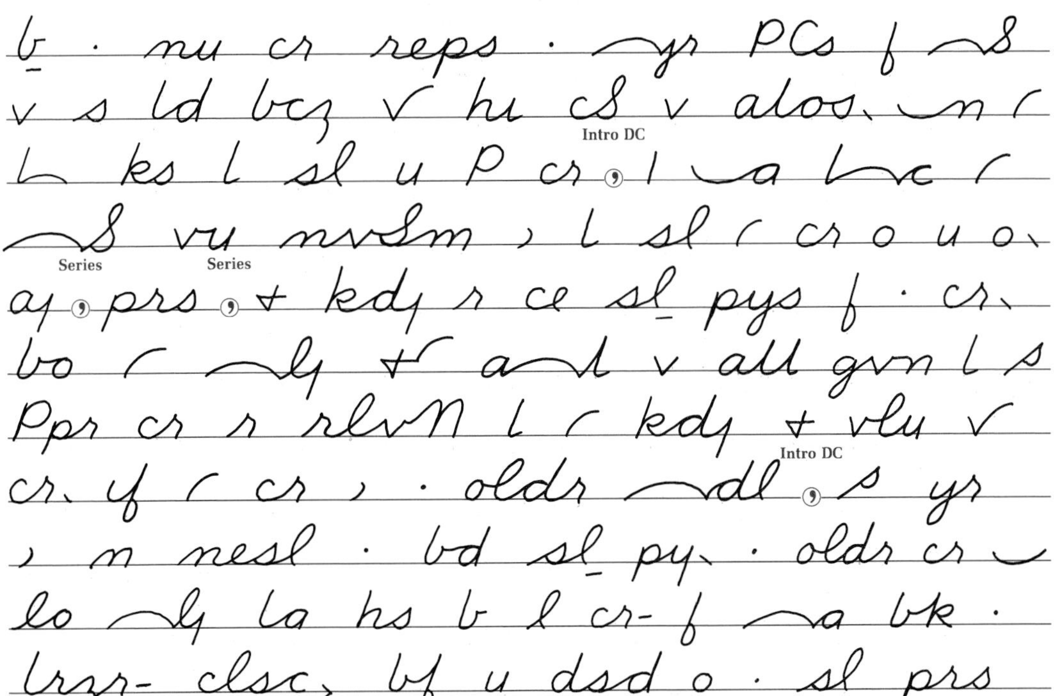

fu cr, (Intro DC) asc u bq or lbrre f plbjs
kln inf o jn ⌒r vlus. q rec cp
l Aso hlp u ⌒c r sl. Pds rses
f ⌒l rprs c nSl lrS + cdb .
⌒pl sl py l r br. sl u old cr
cdb . v ⌒rll ndvr.

2

dr + ⌒rs cr⌒r
⌒ dli- l nf⌒ u
la wb asn- l hNl
u plse. z u lrn-
f⌒, L, (Intro DC) u f⌒r ajN
z P⌒o- l VP. idlc
l A la r P⌒ k n
rcgnj v , olSN
kbjs l r co, Alo
as⌒ , dles lb v
Clnj, (Intro DC) i pln l ku
r P⌒l + lro Svs
crc v ⌒r jnsn. z
. frS Sp idlc l ⌒e
u Psnll + rvu u
plse ldl la r cvrj
⌒es u crN nds,
bcz r ⌒pl f bo vu
lb P du r kvrsj, (Intro DC) l
cl o Wd Ma 27 l
fN . ⌒ kv f E. /
lb . plzr vzl ⌒ u.
⌒ nu lu sle + ilc
fw ⌒c nu frNs. su

3

d ⌒lvn Alo w gvn
⌒C U lu sugj la i
rn f . se w hos v

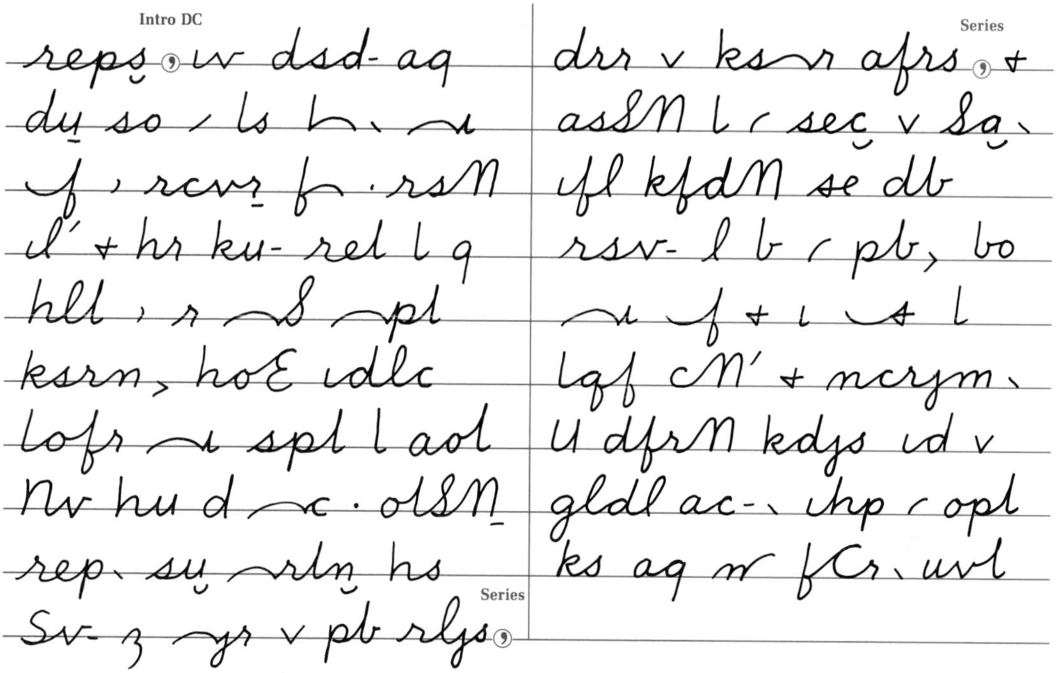

KEY

WRITING ASSIGNMENT

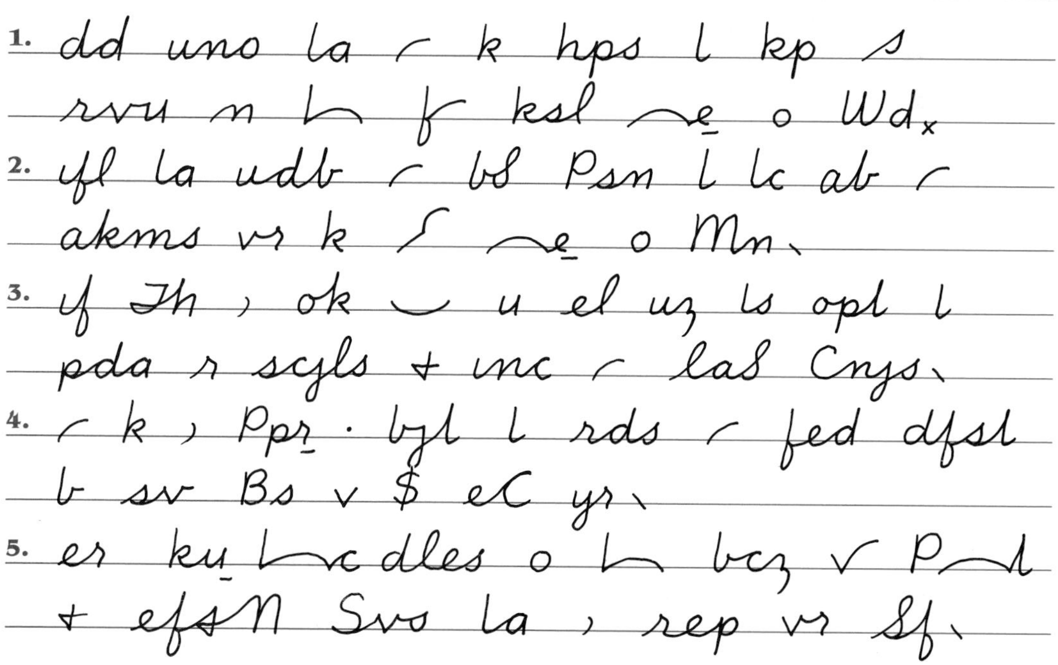

READING AND WRITING EXERCISES

1

Wheels and Good Deals

Buying a new car represents a major purchase for most of us today because of the high cost of autos.[1] When the time comes to sell your present car, one way to make the most of your investment is to sell the car on your[2] own. Age, price, and condition are key selling points for a car. Both the mileage and the amount of attention given[3] to its proper care are relevant to the condition and value of the car. If the car is an older[4] model, its year is not necessarily a bad selling point. An older car with low mileage that has been well[5] cared for may become a treasured classic.

Before you decide on a selling price for your car, ask your bank or[6] library for publications containing information on general market values. Good record keeping will[7] also help you make the sale. Producing receipts for timely repairs can instill trust and could be an important[8] selling point to the buyer. Selling your old car could be a very worthwhile endeavor. (176)

2

Dear Mr. and Mrs. Cramer:

I am delighted to inform you that I have been assigned to handle your[1] policy. As you learned from his letter, your former agent was promoted to vice president. I would like to add[2] that the promotion came in recognition of his outstanding contributions to our company.

Although[3] assuming his duties will be very challenging, I plan to continue the prompt and thorough service characteristic[4] of Mr. Johnson. As a first step, I would like to meet you personally and review your policy[5] to determine that the coverage meets your current needs.

Because it is important for both of you to be[6] present during our conversation, I will call on Wednesday, May 27, to find a time convenient for[7] everyone. It will be a pleasure visiting with you. I am new to your city, and I look forward to making[8] new friends. Sincerely yours, (164)

3

Dear Melvin:

Although I have given much thought to your suggestion that I run for a seat in the House of Representatives,[1] I have decided against doing so at this time. My wife is recovering from a recent illness,[2] and her continued return to good health is our most important concern.

However, I would like to offer my[3] support to another individual who would make an outstanding representative. Sue Martin has[4] served as manager of public relations, director of consumer affairs, and assistant to the Secretary[5] of State. I feel confident she would be received well by the public.

Both my wife and I wish to thank you[6] for your kindness and encouragement. Under different conditions, I would have gladly accepted. I hope the[7] opportunity comes again in the future. Yours very truly, (152)

UNIT 27

Notetaking for Research Projects

You will do many reports and papers while you are in high school and college. These assignments will involve extensive use of the library, and your notetaking ability will help you record facts and summaries quickly and accurately.

First, you must have a thorough understanding of your assignment. Then choose a topic that interests you and is appropriate for carrying out the assignment. After you have chosen a subject, limit it to a workable scope. Then develop a tentative central idea you propose to develop. This central theme and a tentative outline may not emerge until you have done some reading, so the next step is to consult the library.

Many libraries are arranged by the *Dewey Decimal System*, which divides knowledge into ten groups. The main divisions are as follows:

000 General Works	500 Science
100 Philosophy	600 Technology
200 Religion	700 The Arts and Recreation
300 Social Sciences	800 Literature
400 Languages	900 Geography, Biography, and History

To find the decimal numbers under which information may be found on a particular topic, it is necessary to consult the catalogs or indexes under the specific name of the subject. Books are usually listed three times—on an author card, a title card, and at least one subject card. Author, title, and subject indexes take the place of card files in those libraries where computerized catalogs are used. After you have found your sources of information and decided on a central idea, you can begin taking notes.

Follow the good techniques for notetaking that you have been using. The main difference for research papers is one of mechanics and specifics. Take all notes on large index cards rather than in a notebook as you have been doing for your other notetaking activities. It is very easy to add notes on notecards if additional sources are located. It is essential to keep a separate, complete card record of each source of information you use. These cards will provide the specialized information needed for your footnotes and bibliography.

SPEEDWRITING PRINCIPLES

1. When using salutations and closings in context, write them according to the rule.

gentlemen, j-nt-l-men jNlm sincerely, s-n-s-r-ly snsrl

cordially, k-r-j-l-ly crjll

ABBREVIATIONS

advertise av Christmas Xms

BRIEF FORMS

always a prove pv

consider ks note nl

ordinary ord

BRIEF FORM DEVELOPMENT

consideration ksj improvement ꟷpvm

noted nl- approval apvl

ordinarily ordl

COMMONLY MISSPELLED WORDS

opportunity opl

preferred Pfr-

VOCABULARY STUDY

corporate stocks
crprl Scs

Shares in the ownership of a corporation.

search and screen committee
SC + scrn k

Committee appointed to evaluate the credentials of job applicants and recommend candidates for the position. Often used in educational institutions.

PRINCIPLES SUMMARY

1. In context, write salutations and closings according to the rule: gentlemen, j-nt-l-men jNlm .

WORD DEVELOPMENT

Write the following related words in *Speedwriting* in your notebook.

attempt 	-ed	-s	-ing
counsel *ksl*	-ed	-s	-or
state *Sa*	e-	-d	-ment
request *rqS*	-s	-ed	-ing
accommodate *akda*	-d	-s	-ing

WORD CONSTRUCTION

Practice writing these words in *Speedwriting* in your notebook.

considered,
 consider-duh

encounter, en-count-r

requirements,
 re-quire-ment-s

greatness, great-ness

notes, note-s

conversation,
 con-v-r-s-tion

pleasures, p-l-z-r-s

contempt, con-t-m-t

approved,
 a-prove-duh

improving,
 im-prove-ing

WRITING ASSIGNMENT

Write the following sentences in *Speedwriting*.

1. This letter is in response to your inquiry about contributing part of your income to a trust fund.
2. It gives me pleasure to invite you to deliver the main address at the meeting in Boston, Massachusetts.
3. Will you please share your comments with me as soon as you have completed the test and determined the results?
4. The director of field services is coming in from Madison, Wisconsin, and we would like her to visit your plant.

5. Will you please measure the size of the equipment to make certain that it is appropriate for our space requirements?

READING AND WRITING EXERCISES

1

Roses for Everyone

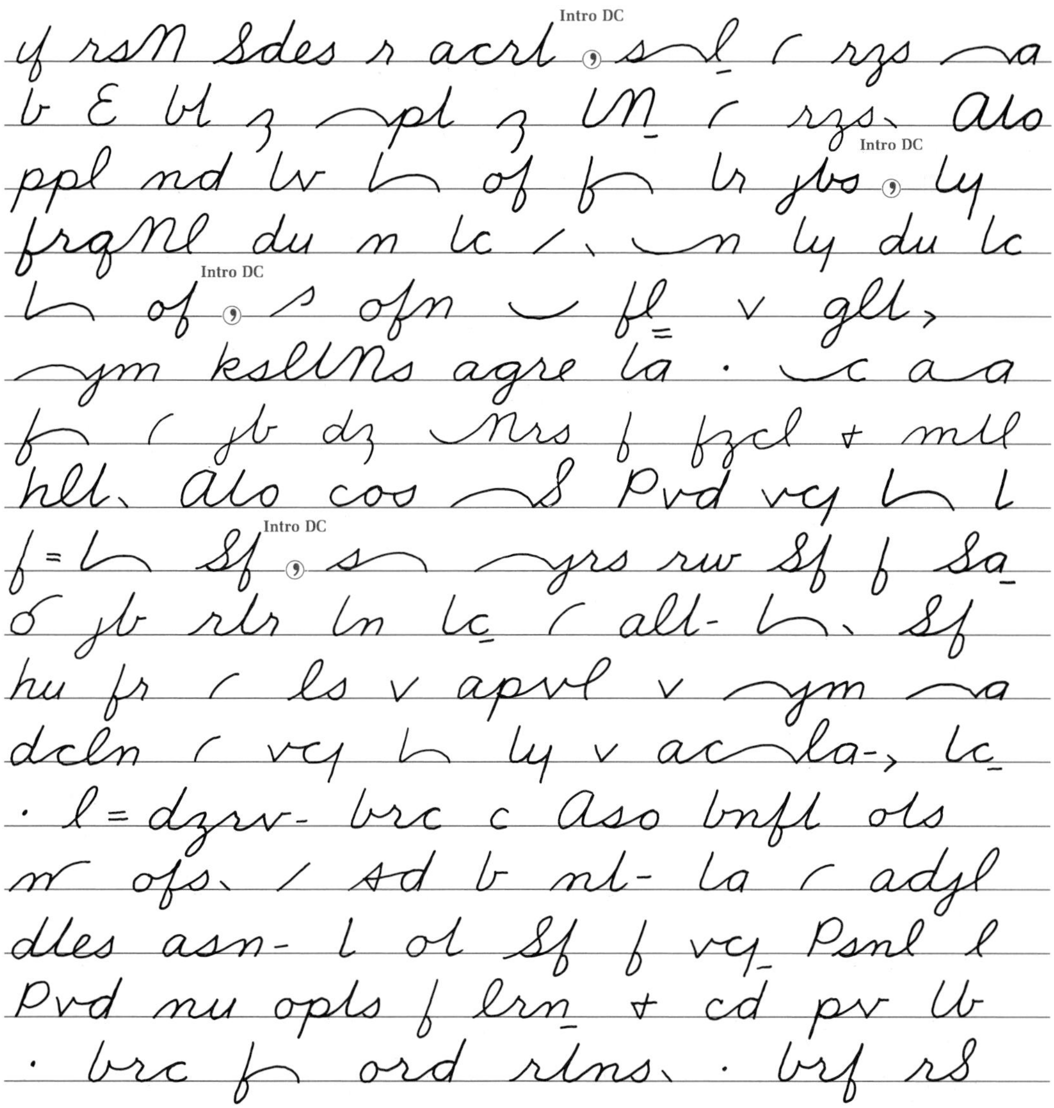

lpcll rzlls n ⌒pv- olpl + ·
hper nvrnm f El.

2

dK Ap 15 , qcl
aprC + e ⌒8 rds
r ntr Sc v nu +
uz- crs. la ⌒ns gr
sv f ⌒z sprs. ls
yr el ofr btr Dks
ln E bf, bgn Fb 3
el rn f=pj nzppr
Avms U ⌒ pb ab r
lo prss b er gv u ·
opl lgl ahd v r+.
er nvr lyl Ks lc
u l lc Avj v lz gr
sv o Fb 2. ul fM ·
Series
⌒d rnj v ⌒cs ⑨
Series
⌒dls ⑨ + prss f⌒
⌒C l Cz, ul Aso
v E ksj n ⌒c ord
cr arms. r Cf cr
ofsr lb o hN du
sl hrs l apv u cr,
rmbr erl sprs
A v ⌒ bs Cyss.
ehp lse u lr. ul

3

dr evns z r vlu-
K uno la r Sr lcs
prd n hNl ol ⌒
bs n jNlms ⌒r. ls
plse hs pv- Lb ⌒
⌒8 ⌒pl rzn Nvs
lc u ku l sp hr, ls
yr ev · Sprz fu. l
so r apj f spl uv
gvn r bs el ofr · bf=
Xs sl f Pfr-Ks, j8

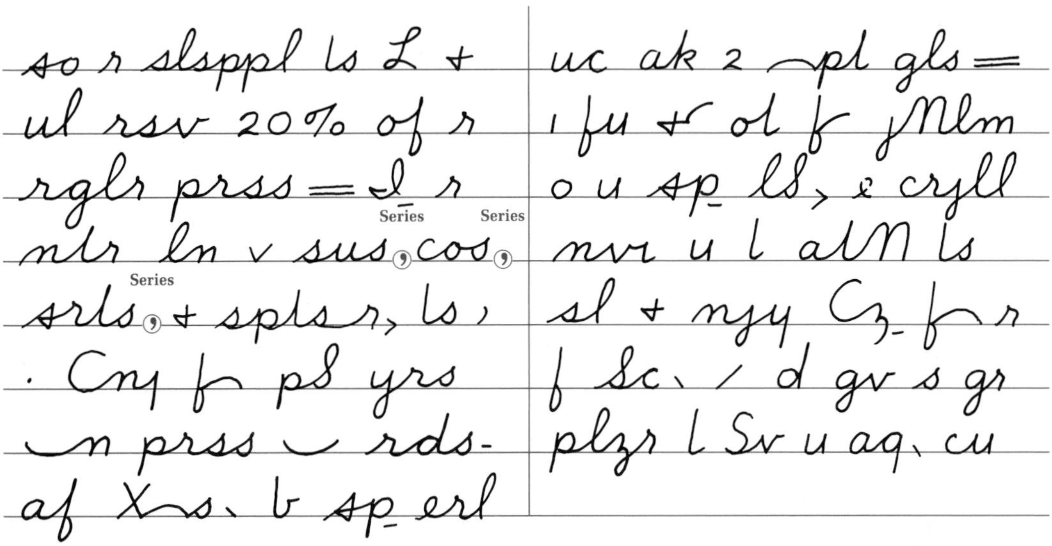

KEY

WRITING ASSIGNMENT

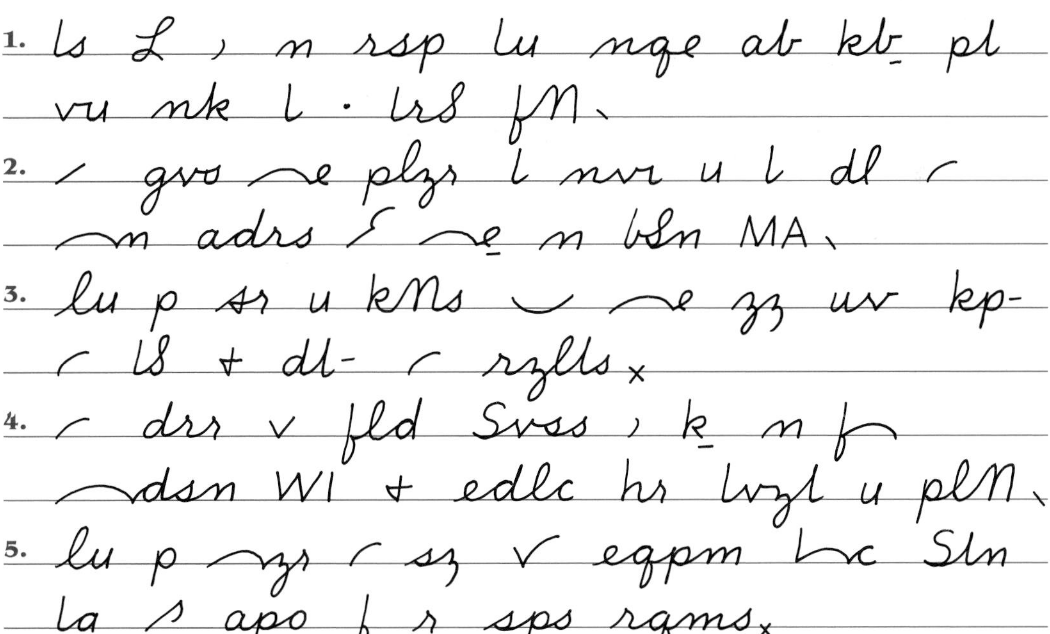

READING AND WRITING EXERCISES

1

Roses for Everyone

If recent studies are accurate, smelling the roses may be every bit as important as tending the[1] roses. Although people need to have time off from their jobs, they frequently do not take it. When they do take time off,[2] it is often with feelings of guilt.

Management consultants agree that a week away from the job does wonders[3] for physical and mental health. Although companies must provide vacation time to full-time staff, some managers[4] reward staff for staying on the job rather than taking the allotted time. Staff who fear the loss of approval[5] of management may decline the vacation time they have accumulated.

Taking a well-deserved break can[6] also benefit others in the office. It should be noted that the additional duties assigned to other[7] staff for vacationing personnel will provide new opportunities for learning and could prove to be a[8] break from ordinary routines. A brief rest typically results in improved output and a happier[9] environment for everyone. (185)

2

Dear Customer:

April 15 is quickly approaching, and we must reduce our entire stock of new and used cars.[1] That means great savings for wise shoppers. This year we will offer better discounts than ever before.

Beginning[2] February 3, we will run full-page newspaper advertisements telling the public about our low prices, but[3] we are giving you an opportunity to get ahead of the rush. We are inviting loyal customers[4] like you to take advantage of these great savings on February 2. You will find a wide range of makes, models,[5] and prices from which to choose.

You will also have every consideration in making ordinary credit[6] arrangements. Our chief credit officer will be on hand during sale hours to approve your credit.

Remember,[7] early shoppers always have the best choices. We hope to see you there. Yours truly, (154)

3

Dear Mr. Evans:

As our valued customer, you know that our store takes pride in handling only the best in[1] gentlemen's wear. This policy has proved to be the most important reason individuals like you continue[2] to shop here.

This year we have a surprise for you. To show our appreciation for the support you have given[3] our business, we will offer a before-Christmas sale for preferred customers.

Just show our salespeople this letter,[4] and you will receive 20 percent off our regular prices—including our entire line of suits, coats,[5] shirts, and sportswear.

This is a change from past years when prices were reduced after Christmas. By shopping early, you can[6] accomplish two important goals—one for you and the other for the gentlemen on your shopping list.

We[7] cordially invite you to attend this sale and enjoy choosing from our full stock. It would give us great pleasure to serve[8] you again. Cordially yours, (165)

UNIT

28

Review and Reinforcement

1. You learned to write the following word beginnings in Units 22–27:

em, im

2. The following word endings were also presented:

quire q

ness

3. The following words illustrate all of the new principles you learned in Units 22–27:

emphasize, em-f-s-z fsz

impress, im-p-r-s prs

image, im-j j

attempt, a-t-m-t at t

promptly, prah-m-t-ly P tl

temptation, t-m-t-tion t t

requirement, re-quire-ment rqm

inquiry, in-quire-e nqe

acquire, a-quire aq

kindness, k-nd-ness cN'

witnesses, w-t-nesses t"

account, a-count ak

common, com-n kn

concern, con-s-r-n ksrn

still, st-l Sl

estate, e-st-ate eSa

most, m-st S

pleasure, p-l-z-r plzr

measure, m-z-r zr

treasure, t-r-z-r trzr

illness, i-l-ness l'

4. Salutations and closings in context are written this way:

sincerely, s-n-s-r-ly *snsrl* cordially, k-r-j-l-ly *cjll*

gentlemen, j-nt-l-men *jNlm*

5. Days of the week are written this way:

Sunday	*Sn*	Thursday	*Th*
Monday	*Mn*	Friday	*Fr*
Tuesday	*Tu*	Saturday	*St*
Wednesday	*Wd*		

6. The names of cities and their state abbreviations are written as follows:

Boston, MA	*bSn* MA	Tulsa, OK	*Usa* OK
Las Vegas, NV	*ls vgs* NV	Dallas, TX	*dls* TX

7. Transcribe the following abbreviations in your notebook:

~dse	*etc*	*fed*
S	*q*	*esp*
gvt	*ok*	*ql*
U	*rep*	*inc*
av	*X~s*	

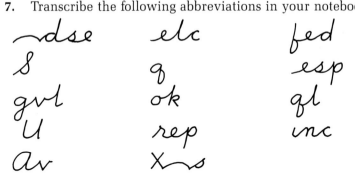

8. Write these brief forms in your notebook:

committee	come	industry
ever	satisfy	continue
other	character	deliver
both	public	satisfactory
individual	important	complete
came	characteristic	every
importance	contribute	opportunity
convenient	convenience	always
note	prove	consider
accomplish	ordinary	

READING AND WRITING EXERCISES

1

Forgotten Presidents

no dol ucd ri . prgrf or 2 6 lf
+ ls v fs Ps b n E P, so
l rmbr-. dd uno la zcre Ulr z
(fr8 r hro l bk P bcz v ,
llre rply× hoE zcre Ulr di- af
Sv f ol 16 os. h lft me Pbls
+ . VP hu z n l Ppr- f ofs.
lrd flr z . Sa rep f bflo
NY. l h z Sv (r8 v Ulrs lr (Intro DC)
flr rds- (prs v Sps f 5¢
l 3¢. flr z n nma- f . sec
lr + , no b8 rmbr- f b (
l8 rmbr- P> frqln prs flo-
flr n ofs + ak- lll n r
nys mre. prs dru Dplzr f , o
plld ple + lft ofs n blr dfe.
nyl cAus ollv- r mres v lz m.
(svl r z ol 1 P aa.

2

dr dvs elb hpe
lsN . njnr lu h⌒
⌒c . kp anlss vu
he + cl sS⌒ , crcs
u dS- O , fn Nca
lau unl , v dfrN
f ⌒S v unls e
se , bcz , n . kn
unl (Intro DC) er sN , r Cf
njnr ⌒c , anlss
Psnll , h l pln , vzl
, u erlS kv + rpl
, fN Pll , ec ln
asr u gs ab rpr or
rpls , unl , if ,
bks nes l od . nu
unl (Intro DC) , eqpm lb dl-
+ nSl- f PCs prs
go- lu orjnll , p cl
r hdglrs ⌒c arms
f anlss , uvl

3

dr jnsn lgf rsp-
l ⌒ rz⌒a + L v
aplc f pzj v rplr ,
iz v hpe l lrn la
⌒ U ksj f . opn o
u bs rz Sf , il gldl
sN u adjl exs v ⌒
rz + ne ol inf u
dzr , z u rqS- (Intro DC) i asc-
2 v ⌒ clj Pfsrs l
ri Ls v rcmj , usd
rsv Ls f dr ⌒s
⌒lsn + dr szn
An ⌒n . fu ds , bcz
v ⌒ bcgroN n bs
+ ecos ifl Sln icd
kb ⌒C z . bs rplr ,
cd e sl p . ⌒e l
Dcs ls frlr , idb
hpe lk l allNa +
dl ⌒ rz exs n

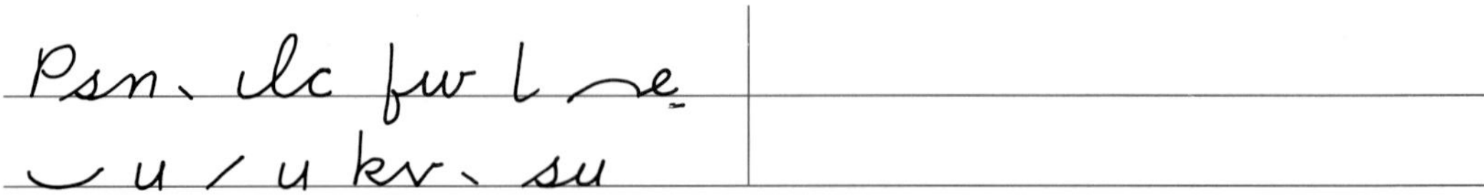

KEY

ABBREVIATIONS

merchandise	et cetera	federal
street	question	especially
government	okay	quart
university	represent, representative	incorporate, incorporated
advertise	Christmas	

BRIEF FORMS

k	k	N
E	sal	ku
ol	crc	dl
bo	pb	sal
Nv	⌢pl	kp
k	crc	E
⌢pl	kb	opl
kv	kv	a
nl	pv	ks
ak	ord	

READING AND WRITING EXERCISES

1

Forgotten Presidents

No doubt you could write a paragraph or two on the life and times of famous Presidents, but not every[1] President is so well remembered. Did you know that Zachary Taylor was the first war hero to become[2] President because of his military reputation? However, Zachary Taylor died after serving for[3] only 16 months. He left many problems and a Vice President who was not well prepared for office. Millard[4] Fillmore was a state representative from Buffalo, New York. While he was serving the rest of Taylor's term, Fillmore[5] reduced the price of stamps from 5¢ to 3¢. Fillmore was not nominated for a second term and is now[6] best remembered for being the least remembered President.

Franklin Pierce followed Fillmore in office and accomplished[7] little more in our nation's memory. Pierce drew displeasure from his own political party and left office[8] in bitter defeat. National issues outlived our memories of these men. The Civil War was only one[9] President away. (184)

2

Dear Mr. Davis:

We will be happy to send an engineer to your home to make a complete analysis[1] of your heating and cooling system. The characteristics you described over the phone indicate that your unit[2] is very different from most of the units we see. Because it is not a common unit, we are sending[3] our chief engineer to make the analysis personally. He will plan the visit at your earliest[4] convenience and report his findings promptly.

We can then answer your questions about repairing or replacing[5] the unit. If it becomes necessary to order a new unit, the equipment will be delivered and[6] installed for the purchase price quoted to you originally.

Please call our headquarters to make arrangements for[7] the analysis. Yours very truly, (147)

3

Dear Mr. Johnson:

Thank you for responding to my resumé and letter of application for the position[1] of reporter.

I was very happy to learn that I am under consideration for an opening[2] on your business writing staff. I will gladly send you additional examples of my writing and any[3] other information you desire.

As you requested, I asked two of my college professors to write letters of[4] recommendation. You should receive letters from Dr. Thomas Wilson and Dr. Susan Allen within a[5] few days.

Because of my background in business and economics, I feel certain I could contribute much as a[6] business reporter. Could we set up a meeting to discuss this further?

I would be happy to come to Atlanta[7] and deliver my writing examples in person. I look forward to meeting with you at your convenience.[8] Sincerely yours, (163)

PART FIVE

Participating in the Dictation Process

Many administrators set aside a certain time of the day for dictation to avoid being interrupted by telephone calls, appointments, or visitors. Others dictate at different times each day, depending upon their schedules. Skilled employees are always ready to record as well as to give dictation. This flexibility makes an individual a more valuable member of the communication team.

RECORDING DICTATION

When you record dictation, focus your attention on the person who is dictating even more sharply than you would in notetaking so that you can hear and accurately record every word. However, if you miss a word, skip a space and ask the person who is dictating to repeat it for you immediately after the dictation.

Your goal is to record dictation completely, quickly, and accurately. By following a few systematic procedures, you will be able to record all information and special details in an organized way without interrupting the thoughts of the person who is dictating. Practice these step-by-step procedures.

1. Assembling materials
   a. Use a rubber band to separate previously recorded dictation from unused pages so that you can immediately open your notepad to a new page.
   b. Attach several paper clips to the back of your *Speedwriting* notepad to flag priority items or to signal special instructions.
   c. Take an extra pen in case the first one stops writing.

d. Use a colored pen to write corrections, to make changes, or to indicate special instructions.

2. Recording dictation

a. Seat yourself comfortably so that you can write easily and hear clearly—possibly across from the person who is dictating or beside his or her desk, using the desk to support your notepad.

b. Date the bottom of the page to identify the day's dictation.

c. If you miss a word or you are not sure about a word, wait until the person dictating has finished the letter or memo. Then ask, "Excuse me, I'm not sure about a word you used. May I read the sentence back to you?"

d. Do not be embarrassed to ask the person who is dictating to speak more slowly if the dictation is faster than you are able to record comfortably. An accurate transcript produced from slightly slower dictation is much more valuable than an inaccurate transcript produced from more rapid dictation. (Note: This fact does not mean that your instructor should not "push you" or encourage you to develop recording speed. A higher recording speed will enable you to take more complete notes during a lecture or a meeting where you may have no control over the presentation speed. Speed potential is just one of many advantages *Speedwriting* has over other alphabetic writing systems.)

e. If the dictation is interrupted, use the time to read your notes. Use your colored pen to insert punctuation, write instructions, or identify any words that are not clear.

f. Flag rush items with a paper clip or colored pen.

Make sure you have all the information you need. If you have additional questions, ask them. If you are uncertain about where to find the spellings of names, addresses, or certain enclosures, ask now. As soon as you return to your desk, review your special notations to clarify details and instructions. Transcribe your notes as soon as time allows, beginning with high-priority items.

GIVING DICTATION

As you assume additional administrative responsibilities, the more dictation you will be giving to one of your assistants. Whether you dictate "live" to another individual or to a machine for transcription at a later time, proper dictation techniques can enhance the quality of the transcription.

In planning for dictation, the material to be transcribed immediately should be designated top priority. Material that could be transcribed at any time within the next few days should be designated low priority.

Prior to responding to correspondence, organize your thoughts by underlining and making marginal notations on the original correspondence regarding the most important points of each letter or memorandum being answered. Also, attach other material to the correspondence being answered when such attachments would help in preparing the response.

Immediately before the actual dictation of each piece of correspondence begins, indicate any special instructions. If there is a special letter style to be used or if more than one file copy is needed, make such notations at this time.

When dictation begins, speak distinctly in a relaxed, natural manner. Give instructions for special capitalization and punctuation such as hyphens, dashes, colons, apostrophes, and paragraph endings. Material to be typed in all capitals or material to be underscored should be designated. Difficult words and "sound-alike" words should be spelled in order to avoid confusion. Unusual spellings should also be dictated; i.e., the name Smythe might be spelled—s-m-y as in yesterday-t-h-e.

At the completion of the dictation, indicate any special mailing instructions; and if other individuals are to receive a copy of the correspondence, give their names and addresses.

Effective dictation and transcription skills are indeed complementary abilities. An employee's ability to dictate competently and transcribe accurately can do much to increase the productivity of any business.

UNIT

29 Preparing Research Papers

When doing research papers, you will be reading from several sources and authors. Notes for your research paper should be in the form of either brief summaries in your own words of the information you gained from your reading or direct quotations taken verbatim from the material you have read. If you are quoting material directly, copy it exactly—word for word. Enclose it in quotation marks if it is a fairly short quote, usually four lines or less; or single space and double indent it in your research paper if it is a lengthy direct quote, usually five lines or more. Indirect citing (referencing material expressed in your own words but taken from a specific source) should also be footnoted; however, quotation marks around such material are not needed.

Whether you are making direct or indirect citations, your notes should be complete and in a form that provides enough reference support so that you will not have to go back later to your original sources to gather reference information.

Take notes on large notecards (5″ x 8″) and use as much *Speedwriting* as possible to accelerate the notetaking process. Here are some tips for creating effective notecards.

1. Write on only one side of the notecards.
2. Limit notes on each card to a single topic.
3. Indicate the source and page number on each card. This information is essential when you begin preparing your footnotes and bibliography.

If you prepare good, clear notecards while researching your topic, writing the paper from your notecards should be fairly easy. Here are some steps to follow when writing the paper from your notecards.

1. Arrange the notecards in groups according to headings.
2. Make a revised outline from the headings on the cards, if necessary.
3. Arrange the cards in the same order as your outline.

4. Write a rough draft of your paper. Using a word processor to draft your paper will greatly facilitate the actual writing process.
5. Make necessary additions, corrections, and deletions.
6. Proofread for all types of errors and make final corrections.

The following questions can serve as a checklist for your use in evaluating present and future research papers.

1. Is the title of your paper original and interesting?
2. Did you limit your subject adequately?
3. Did you locate a sufficient quantity and variety of source material?
4. Did you write your bibliographical information and notes on index cards and copy the bibliographical information exactly as it appears on the title page of each reference?
5. Did you take notes in your own words when not using direct quotations?
6. Did you take notes from your material in phrases and summary statements that were easily understandable?
7. Did you copy direct quotations exactly and enclose them in quotation marks?
8. Did you note the exact page or pages on which a quotation or paraphrased information was found?
9. Do your notecards all have subject headings and contain material relating to the same point?
10. Were you able to arrange your materials in a logical order to facilitate easy writing of your paper?
11. Does your paper read well?
12. Does your paper support your central idea?
13. Do you have sufficient backup material for your central theme?
14. Have you followed the mechanics of the footnote form preferred by your instructor?
15. Is your bibliography in alphabetical order and taken directly from the required information you noted on your cards?
16. Do you have a title page prepared with the title of your paper, your name, the course name and section, and the date?

17. Have you proofread your paper for errors and made the necessary corrections?

SPEEDWRITING PRINCIPLES

1. Write \ for words beginning with the sound of any vowel + x (*aks, eks, iks, oks, uks,* or *eggs*).

accident, x-d-nt vdN

exist, x-st vs

explain, x-p-l-n vpln

examination, x-min-tion vmj

excite, x-ite vi

excellent, x-l-nt vlN

Remember to write x for the medial and final sound of x.

boxes, b-x-s bxs

textbook, t-x-t-b-k txtbc

tax, t-x tx

relax, re-l-x rlx

2. Write X for the word beginnings *extr* and *extra.*

extreme, extr-m Xm

extremely, extr-m-ly Xml

extra X

extraordinary, extra-ordinary Xord

Write these additional words:

express, x-p-r-s vprs

maximum, m-x-mum mxm

exchange, x-chay-n-j vCnj

index, nd-x Nx

extend, x-t-nd vtN

reflex, re-f-l-x rflx

PHRASES

you will find ulfN

as your zu

to call tcl

on you ou

as you zu

on your ou

MORE INTRODUCTORY DEPENDENT CLAUSES

PUNCTUATION STUDY

Introductory dependent clauses beginning with such words as *after*, *while*, and *whether* will be highlighted in your Reading and Writing Exercises.

- □ *After* I study the report, I will write her a memo.
- □ *While* we were reviewing your account, I noticed that your contract renewal is scheduled for next month.
- □ *Whether* you are looking for a specific item or gift ideas in general, you'll find our clerks eager to help.

VOCABULARY STUDY

copy editor cpe edlr — A person employed to edit written material for publication.

unit price unl prs — The price for an individual item selected from a larger quantity of like merchandise.

PRINCIPLES SUMMARY

1. Write \ for words beginning with any vowel + x: explain, x-p-l-n \pln.

   Write x for the medial and final sound of x: boxes, b-x-s bxs.

2. Write X for the word beginnings *extr* and *extra*: extreme, extr-m X; extraordinary, extra-ordinary Xord.

WORD DEVELOPMENT

Write the following related words in *Speedwriting* in your notebook.

relax rlx	-es	-ed	-ation
express \prs	-es	-ed	-ing
explain \pln	-ed	-s	-ing
expand \pN	-s	-ed	-ing
excite \i	-d	-s	-ing

WORD CONSTRUCTION

Practice writing these words in *Speedwriting* in your notebook.

taxes, t-x-s	existing, x-st-ing
accidents, x-d-nt-s	except, x-p-t
mix, m-x	extension, x-t-n-sion
excessively, x-s-v-ly	exception, x-p-tion
export, x-port	extras, extra-s

WRITING ASSIGNMENT

Self-dictate the following letter as you write it in *Speedwriting*.

Dear Howard:

Attached is a copy of a new plan offered by a savings and loan company in town. After[1] reading the brochure, I felt certain you would want to see it. Perhaps we could use the payment plan offered.

Of course,[2] I know we will need much information to determine if the plan is appropriate for our company. Will[3] you let me know if you like the plan? I will be glad to set a time for the manager and us to talk. Very[4] truly yours, (82)

READING AND WRITING EXERCISES

1

A Simple Investment Plan

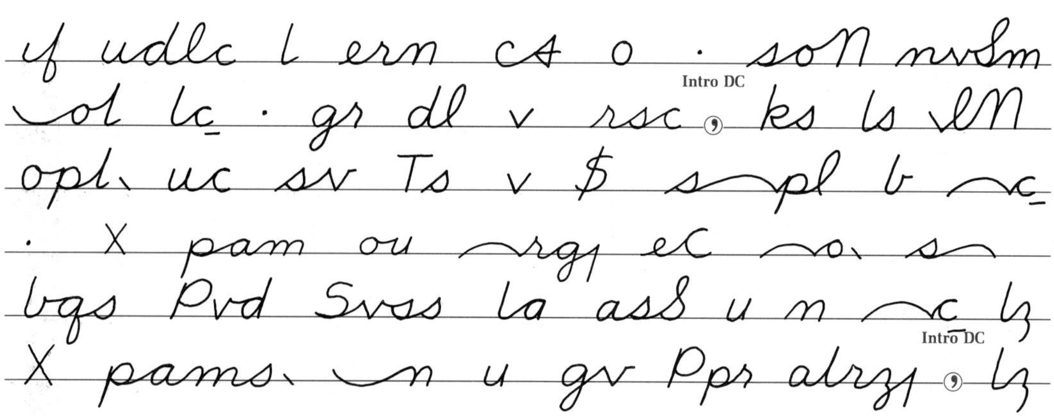

bqs at-lcl -dra fMs f- u ak
+ sN (pam lu -rgj co - (
apo nSrcjs. Alo ls , n . Svs knl
Intro DC
ofs- b A bqs, . gro No r bgn
Intro DC
lz Pgs. if u bq dz n Pvd ls Svs,
asc . ln ofsr l vpln ho -c (
X pam ou -rgj, ls r A -l
Series
-as l spN me=X-s Ap n Dc,
Series
. gr sl n Jl, + -prsv vq lrps
(yr aroN. -n u A jS 50$ l
Intro DC
1H$ eC -o l . -rgj pam, uc
cl sv yrs of . 30=yr ln. las .pln
-rl gv p . fu -ys f.

2

ds edws -
apl f pzj v cpe
edlr - u fr. ulv
ulfN - u bcgroN
apo f dles dS- n
u nzppr Avm. l-
w enc- rz-a , . lS

v bcs w edl-. w
Series
Aso rln Nxs, cvr
Series
cpe, + Av brsrs. du
(lS 4 yrs w -fsz-
Sdes n kpur Pq->
- X-l egr l -e
- u + lrn - ab
u dpl. u co Pdss

lN bcs C rahil
w rpls. a e
Dcs ls pzj n Psn x
l cl o Jn 23 l ar.
apym / u kv, lc
fw l lc u ln vlu

3

f r sm v ofs splis
arv- n lN kdj + o
scyl ls rn. l
e Cc r dse aq r
Intro DC
inv, e Dcvr-. X od
v envs. Alo e rqs-
Intro DC
ol 20 bxs v envs, e
rsv- 21. eC bx kln-

r f and v 2H prN-
envs, e fN no my
v X envs o inv b
e se no rzn l rel
r X pcj + l A / l
r splis. ev dl-la
r Nv unl prs v eC
bx, 8 95 + er enc.
Cc f la and, if u
fl la ls dr rqs
Intro DC
frlr Dcj, p ll e
no. lqf P-d n dl
r gs. er ln sat-
r all gvn r
od. cu

KEY

WRITING ASSIGNMENT

d hord alC- , .
cpe v . nu pln
ofr- b . sv + ln

co n lon. af rd
r brsr i fll Sln
ud N lse / .

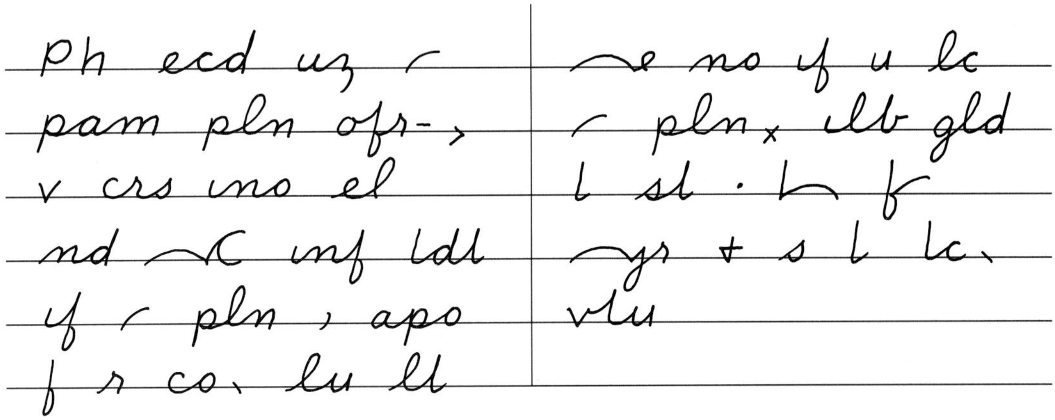

READING AND WRITING EXERCISES

1

A Simple Investment Plan

If you would like to earn cash on a sound investment without taking a great deal of risk, consider this excellent[1] opportunity. You can save thousands of dollars simply by making an extra payment on your mortgage[2] each month. Some banks provide services that assist you in making these extra payments. When you give proper[3] authorization, these banks automatically withdraw funds from your account and send the payment to your mortgage[4] company with the appropriate instructions. Although this is not a service commonly offered by all banks, a[5] growing number are beginning these programs. If your bank does not provide this service, ask a loan officer to[6] explain how to make the extra payment on your mortgage.

There are always tempting ways to spend money—Christmas[7] shopping in December, a great sale in July, and impressive vacation trips the year around. When you add just[8] $50 to $100 each month to a mortgage payment, you can cut several years off a[9] 30-year loan. That's a plan worth giving up a few temptations for. (191)

2

Dear Ms. Edwards:

I am applying for the position of copy editor with your firm. I believe you will[1] find my background appropriate for the duties described in your newspaper advertisement. Included in the[2] enclosed resumé is a list of books I have edited. I have also written indexes, cover copy,[3] and advertising brochures. During the last four years I have emphasized studies in computer programming.

I am[4] extremely eager to meet with you and learn more about your department. Your company produces excellent[5] books which rate highly in the marketplace. May we discuss this position in person? I will call on June 23[6] to arrange an appointment at your convenience.

I look forward to talking with you then. Very truly yours,[7] (140)

3

Gentlemen:

Our shipment of office supplies arrived in excellent condition and on schedule this morning. While[1] we were checking our merchandise against the invoice, we discovered an extra order of envelopes. Although[2] we requested only 20 boxes of envelopes, we received 21. Each box contained the full amount[3] of 200 printed envelopes.

We find no mention of the extra envelopes on the invoice, but we see[4] no reason to return the extra package and will add it to our supplies. We have determined that the[5] individual unit price of each box is $8.95, and we are enclosing a check for that[6] amount.

If you feel that this matter requires further discussion, please let me know. Thank you for your promptness in[7] delivering our goods. We are more than satisfied with the attention given our order. Cordially yours, (159)

UNIT 30

Proofreading and Editing

Proofreading means searching carefully for errors in written communication on a display screen or hard copy. Proofreading is a very important skill. It puts the final polish on any document and requires paying attention to many details. Concentration is needed for proofreading, so you should not attempt to proofread if there are distractions around you.

Proofreading is not to be confused with *editing*. Editing is the process of making changes to improve a written message. Editing is required after you have read and reread your research papers and reports and discovered that some rewriting and revising are required in order to improve the quality of your writing. It is rare that a paper is done perfectly the first time. Even the most experienced writers find that rewriting and editing are always necessary.

Preparing your paper on a word processor greatly facilitates editing because it permits sentences and paragraphs to be inserted, changed, rearranged, or deleted quickly and easily. A word processor also makes proofreading or error correction easier. However, it is not difficult to make corrections on a typewriter either. The goal of proofreading is to find all errors. Whether you produce your papers using a typewriter or a computer keyboard, there are certain basic guidelines to follow when proofreading and editing.

First, look at your document to see if the format is appropriate and attractive. Then proofread and correct the document while it is still on the screen or in the typewriter.

Second, read through the entire document to determine if it makes sense. Then, read it word by word, proofreading for errors and making corrections as you go along. Be sure to check for possible errors or improvements in spelling and word division, punctuation, paragraphing, grammar, spacing and formatting, and content.

It is important when proofreading to know what constitutes an error. Some common types of errors to look for include the following.

1. Spacing Errors; i.e., failure to
   a. provide spacing between words
   b. provide spacing after periods between sentences
   c. provide spacing after colons within a sentence

d. provide spacing after a comma or semicolon
e. double space the contents of a report
f. single space long quotations
g. single space footnotes
h. double space between footnotes

2. Content Errors; i.e., failure to
a. spell words correctly
b. punctuate correctly
c. have sentences and paragraphs make sense
d. use correct grammar

3. Keying Errors, including

	Example	**Correction**
a. omitting letters in words	*atitudes*	*attitudes*
b. adding letters to words	*exampple*	*example*
c. reversing letters	*reveiw*	*review*
d. using incorrect letters	*avout*	*about*

Word division should be used judiciously. Do not divide a word unless it is necessary and desirable. A slightly irregular right margin is better than an overabundance of hyphenated words.

SPEEDWRITING PRINCIPLES

1. Write *q* for the medial or final sound of any vowel + *ng* when the sound is part of the root word and is not a suffix (*ang, eng, ing, ong, ung*).

sang, s-ang *sq*
single, s-ing-l *sgl*
thing, ith-ing *lq*
nothing, n-ith-ing *nlq*
long, l-ong *lq*
young, y-ung *yq*

BRIEF FORMS

already *ar*
immediate *m*
approximate *apx*
next *nx*
experience *xp*

BRIEF FORM DEVELOPMENT

immediately ml approximately apxl

COMMONLY MISSPELLED WORDS

accept ac To receive:

□ Tom will be happy to *accept* our service award.

except vpl Not including:

□ Jane has completed everything *except* the monthly report.

VOCABULARY STUDY

item breakdown im brcdon A classification or division of items within a group or category.

PRINCIPLES SUMMARY

1. Write q for the medial or final sound of any vowel + *ng* when the sound is part of the root word and is not a suffix (*ang, eng, ing, ong, ung*): long, l-ong lq.

WORD DEVELOPMENT

Write the following related words in *Speedwriting* in your notebook.

long lq	a-	-er	-est
young yq	-er	-est	-ster
distinguish Dlgs	-ed	-es	-ing
experience vp	-d	-s	-ing
sing sq	-s	-er	-le

WORD CONSTRUCTION

Practice writing these words in *Speedwriting* in your notebook.

bring, b-r-ing strong, st-r-ong

things, ith-ing-s rings, r-ing-s

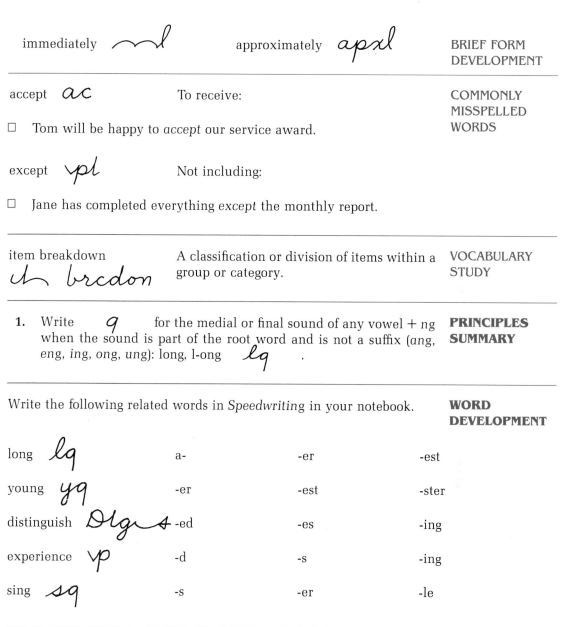

among, a-m-ong belonging, b-l-ong-ing

longing, l-ong-ing	brings, b-r-ing-s
spring, sp-r-ing	strongly, st-r-ong-ly

WRITING ASSIGNMENT

Self-dictate the following letter as you write it in *Speedwriting*.

Dear Mr. Brown:

We are happy to say we are enclosing a check for the money we owe you. We did indeed[1] discover a mistake in your hotel bill and are glad to return your money. We would like you to accept the[2] enclosed gift certificate for a free visit to our hotel. We hope to hear from you soon. When making your[3] travel plans, be certain to give us a call. Sincerely yours, (70)

READING AND WRITING EXERCISES

1

Canada

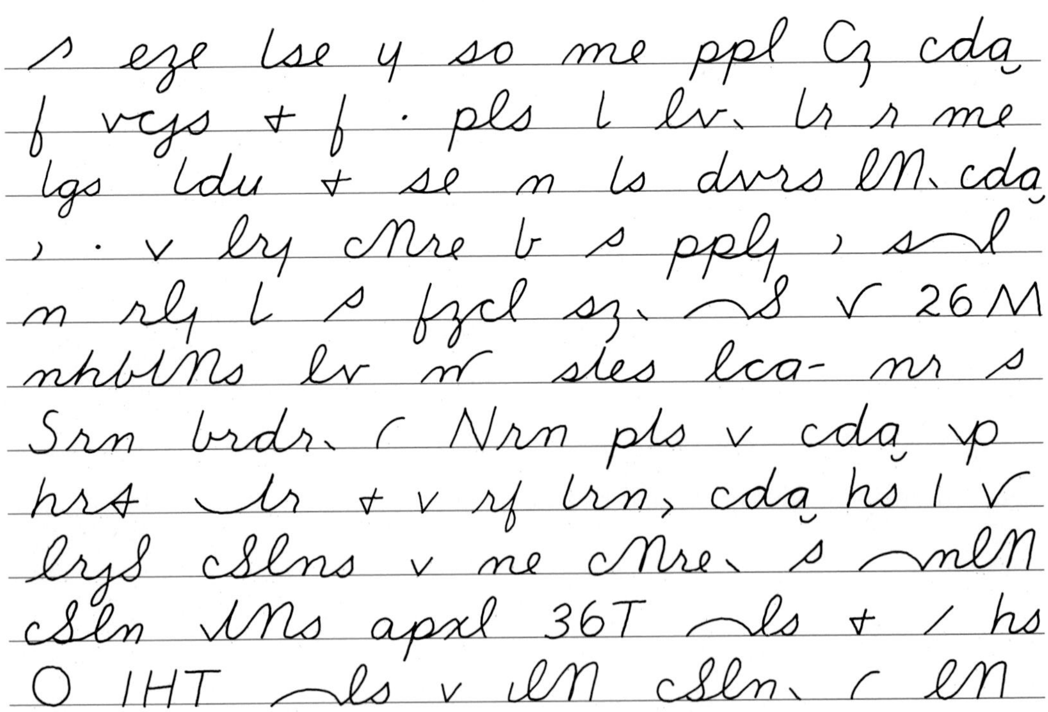

n bln (psfc + allNc ojs [Series] Ss ([Series]
vS rce, onNn rny, hve fSs, [Series]
Hs v lcs + rvrs, + gr prres,
yr sles Sv z clCrl + Nl sNrs.
cda) . yr fA ny bcz v s me
bdes [Series] v [Series] ls. s aso . yr splis v
e, yl, + lbs. s nCrl SoN
kbn- s v sles rc cda .
plzN pls l lv + . Cr lN lvzl.

2

dr Svns ls) yS .
rms l ll uno u
a no fl . vy ou
Sa prp lxs. n od
l lc avj v ls opl
u S fl b Ms 1,
if uv n h p fl f
. rgj [Intro DC] vy, ulfN (
Pss lb qi eze. lc (
enc- f lu ke lx
assr. (nlr Pss
lcs apxl 15 mls l
kp + l rzll n .
yr sv aq nx yrs
lxs, a l fsz aq
(pl v fl b Ms 1.
alo (vy aplis l
nx yrs lxs, [Intro DC] (S
b fl- ls yr, p cl o
e nE icb v
hlp. cu

3

mo l ⌒r + sls
Psnl erp- l a 2
nu mbrs l r Sf.
⌒r hrld sd + ⌒s
ble ⌒dsn jyn- r
dvj o Jl 15, bo v lz
ppl as ⌒ pz v
rjnl ⌒yr f eqpm
sls + Svs. hrld l
cvr ⌒ NE pl v
cMre + ble l cvr
⌒ W cs, hrld spM
9 yrs w US ar fs z
Cf nynr n Cq v ls
Pq. ble hs ⌒- sls
Pgs n CA, WA, + OR,
ble , ar op ol v hr
ofs n sn frnssco
+ hrld lb ⌒v nl
, bln ofs ⌒l. p
jyn ⌒e n lk lz v
nu ppl l r co.

KEY

WRITING ASSIGNMENT

dr bron er hpe
lsa er enc .
Cc f me e o u.
e dd ndd Dcvr
. Mlc n u hll bl
+ r gld l rel u
me. edlc u l
ac ⌒ enc- gfl
Slfcl f . fre vzl
l r hll. ehp
Uhr f u sn.
⌒n ⌒c u lrvl
plns b Sln lgv
s . cl. su

READING AND WRITING EXERCISES

1

Canada

It is easy to see why so many people choose Canada for vacations and for a place to live. There are[1] many things to do and see in this diverse land. Canada is a very large country, but its population[2] is small in relation to its physical size. Most of the 26,000,000 inhabitants live in the cities[3] located near its southern border. The northern parts of Canada experience harsh weather and have rough terrain.[4]

Canada has one of the largest coastlines of any country. Its mainland coastline extends approximately[5] 36,000 miles, and it has over 100,000 miles of island coastline. The land in between[6] the Pacific and Atlantic Oceans includes the vast Rocky Mountain range, heavy forests, hundreds of lakes and[7] rivers, and great prairies.

Major cities serve as cultural and industrial centers. Canada is a major[8] fishing nation because of its many bodies of water. It is also a major supplier of wheat,[9] oil, and timber. Its natural surroundings combined with its exciting cities make Canada a pleasant place[10] to live and a charming land to visit. (207)

2

Dear Mr. Stevens:

This is just a reminder to let you know you may now file an exemption on your state[1] property taxes. In order to take advantage of this opportunity, you must file by March 1.

If you have[2] not had experience with filing for a mortgage exemption, you will find the process to be quite easy. Take[3] the enclosed form to your county tax assessor. The entire process takes approximately 15 minutes to[4] complete and will result in a major savings against next year's taxes.

May I emphasize again the importance[5] of filing by March 1. Although the exemption applies to next year's taxes, it must be filed this year.

Please call[6] on me whenever I can be of help. Cordially yours, (130)

3

MEMO TO: Marketing and Sales Personnel

We are pleased to add two new members to our staff. Mr. Harold Smith[1] and Ms. Betty Madison joined our division on July 15.

Both of these people assume the position[2] of regional manager for equipment sales and service. Harold will cover the northeast part of the country,[3] and Betty will cover the West Coast.

Harold spent nine years in the U.S. Air Force as chief engineer in charge of[4] the testing program. Betty has managed sales programs in California, Washington, and Oregon.

Betty[5] is already operating out of her office in San Francisco, and Harold will be moving into his[6] Boston office immediately. Please join me in welcoming these exciting new people to our company.[7] (140)

UNIT 31

Notetaking for Minutes of a Meeting

Minutes of a meeting are a record of when and where a meeting was held and who attended. It is a record of reports given, agenda items discussed, and motions proposed, discussed, and decided upon. Summary statements are made of the important points of all discussions. Motions are recorded word for word, and the minutes indicate who made them, who seconded them, and what decisions were made on the motions. Finally, minutes contain the future meeting date, if known, and the time of adjournment. An agenda for a meeting usually includes these basic elements:

1. Call to order
2. Roll call
3. Reading of the minutes
4. Treasurer's report
5. Old business
6. New business
7. Adjournment

Whether your role is that of an officer or simply a member of a club, committee, or organization, your notetaking abilities can be very useful. As a member of any organization, your notetaking skills enable you to take notes for your personal use. If you are a president or a chairperson, notetaking is useful in drafting an agenda and making reminders to yourself during the meeting. As secretary of an organization or a person designated to take the minutes of a meeting, your job is easier because you are proficient in listening and recording essential information.

Selective notes taken at the point of origin are far easier and less time consuming to process than notes from a tape recorder, but a tape recorder may be used as a backup to verify information, if needed. All of your *Speedwriting* shortcuts will become valuable aids in the recording of minutes.

SPEEDWRITING PRINCIPLES

1. Write B for the word endings *bil, ble* (bul), or *bly.*

table, t-ble	tB	mobile, m-ble	~B
double, d-ble	dB	eligible, e-l-j-ble	eljB
possible, p-s-ble	psB	assembly, a-s-m-bly	as~B
possibly, p-s-bly	psB	available, a-v-l-ble	avlB

2. Omit the final *t* of a root word after the sound of *k.*

act, a-k	ac	object, o-b-j-k	objc
elect, e-l-k	elc	deduct, d-d-k	ddc
instruct, in-st-r-k	nSrc	effect, e-f-k	efc

Write these additional words:

responsible, response-ble	rspB	expect, x-p-k	xpc
deductible, d-d-k-ble	ddcB	elected, e-l-k-ed	elc-
probably, prah-b-bly	PbB	impact, im-p-k	~pc
product, prah-d-k	Pdc	protected, pro-t-k-ed	Ptc-

3. Indicate time in the following way:

ten o'clock	10°	8:30 a.m.	8^{30}a
12 noon	12 nn	9:30 p.m.	9^{30}p

PHRASES

as I *zi*

has been *hsb*

should be *Adb*

thank you *lqu*

would like *dlc*

PUNCTUATION STUDY

USE COMMAS WITH NOUNS OF DIRECT ADDRESS.

A direct address is a specific referral to a person's name, title, and/or other designation. When the direct address occurs in the middle of the sentence, place a comma before and after it. If the direct address occurs at the beginning or at the end of the sentence, use only one comma.

□ We know, Mary, that you are an excellent administrative assistant.
□ Professor Jefferson, will you be able to attend the meeting?
□ You will enjoy working in Washington, Mr. President.

In the Reading and Writing Exercises, the abbreviation **Dir Ad** will be used to highlight nouns of direct address.

VOCABULARY STUDY

trust account *lrS ak* An account established by an individual or organization in the name of another individual or organization to be administered by a trustee (trust company or bank, for example).

PRINCIPLES SUMMARY

1. Write *B* for the word endings *bil, ble* (bul), or *bly*: table, t-ble *lB*.
2. Omit the final *t* of a root word after the sound of *k*: act, a-k *ac*.
3. Indicate time: 7:30 p.m. *7 30 p* .

WORD DEVELOPMENT

Write the following related words in *Speedwriting* in your notebook.

contact *klc*	-ed	-s	-ing
project *Pjc*	-s	-ed	-or
affect *afc*	-ed	-s	-ing

inspect	nspc	-s	-ed	-or
correct	crc	-ed	-s	-ing

WORD CONSTRUCTION

Practice writing these words in *Speedwriting* in your notebook.

trouble, t-r-ble

applicable, a-p-l-k-ble

selected, s-l-k-ed

respect, re-s-p-k

cablegram, k-ble-gram

collect, k-l-k

reasonable, re-z-n-ble

reject, re-j-k

effects, e-f-k-s

comfortable, com-for-t-ble

WRITING ASSIGNMENT

Self-dictate the following letter as you write it in *Speedwriting*.

Dear Miss Henry:

Attached are the copies you need. Because our files have grown so large and are used by so many[1] people, it is necessary to use a different filing method. Currently, all legal documents are[2] being kept in our legal office. When you need an item, a filing clerk will be glad to get it for you. This[3] method should reduce filing mistakes and also allow you to get information rapidly. We hope it serves you[4] well from now on. Cordially, (85)

READING AND WRITING EXERCISES

1

Lengthening the Lifetime of This Year's Model

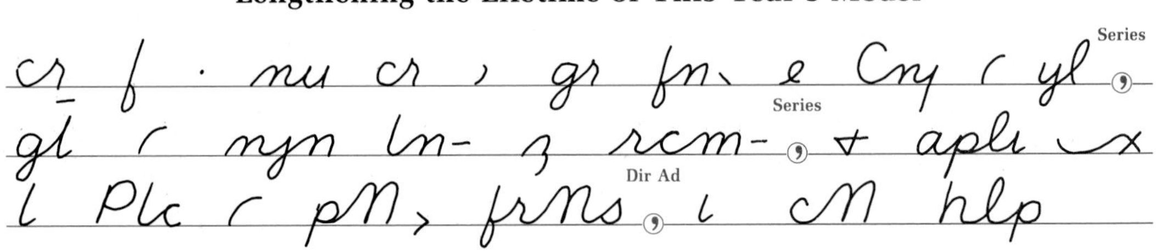

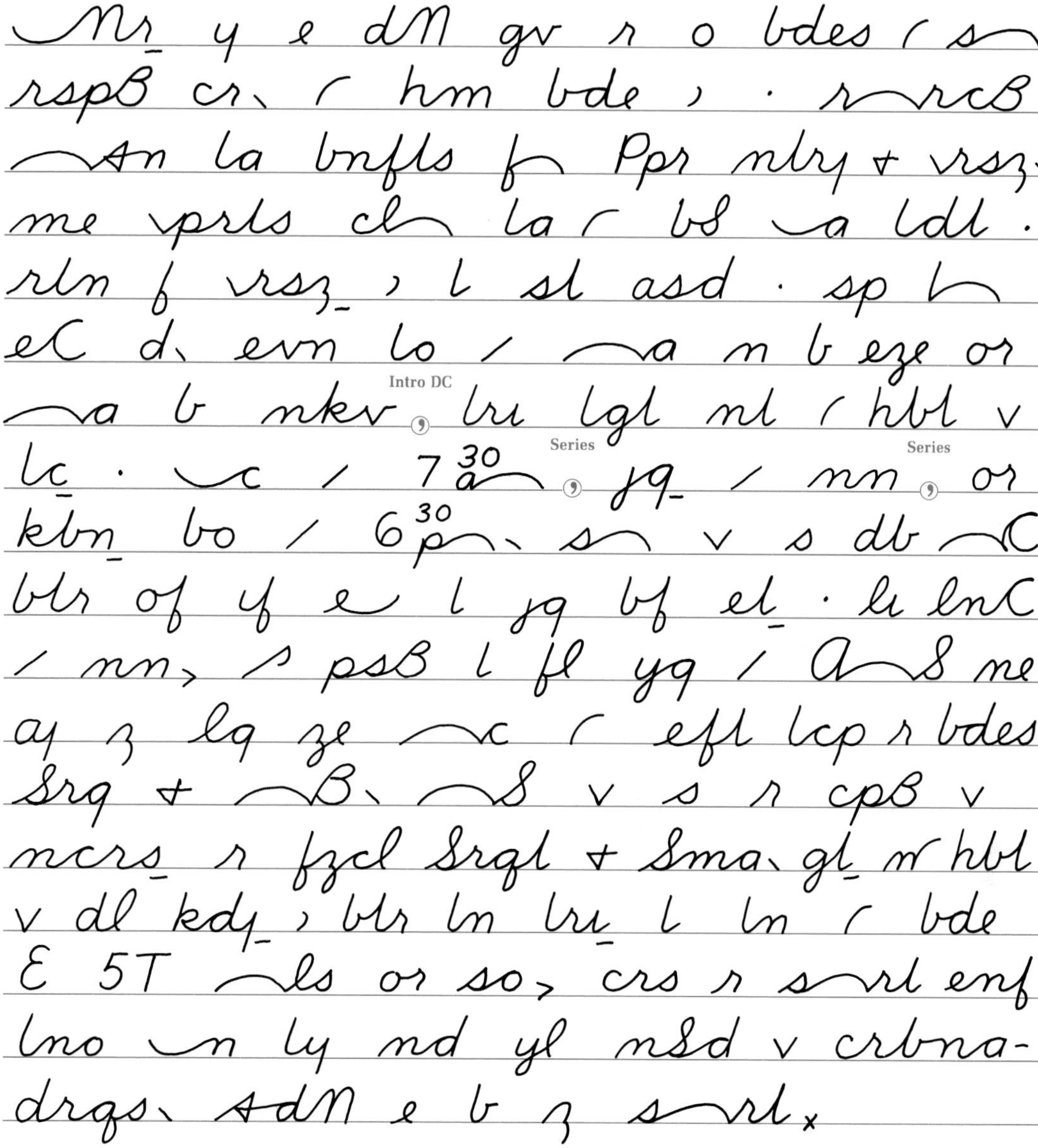

2

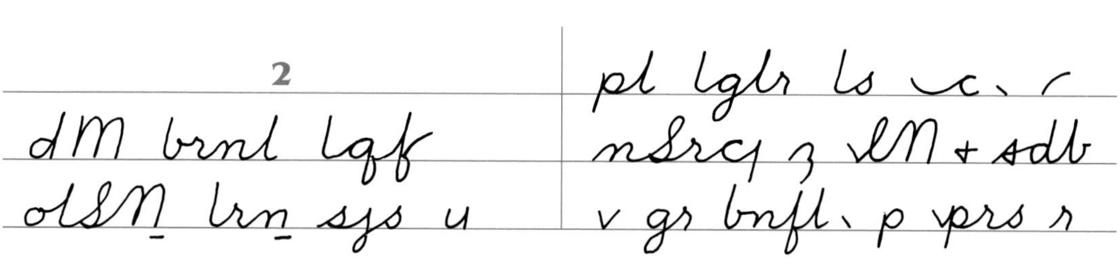

apj l E, hu hlp-mc
sC . plzN vp f s, (
Pq nd sC . Srq npc
o r Sf lae ust l pln
. slr evN f nx yr.
e vpc lv apxl 2H
ppl elyB f Pq. du
ks brq u lrn grp l
r sle, ed flo u
efsN LIB. b Srl (
me Pdl / 8:30 am +
N / 5 pm ecd kp (
sjs n 3 ds. if u

Intro DC

apv, il bgn mc
arms no. e Ar v
sn sugjs n m,
ilc fw ls rpli. aq
uv r lqs f . jb l
dn. vlu

3

dr r bron vu ks-

opn . lrS ak u r
bq, lrS aks ofr
me avjs l ppl n
ndl=l=hi nk rn,.
ly Pvd . lq=lr sv
pln uC cb uz- f
dfrN Ppss. f ex .
lrS fN fu Cldrn
Plcs lr fCr. z (ak

Intro DC

gros, / bks . bss f
lr cly ejcj or / c
fN aol nvSm lgv
L . esp soN Srl
n lf, lr r lN lx
bnfts aco lrS fNs.
edb hpe l vpln L
n dtl. y n mc .
apym ld l lrn
ho lz plns op,
e ofr me Svss dzn-
l hlp u fl + eSa
pln. ehp ul lc

avy v s⌒ v opjs (Dir Ad)	bron, vlu
la r avlB , ⌒r	

KEY

WRITING ASSIGNMENT

d M hnre alC- r	⌒n und . l⌒
r cpes und,	. fl clrc lb gld
bcz r fls v grn	lgl / fu, ls
so lry + r uz-	⌒ld +d rds
b so me ppl s	fl Mlcs + aso
nes luz . dfrN	alo u lgl inf
fl ⌒ld, crNl a	rpdl, ehp /
lgl dcms r b	Svs u l f⌒ no
cpl n r lgl ofs,	o, c

READING AND WRITING EXERCISES

1

Lengthening the Lifetime of This Year's Model

Caring for a new car is great fun. We change the oil, get the engine tuned as recommended, and apply wax to[1] protect the paint.

Friends, I can't help wondering why we don't give our own bodies the same responsible care. The human[2] body is a remarkable machine that benefits from proper nutrition and exercise. Many experts[3] claim that the best way to determine a routine for exercising is to set aside a specific time[4] each day. Even though it may not be easy or may be inconvenient, try to get into the habit of[5] taking a walk at 7:30 a.m., jogging at noon, or combining both at 6:30 p.m. Some of[6] us would be much better off if we were to jog before eating a light lunch at noon.

It is possible to feel[7] young at almost any age as long as we make the effort to keep our bodies strong and mobile. Most of us are[8] capable of increasing our physical strength and stamina. Getting in the habit of daily conditioning[9] is better than trying to tune the body every 5,000 miles or so.

Cars are smart enough to know[10] when they need oil instead of carbonated drinks. Shouldn't we be as smart? (213)

2

Dear Miss Barnett:

Thank you for the outstanding training sessions you put together this week. The instruction was[1] excellent and should be of great benefit. Please express our appreciation to everyone who helped make such[2] a pleasant experience for us.

The program made such a strong impact on our staff that we wish to plan a[3] similar event for next year. We expect to have approximately 200 people eligible for the[4] program. Would you consider bringing your training group to our city?

We would follow your efficient timetable. By[5] starting the meetings promptly at 8:30 a.m. and ending at 5 p.m., we could complete the sessions in[6] three days. If you approve, I will begin making arrangements now. We already have some suggestions in mind.

I[7] look forward to your reply. Again, you have our thanks for a job well done.

Very truly yours, (156)

3

Dear Mr. Brown:

Have you considered opening a trust account with our bank?

Trust accounts offer many[1] advantages to people in the middle-to-high income range. They provide a long-term savings plan which can be used[2] for different purposes. For example, a trust fund for your children protects their future. As the account grows,[3] it becomes a basis for their college education, or it can fund another investment to give them an[4] especially sound start in life.

There are excellent tax benefits accompanying trust funds. We would be happy[5] to explain them in detail. Why not make an appointment today to learn how these plans operate?

We offer[6] many services designed to help with family and estate planning. We hope you will take advantage of some[7] of the options that are available, Mr. Brown. Very truly yours, (152)

UNIT 32 Creative Uses for Notetaking

Personal notetaking has many possibilities and may serve you in a variety of ways. You will also like the convenience and time-saving aspects of *Speedwriting*.

Included in this unit are several suggestions for applying *Speedwriting* for personal use.

Diary. A diary is a daily record of a person's experiences, thoughts, and observations. The privacy afforded in making diary entries in *Speedwriting* provides added appeal.

Journal. A journal differs from a diary in that it usually focuses on particular events in a person's life. Journal entries are typically records of thoughts and observations on a variety of topics. Like diaries, journals are often kept on a daily basis; however, journals are usually a more objective record of events and are frequently used as material for future writing projects.

Telephone. Notetaking in preparation for making phone calls is a valuable personal management activity. Having a list of topics and information ready before phoning conserves time, energy, and money. *Speedwriting* also enables you to take phone messages neatly, accurately, and rapidly.

Speeches and Speakers. You may have many occasions to make informal presentations or formal speeches before groups. Avoid having a typewritten script that you will have a tendency to read. A more effective approach is to know your subject well and have a few 5″ x 8″ numbered index cards with well-chosen key words for memory joggers. At other times, your assignment may be to introduce a speaker. Ask the speaker for a brief written introduction that you can deliver. Make notes from this introduction and speak in a personal, friendly manner—not as though you are presenting a resumé.

Films, Radio, Video, or Television. You may be asked to review or critique programs, films, or video presentations (or you may simply want to write down addresses and information quickly from radio or television for your own information). Your *Speedwriting* and notetaking skills will be very useful for any of these purposes. Listen or observe and note the central theme and important supporting material of audio and video presentations; then take notes as you would in other situations.

Tours of Museums and Galleries. A small notepad is useful in which to record impressions and information gathered from tours through exhibits of any kind.

Other notetaking possibilities include such activities as indexing a favorite book, listing unfamiliar vocabulary words with their definitions, using weekly planners, making "to do" lists, logging travels, taking directions, composing New Year's resolutions, and noting instructions, in addition to countless other uses. Your creativity in applying your listening, notetaking, and *Speedwriting* skills is unlimited in providing a written record of personal creations or applications.

SPEEDWRITING PRINCIPLES

1. Write a small, disjoined, and slightly raised *t* ^{t} for the word ending *ity* (pronounced *uh-tee*).

quality, q-l-ity	ql^{t}	facilities, f-s-l-ity-s	fsl^{ts}
possibility, p-s-bil-ity	psB^{t}	authority, a-ith-r-ity	alr^{t}
majority, m-j-r-ity	$\frown jr^{t}$	security, s-k-r-ity	scr^{t}

2. Write ( ) to indicate parentheses.

Most of our staff (80%) have had their vacations.

⌒8 vr Sf (80%) vh lr vcjs.

BRIEF FORMS

able	B	difficult	dfc
opinion	opn	contract	kc
employ	⌒p		

BRIEF FORM DEVELOPMENT

difficulty	dfce	enable	nB
responsibility	$rspB^{t}$	ability	B^{t}

COMMONLY MISSPELLED WORDS

excellent xln

correspondence cor

VOCABULARY STUDY

term policy tr plse — In life insurance, a contract providing benefits for a limited number of years. It pays face value if the owner's death occurs during the time specified in the contract.

PRINCIPLES SUMMARY

1. Write a small, disjoined, and slightly raised *t* for the word ending *ity (uh-tee)*: quality, q-l-ity qlt.
2. Write ⸨ ⸩ to indicate parentheses.

WORD DEVELOPMENT

Write the following related words in *Speedwriting* in your notebook.

employ mp	-s	-ed	-ment
secure scr	-d	-ing	-ity
deduct ddc	-s	-ible	-ibility
contract kc	-ed	-s	-ing
suit su	-ed	-able	-ability

WORD CONSTRUCTION

Practice writing these words in *Speedwriting* in your notebook.

community, com-n-ity

capacity, k-p-s-ity

personality, per-s-n-l-ity

quantities, q-nt-ity-s

locality, l-k-l-ity

electricity, electr-s-ity

necessity, n-s-s-ity

probability, prah-b-bil-ity

eligibility, e-l-j-bil-ity

possibilities, p-s-bil-ity-s

WRITING ASSIGNMENT

Self-dictate the following letter as you write it in *Speedwriting*.

Gentlemen:

As the head of this hospital, I was happy to hear that a new children's unit is being proposed.[1] As part of this proposal, parents will be allowed to remain here in the hospital with their children.[2] Generally, such an arrangement provides a great benefit to the parents as well as the patients.

To determine[3] a need for this unit, a survey was made with local residents. Of the total surveyed, 80 percent were[4] in favor of this unit. I feel happy and proud to see this matter finally receiving the attention[5] it needs. As members of the hospital board, you will no doubt wish to receive a full report on this new plan.[6] Very truly yours, (124)

READING AND WRITING EXERCISES

1

Putting Your Best Foot Forward

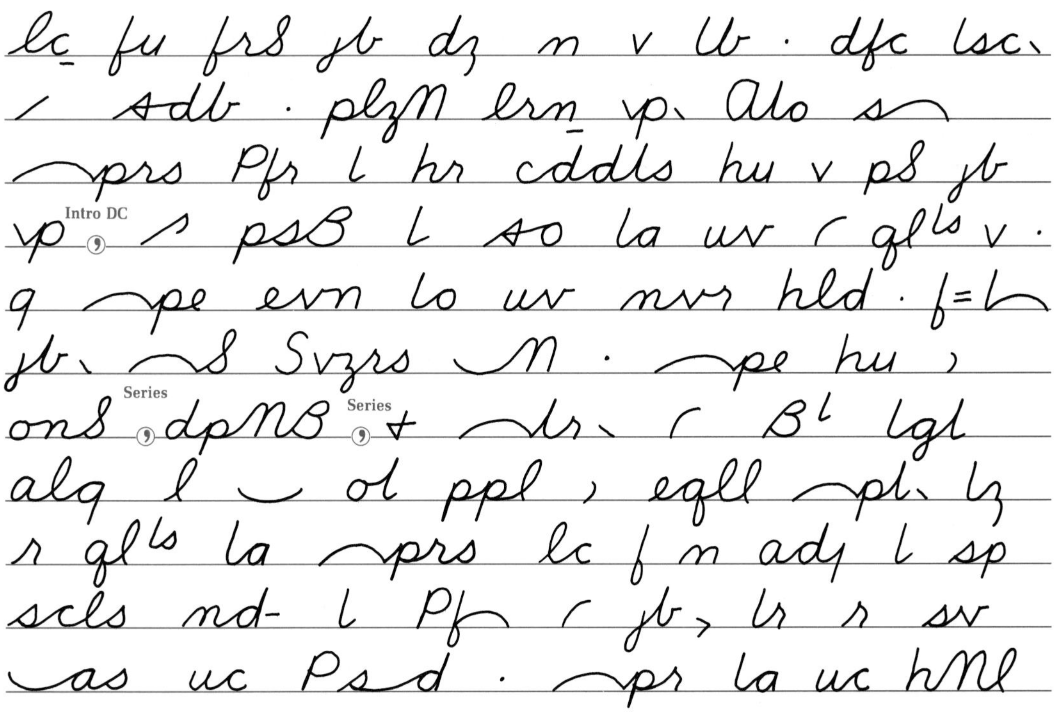

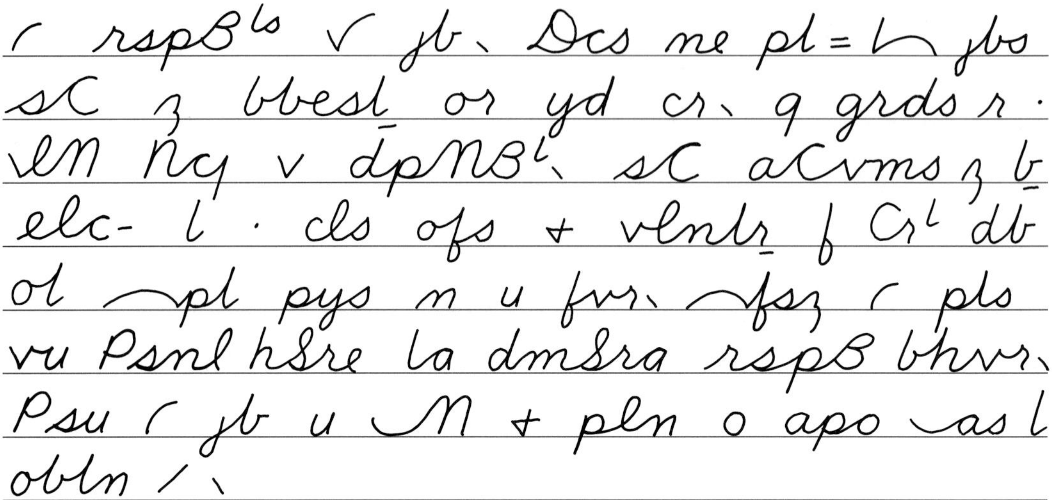

2

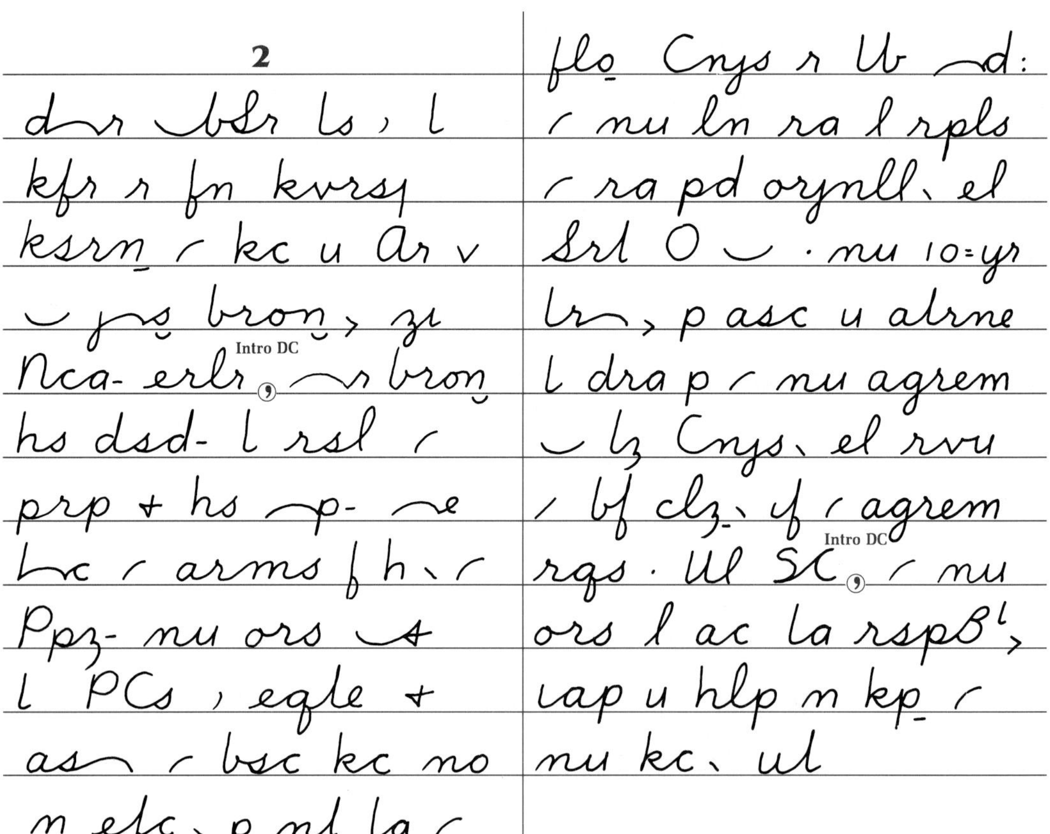

3

d ed p- lsa lb
vzt llsa evn snr
ln e vpc-, i pln l
brq r nu sls yrs
o . lrp lru r Wrn
plNs du r c v
Mr 6. i N l so
r lN fsl ls +
Pgs crNl n efc.
el arv o flt 519 /
5 30 p o Wd. cd u
e s + v dnr
s la evn x, idap

Series
e Th rn u,
Series
r nu pes, + ne i
els u lq ly sd e,
Intro DC
if r n l dfc l ar,
Dir Ad
ed, idlc r g8s lq
lru A v plNs. e
i ks r psBl v
rN . bs f Th afnn.
I du u lq? u
opns A kb grl
l r efls, e pln l
lv / ab 9° r nx
rn. u hlp, Slnl
ap-. s

KEY

WRITING ASSIGNMENT

1 z r hd v ls hsp
iz hpe lhr la .
nu Cldrns unl
, b Ppz-. z pl v ls
Ppzl prNs lb alo-

l r n hr r hsp
ls Cldrn. jnl
sC . arm Pvds .
gr bnfl l r prNs
zlz r pNs, ldl

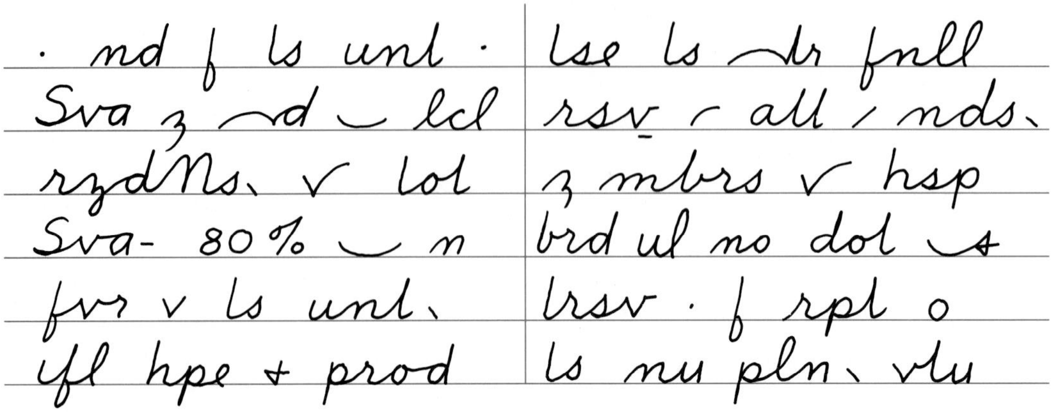

READING AND WRITING EXERCISES

1

Putting Your Best Foot Forward

Looking for your first job does not have to be a difficult task. It should be a pleasant learning experience.[1] Although some employers prefer to hire candidates who have past job experience, it is possible to[2] show that you have the qualities of a good employee even though you have never held a full-time job. Most[3] supervisors want an employee who is honest, dependable, and mature. The ability to get along[4] well with other people is equally important. These are qualities that employers look for in addition to[5] specific skills needed to perform the job.

There are several ways you can persuade an employer that you can[6] handle the responsibilities of the job. Discuss any part-time jobs such as babysitting or yard care.[7] Good grades are an excellent indication of dependability. Such achievements as being elected[8] to a class office and volunteering for charity would be other important points in your favor. Emphasize[9] the parts of your personal history that demonstrate responsible behavior. Pursue the job you want[10] and plan on appropriate ways to obtain it. (209)

2

Dear Mr. Webster:

This is to confirm our phone conversation concerning the contract you already have with[1] James Brown.

As I indicated earlier, Mr. Brown has decided to resell the property and has[2] employed me to make the arrangements for him. The proposed new owners wish to purchase his equity and assume the[3] basic contract now in effect.

Please note that the following changes are to be made: The new loan rate[4] will replace the rate paid originally. We will start over with a new ten-year term.

Please ask your attorney to[5] draw up the new agreement with these changes. We will review it before closing. If the agreement requires a[6] title search, the new owners will accept that responsibility.

I appreciate your help in completing[7] the new contract. Yours truly, (145)

3

Dear Ed:

I am pleased to say I will be visiting Tulsa even sooner than we expected.

I plan to bring[1] our new sales managers on a trip through our western plants during the week of March 6. I want to show them our[2] excellent facilities and the programs currently in effect. We will arrive on Flight 519 at[3] 5:30 p.m. on Wednesday. Could you meet us and have dinner with us that evening?

I would appreciate meeting[4] Thursday morning with you, our new employees, and anyone else you think they should meet.

If it is not too difficult[5] to arrange, Ed, I would like our guests to go through all of the plants. We might consider the possibility of[6] renting a bus for Thursday afternoon. What do you think? Your opinions always contribute greatly to our efforts.[7]

We plan to leave at about 9 o'clock the next morning. Your help is certainly appreciated. Sincerely,[8] (160)

UNIT 33 Notetaking and College Applications

The manner in which you complete your college and scholarship applications is very important. In many cases, the application is the only information the admissions or selection committee has about you. Here are some rules to follow for completing your application forms.

1. Read through the entire application first and be sure you understand what information is requested.
2. Think about all your answers and make notes on what you are going to say on a separate worksheet.
3. Follow directions carefully and answer all questions accurately and completely.
4. Be neat and accurate. If you type well, the application should be typed; otherwise, print or write neatly with blue or black ink.
5. Check all dates, addresses, financial information, and spelling for accuracy.
6. Select your references carefully and ask for permission to use their names before listing them on the application form. If the college requests that you ask your references to submit letters of recommendation directly to the school, provide your references with stamped, addressed envelopes for all requested letters.
7. Complete your application from the notes you have made and check for accuracy and completeness. Allow yourself plenty of time to do a good job.
8. Sign your name with a pen in all designated places and have your parents sign where it is requested on the form.
9. Have the required fee and all other enclosures together.
10. Draft a thank you letter to the people you asked for letters of recommendation.

When you apply for college admission, many colleges will ask you to write an essay. Admissions personnel use the essay to get to know you better than they can from just your high school transcript and recommendations. Thus, the essay topic, indicated by the college, is usually autobiographical in nature. The essay is also viewed as an example of your writing skills, so invest the same amount of time and care that you would use in completing an essay examination or composition.

SPEEDWRITING PRINCIPLES

1. Write *u* for the word beginning *un*.

until, un-t-l	*ull*	unfair, un-f-r	*ufr*
unpaid, un-p-d	*upd*	unchanged, un-chay-n-j-duh	*uCnj-*
unless, un-l-s	*uls*	uncover, un-k-v-r	*ucvr*

BRIEF FORM DEVELOPMENT

Use this principle to develop words from brief forms and abbreviations.

unable	*uB*	unfortunate	*ufCnl*
unsatisfactory	*usal*	unnecessary	*unes*

MORE ABOUT PHRASING

An easily recognized word may be omitted from common phrases or compound words. In the following examples, the boldface word has been omitted in the *Speedwriting* phrase.

never**the**less	*nvrls*	time **to** time	*ltl*
none**the**less	*nnls*	up **to** date	*pda*

PUNCTUATION STUDY

USE COMMAS WITH APPOSITIVES.

An appositive is a word or group of words that explains, renames, or identifies someone or something that immediately precedes it in the sentence.

Appositives are usually set off by commas from the rest of the sentence. The following are examples of appositives:

- His new textbook, *Business English*, has now been published.
- Please see our sales manager, Sally Stanfield.
- Mr. Ronald Jackson, the Secretary of State, will deliver our commencement address.

Appositives will be highlighted in the Reading and Writing Exercises by the abbreviation **Ap**.

VOCABULARY STUDY

computer terminal 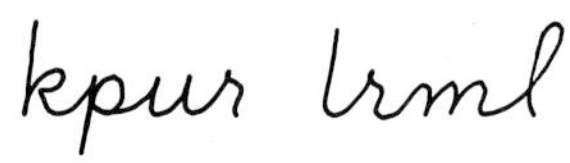
A device usually consisting of a keyboard and a screen that is used to input data to and output data from a computer. Also called a work station.

questionnaire 
A set of questions assembled for the purpose of making a survey.

PRINCIPLES SUMMARY

1. Write  for the word beginning *un*: until, un-t-l .

WORD DEVELOPMENT

Write the following related words in *Speedwriting* in your notebook.

able 	en-	dis-	un-
bound 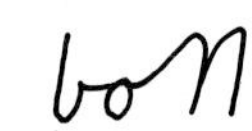	re-	un-	-ary
bend 	-s	-ing	un-
cover 	-ed	-ing	un-
willing 	-ly	-ness	un-

---

WORD CONSTRUCTION

Practice writing these words in *Speedwriting* in your notebook.

unlike, un-l-k

unreasonable, un-re-z-n-ble

unearned, un-e-r-n-duh

unloaded, un-l-d-ed

uncut, un-k-t

undivided,
un-d-v-d-ed

undue, un-d-u

unlisted, un-l-st-ed

unemployed,
un-employ-duh

unwelcome,
un-wel-come

WRITING ASSIGNMENT

Self-dictate the following memo as you write it in *Speedwriting*.

MEMO TO: Manager of Boy's Wear

We will offer savings of between 20 and 30 percent on all[1] back-to-school needs—clothing, as well as supplies. All clothing should be marked down 20 percent. All school supplies will be[2] displayed between the boy's and girl's departments.

We will accept payment in the form of cash, credit cards, and personal[3] checks. Those persons wishing to cash payroll checks should be sent to the credit office. All personal checks should be[4] seen by the department manager.

We suggest your clerks remind all shoppers that clothing items may be returned[5] within one week following the purchase. (107)

READING AND WRITING EXERCISES

1

The National Checking Account

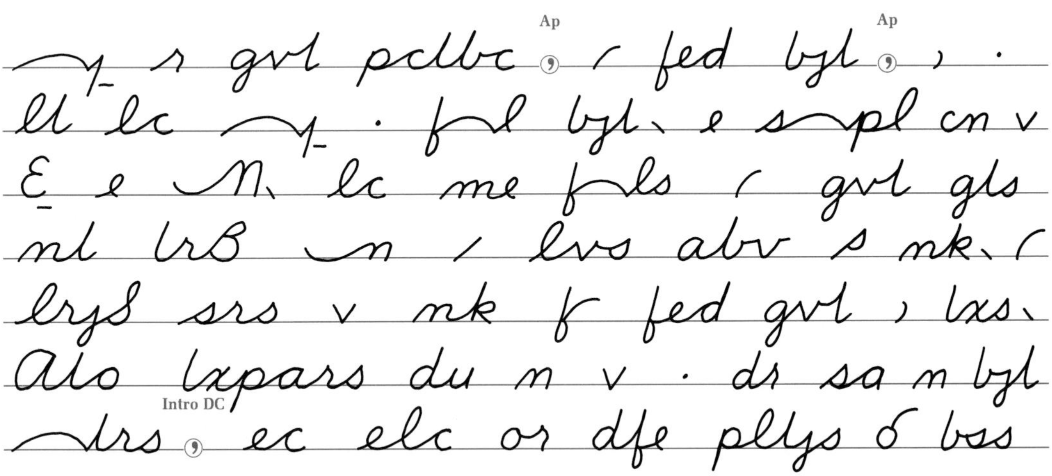

v ho ly spN r lx $, rz lxs, so
uppl r la (gvl d rlr bro ln c
Ap
lxpars uhpe. la , vcl ho (nyl dl,
Ap
(me o- l crrs, gru lb so ly.
nk lxs r bs- po (Bl lpa. hoE
lr r sv Pbls n zr (Bl lpa
+ loz hu pa (S A fl la (
sS , ufr. n i gl lr- v pa
Intro DC
lxs, i Cc ol · bc f i ke lbrre
or vzl · nyl prc la , Plc- lru lx
$.

2

d rdr ev Ar sN
Ap
sv bls f r gzn,
Ap
arl nz, od- n u m.
so fr ev n rsv- me
pam or plny, r n
r cS l asc f pams
ods. e lq r rdrs
ap (kv v b B lc
pams nE ly sll
lr ol hoshld or ofs
aks. e ks r rdrs lb
nf- Nvs hu ac
rspBl f kcs ly v
d, eno la lr ,
· q rzn fu dla n
c pam. (l lc ol
· fu mls l sll ls
lr = elr · Cc
or · fu rds pln

(dla. p rel u
rsp ‿ (inv n
aco env. su

3

d dvd lqf opl l
rcm ‿ asSN ‿yr, Ap
jnfr yq, Ap f pzi
v pb rlys drs. idu
so ‿ plzr, jnfr hs
me fn ql^{ls} rep v q
‿ym. 1 Srq py, hr
B^{l} l vprs hr opns bo
n spC + n ri. se

sos. USN v co gls
alq ‿ . snsr ksrn
f r ol ‿pes, jnfr
as‿s f rspB^{l} f ne
jb no ‿dr ho dfc.
ull se k l (Av
dpl, Intro DC jnfr h no vp
n ‿ym. nvrls se
Svz- sv Pjcs n
‿nr v . vp- dpl
hd, n ‿ opn jnfr
, rde f ncrs- rspB^{l}.
se l brq me fn ql^{ls}
l (pzi U ksi. ul

KEY

WRITING ASSIGNMENT

mo l ‿yr v bys ‿r
el ofr sv v bln
20 + 30 % o A bc=l=
scl nds = cl zlz
splis. A cl sdb

‿rc- don 20%. A
scl splis lb Dpla-
bln (bys + grls dpls,
el ac pam n f
v c4 cr crds + Psnl

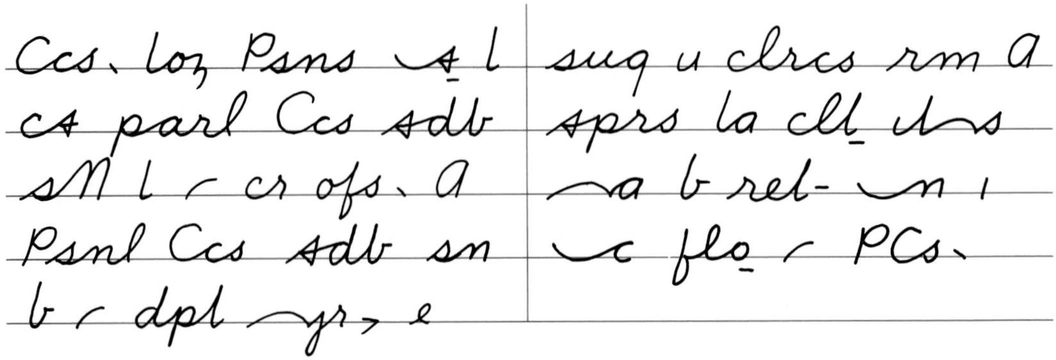

READING AND WRITING EXERCISES

1

The National Checking Account

Managing our government pocketbook, the federal budget, is a lot like managing a family budget.[1] We simply cannot have everything we want. Like many families, the government gets into trouble[2] when it lives above its income. The largest source of income for the federal government is taxes. Although[3] taxpayers do not have a direct say in budget matters, we can elect or defeat politicians on the[4] basis of how they spend our tax dollars.

Raising taxes is so unpopular that the government would rather[5] borrow than make taxpayers unhappy. That is exactly how the national debt, the money owed to creditors,[6] grew to be so large. Income taxes are based upon the ability to pay. However, there are several[7] problems in measuring the ability to pay, and those who pay the most always feel that the system is[8] unfair. When I get tired of paying taxes, I check out a book from my county library or visit a[9] national park that is protected through tax dollars. (189)

2

Dear Reader:

We have already sent several bills for our magazine, *Art News*, ordered in your name. So far we[1] have not received any payment or explanation.

It is not our custom to ask for payments with orders. We[2] think our readers appreciate the convenience of being able to make payments whenever they settle their[3] other household or office accounts. We consider our readers to be informed individuals who accept[4] responsibility for contracts they have made.

We know that there is a good reason for your delay in making[5] payment. It will take only a few minutes to settle this matter—either with a check or a few words explaining[6] the delay. Please return your response with the invoice in the accompanying envelope. Sincerely yours,[7] (140)

3

Dear David:

Thank you for the opportunity to recommend my assistant manager, Jennifer Young, for[1] the position of public relations director. I do so with pleasure.

Jennifer has many fine qualities[2] representative of good management. One strong point is her ability to express her opinions both in[3] speech and in writing. She shows an understanding of company goals along with a sincere concern for our[4] other employees.

Jennifer assumes full responsibility for any job, no matter how difficult.[5] Until she came to the advertising department, Jennifer had no experience in management.[6] Nevertheless, she supervised several projects in the manner of an experienced department head.

In my[7] opinion, Jennifer is ready for increased responsibility. She will bring many fine qualities to the[8] position under consideration. Yours truly, (169)

UNIT 34 The Secret to College Success

What is the secret to success in college? Efficient and sufficient study! Well-organized study skills can help ensure the success of most college students.

Even excellent high school students are sometimes disappointed with their college performance. The main reason for this disappointment is that they do not know how to study for college classes or how to manage their time effectively. Establishing a proper study environment and an efficient study schedule can help improve study habits.

Study Environment. Just as in high school, you need a place where you can concentrate and avoid distractions. The library may be a wise choice, or you can create an environment conducive for studying in your own room. Your study environment should be functional and comfortable, but not too comfortable. The purpose is to keep alert, comprehend, and learn—not to be entertained or fall asleep.

Study Schedule. Creating and following a study schedule is an important step to your success. Colleges have definite schedules of obligations and events. You will have a schedule for registration, classes, tests, sports events, and work, if you have a job.

As a general rule, the average college student should spend four to six hours studying each day. Postponing studying until the week before exam time is counterproductive for accomplishing your college goals.

High school students have become accustomed to classes that meet five days per week with relatively small daily assignments. In college, classes may meet only one, two, or three times per week, but the assignments may be quite lengthy. Students often make the mistake of feeling there is much preparation time available between class meetings; however, beware of those appealing yet time-wasting opportunities in college. Time vanishes rapidly, and you can easily find yourself poorly prepared for the next class session. Since college classes meet less frequently, regular and punctual class attendance is very important.

Develop a daily study timetable for each of your classes (based on the class syllabus) and then follow it. You may need to make adjustments in your schedule to allow extra time for term papers or exams, but following a regular schedule will help you develop good study habits and will make preparing for tests easier. Developing a schedule for all activities and following it will make studying a high priority, but such a schedule will also include time for other activities and socializing.

You can make productive use of even short periods of unscheduled time. Those few minutes before a class begins are perfect for a quick review of your notes or text. A few minutes after class spent going over lecture notes while they are fresh in your mind can be as valuable as a much longer review later.

Tailor your schedule to fit your needs. When is the best time of day for you to study? That will depend on your program, other obligations, and personal habits. If possible, try to schedule some study time in the morning. The more you accomplish early in the day, the more time you will have available for other activities in the evenings. Remember, however, that sufficient rest is essential for optimum academic performance. To maintain a healthy attitude and a healthy body throughout your academic career, pay careful attention to what you eat and try scheduling some time for exercise. When caught up in college life, it is often easy to overlook desirable daily routines of proper diet, exercise, and rest.

SPEEDWRITING PRINCIPLES

1. Write *sl* for the word ending *cial* or *tial* (shul, chul).

official, o-f-ish-l *ofsl*	financial, f-n-n-ish-l *fnnsl*
special, s-p-ish-l *spsl*	potential, p-t-n-ish-l *ptnsl*
initial, i-n-ish-l *insl*	social, s-ish-l *ssl*

ABBREVIATIONS

volume *vol*	America, American *a*
literature *lit*	

BRIEF FORMS

develop *dv*	acknowledge *ak*
organize *og*	associate *aso*
success *suc*	congratulate *kg*
standard *Sd*	

BRIEF FORM DEVELOPMENT

acknowledgment	acjm	associations	asojs
organizations	ogjs	development	dvm
organizing	og-	congratulations	kgjs
standards	Sds	developing	dv-

COMMONLY MISSPELLED WORDS

cites sis

questionnaire qr

VOCABULARY STUDY

group retirement plan grp rtrm pln — A plan to provide income for retired employees; premiums may be paid entirely by the employer or partly by the employer and partly by the employee.

accordingly acrdl — Within (according to) a special way.

PRINCIPLES SUMMARY

1. Write sl for the word ending *cial* or *tial* (shul, chul): official, o-f-ish-l ofsl; financial, f-n-n-ish-l fnnsl.

WORD DEVELOPMENT

Write the following related words in *Speedwriting* in your notebook.

initial insl	-s	-ed	-ly
social ssl	-s	-ly	-ize
special spsl	-s	-ly	-ize
develop dv	-s	-ed	-ments
acknowledge acj	-d	-s	-ments

WORD CONSTRUCTION

Practice writing these words in *Speedwriting* in your notebook.

commercial, com-r-ish-l

residential, r-z-d-n-ish-l

officially, o-f-ish-l-ly	sequential, s-q-n-ish-l
essential, e-s-n-ish-l	developer, develop-r
financially, f-n-n-ish-l-ly	associated, associate-d
potentially, p-t-n-ish-l-ly	congratulating, congratulate-ing

WRITING ASSIGNMENT

Self-dictate the following letter as you write it in *Speedwriting*.

Dear Senator Martin:

As you know, some members of our group have been involved in a fight to prevent increases[1] in oil and gasoline rates. We invite you to help by voting to defeat this gasoline bill.

This bill would[2] allow companies to determine their own rates. It would also provide new policies for locating oil on[3] properties near the sea. Those new policies could be very damaging to a great number of people in many[4] ways. We hope that you will join our cause. Help us win this fight. Yours truly, (92)

READING AND WRITING EXERCISES

1

What Kind of Coach Are You?

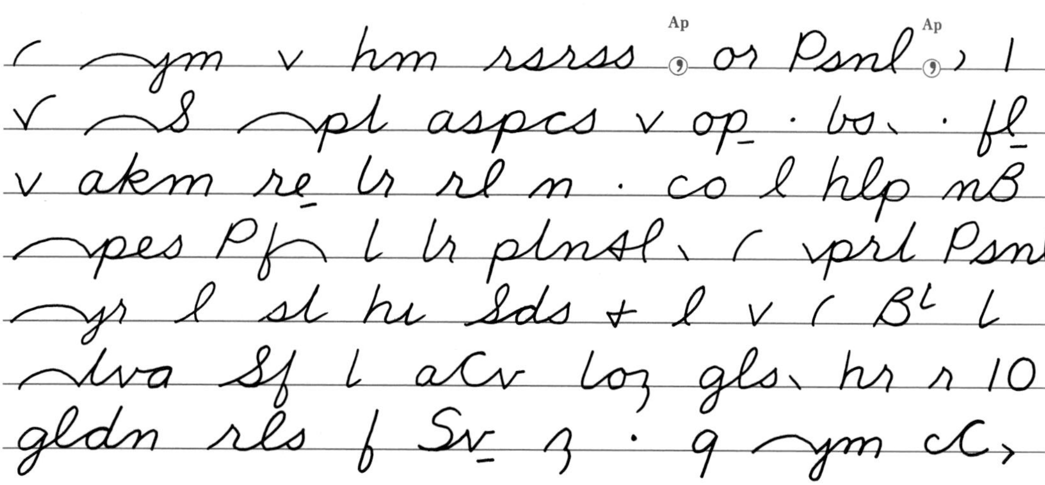

1. sl u ⌒pes o gls vu ogj. 2. sl gls lau Sf c aCv. 3. dlga s⌒ dsjs lu Sf. 4. avyd (h/y l d⌒p A (uplzN lscs ou Sf. 5. kq ⌒pes + gv Ppr cr f lr sugjs + aCvms. 6. lsn lu ⌒pes + ll h no u hr ⌣l ly r sa̲. 7. so rspc l ⌒pes / a jb lvls / a hs. 8. rmbr la ⌣n u ⌒8 crlsz du so ⌣ grs + USN̲. 9. flo lru o P⌒ss u ⌒c. 10. ncrj · fl̲ v frN+ + h sprl n ofs.

2

ddr ⌣lyns / gvs ⌒e gr saly l rcm dr elzbl̆ crlr̆ f rq v aso Pfsr. z spl f ls acj ı ofr (alC- fl kln̲ · s⌒re v hr p. ⌣n aso ⌣l̲ 2 arlcls se rsNl pbl+- alq ⌣ opns v SdNs + ol fclle. elzbl̆ jyn- r Sf 3 yrs aq. se hs dv- nu crss n A⌒ hSre ⌣C v kb- ⌒C l r Pq. se sos · re f hu lC̲ Sds + Pvds · ⌣lN ex f SdNs +

ol fclle, elzbl , .
lCr ⌣ gr plnsl +
. P~s fCr. / s~s
ol apo lae acj hr
kbjs ⌣ ls P~j.
vlu

3

d~r dvdsn kgjs
r n od fu + u f~l.
u n~ hsb slc-f
nx vol v yq ppl
n a~ (Ap) . v spsl
pbj, ls Dlg s-

bc lSs Nvs U r aj
v 40 hu r ern
olSN rcgnj. / sis
r sucs v yq ppl
n a ⌣cs v lf=bs, (Series)
N, (Series) ejcj, (Series) gvl, (Series) spls, (Series)
la, (Series) + ~dsn, r enc-
dla se sps Psnl
+ Pfyl inf Ub d- n
r nx vol. p rd +
rel r inf ⌣ ne
crcjs u ⌣s bc,
aq kgjs o rsv ls
spsl aw. cu

KEY

WRITING ASSIGNMENT

d snlr ~rln z
uno s~ mbrs vr
grp vb nvlv- n .
fu l PvN ncrss n
yl + gsln ras. e

nvi u l hlp b vo l
dfe ls gsln bl, ls
bl d alo cos ldl
lr o ras. / d aso
Pvd nu plses f lca

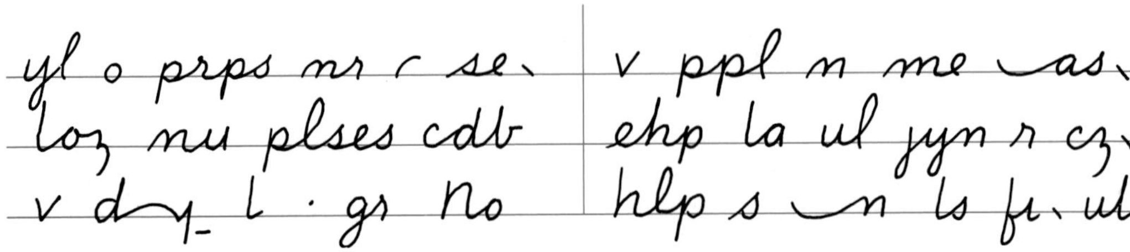

READING AND WRITING EXERCISES

1

What Kind of Coach Are You?

The management of human resources, or personnel, is one of the most important aspects of operating[1] a business. A feeling of accomplishment regarding their role in a company will help enable employees[2] perform to their potential. The expert personnel manager will set high standards and will have the ability[3] to motivate staff to achieve those goals. Here are ten golden rules for serving as a good management coach.[4]

1. Sell your employees on the goals of your organization.
2. Set goals that your staff can achieve.
3. Delegate[5] some decisions to your staff.
4. Avoid the temptation to dump all the unpleasant tasks on your staff.
5. Congratulate[6] employees and give proper credit for their suggestions and achievements.
6. Listen to your employees[7] and let them know you hear what they are saying.
7. Show respect to employees at all job levels at all[8] times.
8. Remember that when you must criticize, do so with grace and understanding.
9. Follow through on the[9] promises you make.
10. Encourage a feeling of friendship and team spirit in the office. (196)

2

Dear Dr. Williams:

It gives me great satisfaction to recommend Dr. Elizabeth Carter for the rank[1] of associate professor. As support for this action, I offer the attached file containing a summary[2] of her experience. I am also including two articles she recently published, along with opinions[3] of students and other faculty.

Elizabeth joined our staff three years ago. She has developed new[4] courses in American history which have contributed much to our program. She shows a regard for high[5] teaching standards and provides an excellent example for students and other faculty.

Elizabeth is[6] a teacher with great potential and a promising future. It seems only appropriate that we acknowledge[7] her contributions with this promotion. Very truly yours, (151)

3

Dear Mr. Davidson:

Congratulations are in order for you and your family. Your name has been selected[1] for the next volume of *Young People in America,* a very special publication.

This distinguished[2] book lists individuals under the age of 40 who are earning outstanding recognition. It cites the[3] successes of young people in all walks of life—business, industry, education, government, sports, law, and[4] medicine.

The enclosed data sheet specifies personal and professional information to be included[5] in our next volume. Please read and return the information with any corrections you wish to make.

Again,[6] congratulations on receiving this special award. Cordially yours, (133)

UNIT

35 Review and Reinforcement

1. In Units 29–34, you learned to write the following word beginnings:

extr and extra X

aks, eks, iks, oks, uks, eggs \

un u

2. These word endings were presented:

bil, ble *(bul)*, or bly B

ity *(uh-tee)* l

cial, tial *(shul, chul)* Al

3. These words illustrate all of the new principles studied in Units 29–34:

accident, x-d-nt vdN

long, l-ong lg

facilities, f-s-l-ity-s fsl^{ls}

exciting, x-ite-ing vi

exist, x-st vS

until, un-t-l ull

double, d-ble dB

relaxing, re-l-x-ing rlx

extremely, extr-m-ly Xml

effect, e-f-k efc

financial, f-n-n-ish-l fnnAl

social, s-ish-l sAl

4. You learned to indicate time in the following way:

one o'clock 1°

11:30 a.m. $11^{30}a$

12 noon 12 nn

10:30 p.m. $10^{30}p$

5. Easily recognized words are omitted from common phrases:

never*the*less	nvrls	time *to* time	Ltl
none*the*less	nnls	up *to* date	pda

6. Transcribe the following abbreviations in your notebook:

vol lil a

7. How quickly can you write these brief forms in your notebook?

always	prove	immediate
consider	next	note
experience	already	approximate
able	opinion	difficult
contract	employ	standard
develop	organize	associate
acknowledge	success	congratulate

READING AND WRITING EXERCISES

1

South of the Border

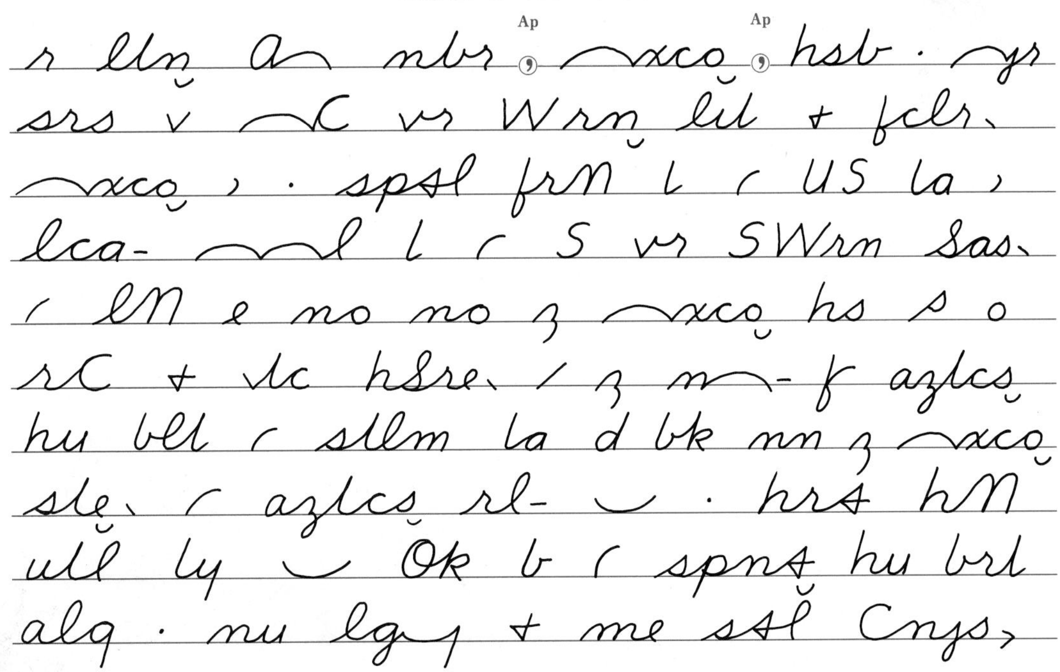

lr r me spcldr lgs lse n
⌒xco = f⌒ lrpcl rn fSs w S
l X⌒l dri + brn dzrls w N.
(⌒oNns w sNrl pl v cNre
r f⌒s f lr gld + slvr ⌒ns.
Ap
⌒xco sle, (lrgS sle n ⌒xco,
Ap
, . u Nl sNr ppla- b ⌒ ln
25M ppl. me lrvlrs vzl ⌒xco
sle zlz (rzrl lons w ⌒oNns
+ alq (cS.

2

dS hr r 4 rzns y
usd cp rd, 1. ur
. ejca- Psn, 2. uno
. brgn ⌒n u se /,
3. u blv n sv me
⌒n uc, 4. uno ho
l lc avq v . rr opl,
y und . 5l rzn ks
ls. ur a⌒q ol 1H ppl
lrsv ls ofr. z pl v
. rr ⌒r Pq u + 99
ols vb slc- l lri r
vcq h⌒s, vlq h⌒s,
, . pln- nbrh ar
U kSrcq. r Pfc f
yq f⌒ls. vlq h⌒s,
hs E ul ⌒N + ⌒.
⌒n u se (kcs la
Intro DC
r avlS, ul PbS sa
u cN afd n l b!,
ll s pv /. njy!

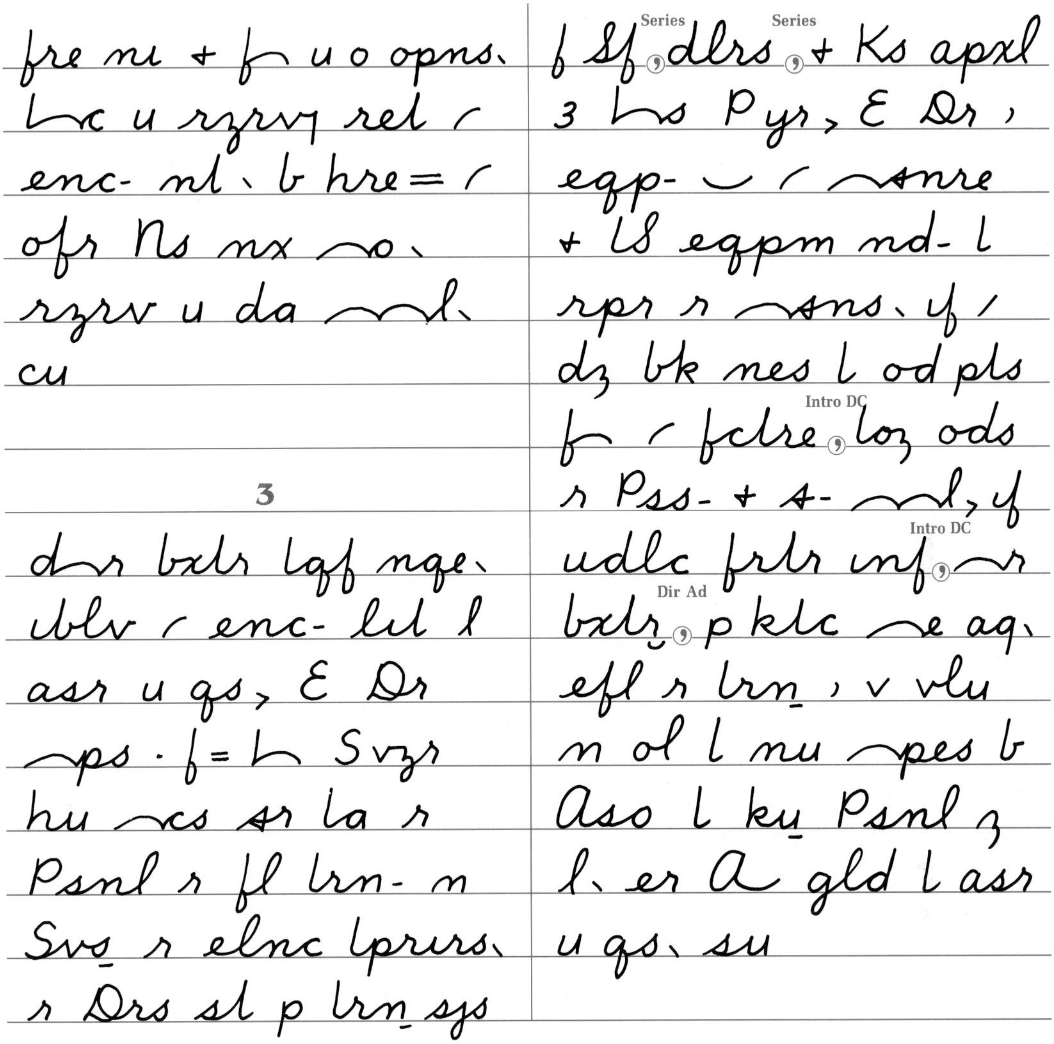

KEY

volume	literature	America, American	**ABBREVIATIONS**

BRIEF FORMS

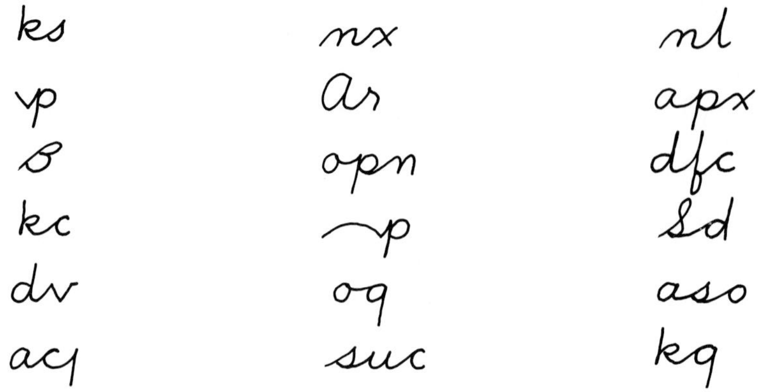

READING AND WRITING EXERCISES

1

South of the Border

Our Latin American neighbor, Mexico, has been a major source of much of our Western literature[1] and folklore. Mexico is a special friend to the U.S. that is located immediately to the south[2] of our southwestern states. The land we now know as Mexico has its own rich and exotic history. It was[3] named for the Aztecs, who built the settlement that would become known as Mexico City. The Aztecs ruled with a[4] harsh hand until they were overcome by the Spanish, who brought along a new language and many social changes.[5]

There are many spectacular things to see in Mexico—from tropical rain forests in the south to[6] extremely dry and barren deserts in the north. The mountains in the central part of the country are famous for their[7] gold and silver mines. Mexico City, the largest city in Mexico, is an exciting industrial[8] center populated by more than 25,000,000 people. Many travelers visit Mexico City[9] as well as the resort towns in the mountains and along the coast. (191)

2

Dear Sir:

Here are four reasons why you should keep reading.

1. You are an educated person.
2. You know a bargain[1] when you see it.
3. You believe in saving money when you can.
4. You know how to take advantage of a[2] rare opportunity.

If you need a fifth reason, consider this. You are among only 100 people[3] to receive this offer. As part of a rare marketing program, you and 99 others have been selected[4] to try our vacation homes.

Village Homes is a planned neighborhood already under construction. It is perfect[5] for young families. Village Homes has everything you will want and more. When you see the contracts that are available,[6] you will probably say you can't afford not to buy!

Let us prove it. Enjoy one free night and form your own[7] opinions. To make your reservation, return the enclosed note. But hurry—the offer ends next month. Reserve your[8] date immediately. Cordially yours, (167)

3

Dear Mr. Baxter:

Thank you for your inquiry. I believe the enclosed literature will answer your questions.[1]

Every distributor employs a full-time supervisor who makes sure that our personnel are fully trained in[2] servicing our electronic typewriters. Our distributors set up training sessions for staff, dealers, and[3] customers approximately three times per year.

Every distributor is equipped with the machinery and test[4] equipment needed to repair our machines. If it does become necessary to order parts from the factory,[5] those orders are processed and shipped immediately.

If you would like further information, Mr. Baxter,[6] please contact me again. We feel our training is of value not only to new employees but also to[7] continuing personnel as well. We are always glad to answer your questions. Sincerely yours, (156)

Applying Your *Speedwriting* and Notetaking Skills

PART SIX

When you transcribe *Speedwriting* notes, your goal is to produce an attractive printed document that speaks well of you and of your business.

BEFORE BEGINNING TO TYPE OR TRANSCRIBE

The following step-by-step procedures provide an efficient, reliable method of producing an acceptable transcript.

1. Determine the order in which each document should be completed. Which one should be done first, second, and so on? Then transcribe each document according to its order of priority.
2. Determine the style, the format, and the margin settings for each document.
3. Verify the spellings of any words that you are not certain of by checking a dictionary. Learn to watch for commonly misspelled words that often slip by unnoticed.
4. Elevate your notepad for convenient reading before beginning to type or keyboard.

BEFORE PRINTING OR REMOVING THE DOCUMENT

Follow these simple yet very important steps before printing or removing your document from the typewriter.

1. Proofread carefully—not once, but twice. Read first against your notes to be certain that your copy is complete and accurate; then read again for typographical, spelling, punctuation, or grammatical errors you might have overlooked.
2. Make any necessary corrections before you print the document if you are using a word processor or while the document is in the machine if you are using a typewriter.

BEFORE PRESENTING THE DOCUMENT

The following procedures should be followed before submitting any document.

1. Draw a line through the *Speedwriting* notes that you have transcribed to indicate that you no longer need them.
2. Look at your transcript carefully. Is it attractively arranged on the page? Does it contain noticeable corrections? When your transcribed copy is neat, free of errors, and shows no evidence of correction, it is ready to be submitted or, if it is a letter, signed and mailed.
3. If you are typing a letter, type the envelope, giving it the same careful attention you gave the letter.
4. If the letter calls for enclosures, assemble them now to be included with the letter.
5. If the document is being presented for another's signature, present the envelope and any specified enclosures along with the transcript.

A WORD ABOUT EQUIPMENT AND SUPPLIES

Some supplies and procedures will vary slightly depending upon the printing equipment that you use. However, you should always have the following items available:

1. A dictionary
2. A list of commonly misspelled words
3. An office procedures manual
4. An English usage manual.

Electric or electronic typewriters usually provide correcting features. Word processors allow you to make corrections in the copy displayed on the video screen before the document is printed. If your machine does not have a correcting feature, choose the most effective agent available—correction film, tape, or fluid. Master the use of the correcting agent so that your transcript will not show any sign of correction.

UNIT

36

Planning a Job Search

Whether you are looking for a part-time job now while you are still in school or for a full-time job after high school or college graduation, you may find the suggestions in this and following units to be very helpful.

Before you begin a job search, it is important to identify your interests, abilities, skills, and goals. Doing so will enable you to match your traits with specific job requirements. Formulate specific answers in your mind as you read the following questions.

1. What type of job am I looking for? Be specific.
2. What skills and qualities are needed to do well in this job?
3. What skills have I developed that would be useful to an employer? Include such skills as word processing, computer operations, and any other tools or equipment you are adept in using. You should also include traits and skills such as organizational ability, trustworthiness, neatness, and the ability to get along well with others.
4. What is my most important reason for wanting a job?
5. What is my second most important reason for wanting a job?
6. Where do I want to work?
7. Is transportation available to where I want to work?
8. What educational background do I have that would be helpful preparation for the job I want?
9. What are my most important successes?
10. What job experience have I had?
11. Am I able to work without close supervision?
12. Do I like to be around people, or do I prefer to work alone?
13. Am I a reliable person? Have I had a good attendance record at school and on previous jobs? Am I punctual?
14. Do I make a good impression? Is my appearance neat?

15. What else about me would an employer find valuable?

This is not a time to be overly modest about describing yourself. Assess your skills, experience, goals, circumstances, interests, and habits realistically but in a positive manner.

SPEEDWRITING PRINCIPLES

1. Write N for the sounds of *ance, ence, nce,* and *nse* (pronounced *ence*).

dance, d-nce dN	since, s-nce sN
balance, b-l-nce blN	defense, d-f-nse dfN
expense, x-p-nse vpN	advance, ad-v-nce avN
agency, a-j-nce-e ajNe	efficiency, e-f-ish-nce-e efsNe

2. Write s for the word beginning *sub.*

submit, sub-m-t s-t	subway, sub-w-a s-a
subscribe, sub-scribe sS	substantial, sub-st-n-ish-l sSnsl
subscription, sub-scrip-tion sSj	subject, sub-j-k sjc

PHRASES

that you are laur   that you will laul

COMMONLY MISSPELLED WORDS

congratulate kq

already ar

VOCABULARY STUDY

unpaid balance — The total amount of money remaining to be paid on a bill or loan.

upd blN

PRINCIPLES SUMMARY

1. Write  for the sound of *ance, ence, nce, nse*: dance, d-nce  .
2. Write  for the word beginning *sub*: submit, sub-m-t  .

WORD DEVELOPMENT

Write the following related words in *Speedwriting* in your notebook.

accept 	-ed	-ing	-ance
subject 	-ed	-s	-ing
assist 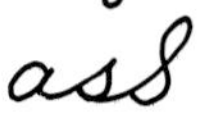	-ed	-ing	-ance
submit 	-ted	-s	-ting
accord 	-ed	-ing	-ance

---

WORD CONSTRUCTION

Practice writing these words in *Speedwriting* in your notebook.

chance, chay-nce	confidence, con-f-d-nce
density, d-nse-ity	remittance, re-m-t-nce
evidence, e-v-d-nce	performance, per-for-m-nce
instance, in-st-nce	substandard, sub-standard
finance, f-n-nce	subcommittee, sub-committee

WRITING ASSIGNMENT

Self-dictate the following letter as you write it in *Speedwriting*.

Dear Ms. Jackson:

Thank you for your answer to my letter. The booklets you sent will greatly help me in doing a[1] research paper due this term.

I anticipate finishing the paper in two weeks. The only problem I've had[2] is obtaining data from companies located out of town. Out of a total of seven, I have heard from[3] only four. I am now waiting for responses from the remaining three before analyzing the final[4] results.

You will certainly receive a copy of my finished report. Yours truly, (94)

READING AND WRITING EXERCISES

1

The 1960s

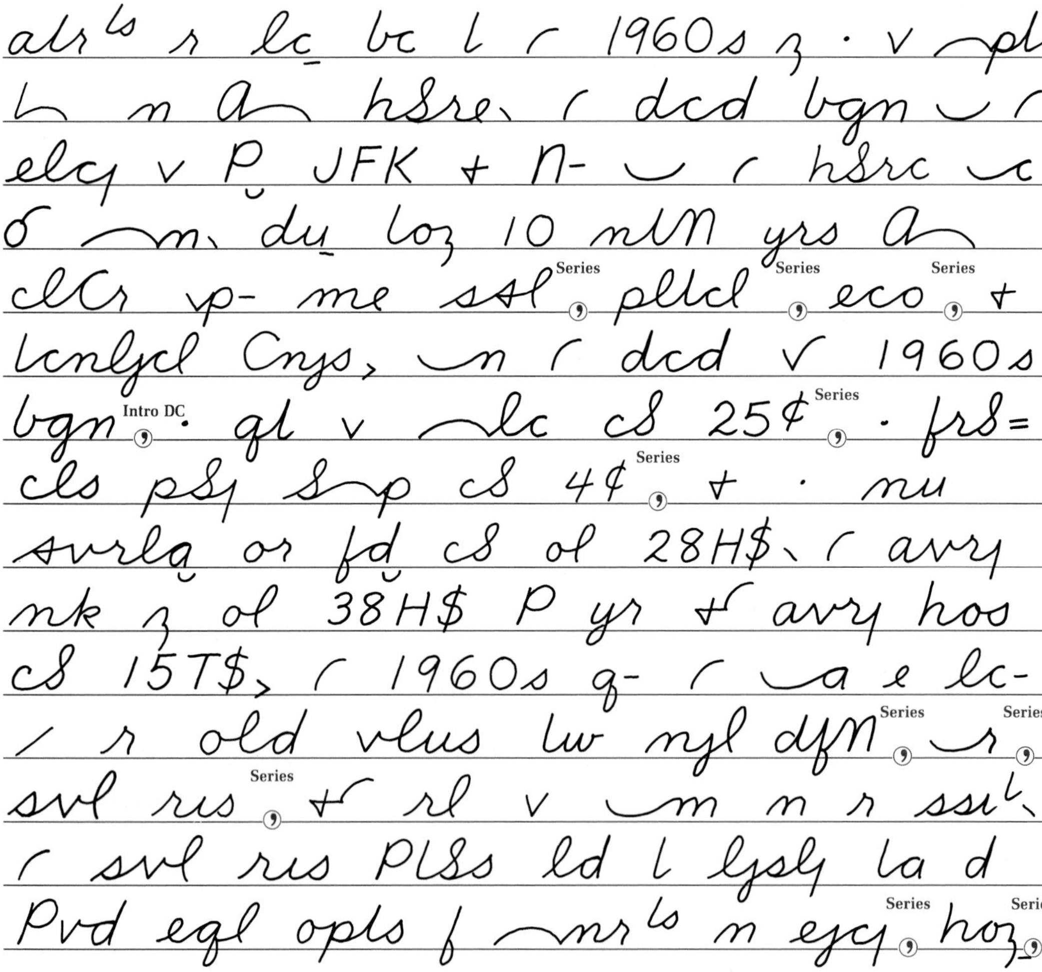

Ap
+ pm. l olSN dvm v ls era ,
Ap
(nvlvm v ul n brq ab Cnj , h
lS efcs. f frS (pllcl + sAl
lAus n sycs rzrv- f eldr
Sasm. n SdNs n sSnAl Noo Clnj-
Intro DC
loz n alr , aloNs f grr Nv fred
fl f + n, ls dcd hsb dS- z.
n C ms hr gru lq + ms
h lns gru Arl z yq ppl dN-l (
rc zc v sC grps z (blls +
rl Sns hu inc sAl kN nl lr sgs.

2

drs s ev
rzrv- . efANe
aplm fu n lq bC.
(aplm hs . lN
vu v oq + a v fsl ls
u rqS-, sN u vq
Intro DC
fls du (bze szn ,
e rcm lau kfr u
rzrvj. / db z

lcl i c n avN,
p sN . 50$ dpzl
no l rzrv ls
aplm. if u A s
Intro DC
l hNl a arms fu ,
elb hpe l fw u
Cc. el aso kfr (
das vu Sa, efl
Sln laul nzy lv-
n ls Cr aplm

o bC. lqf alo s
l asSun ...c u
lrvl plns. cu

3

drs bxlr edlc l
rm u lau ak,
pS du. d u lc .
ml no l ...l s .
Cc, f ... e A
Olc . pam. sNuv
A pd u bls o ..., Intro DC
er Sln ls dla ...S
b c rzll v . Osi.

uf ls, s... ol rzn Intro DC
y ev n hrd f u,
d u drp s . nl v
plnj, Ph esd py
ol aq laul sv me
b s... u pams n
AvN. ...n u pam
arvs la, . fe, G- Intro DC
aq c upd blN,
lqf all l ls ...r.
uf u pam, Ar r
...l, p Dre ls nls. Intro DC
su

KEY

WRITING ASSIGNMENT

drs jcsn lqf asr
l ...i L. c bclls u
sN l grl hlp ...e
n du . rSC ppr
du ls lr, i alspa

fn c ppr n 2 ...cs.
c ol Pb... iv h,
obln dla f cos
lca- ol v lon. ol v
. lol v 7 iv hrd

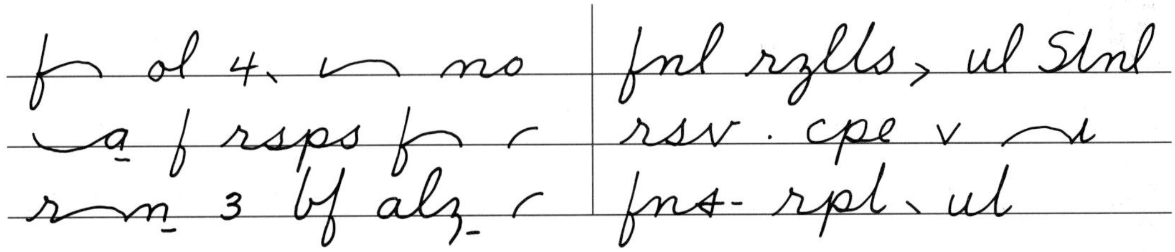

READING AND WRITING EXERCISES

1

The 1960s

Authorities are looking back to the 1960s as a very important time in American[1] history. The decade began with the election of President John F. Kennedy and ended with the[2] historic walk on the moon. During those ten intense years, American culture experienced many social,[3] political, economic, and technological changes.

When the decade of the 1960s began, a[4] quart of milk cost 25¢, a first-class postage stamp cost 4¢, and a new Chevrolet or Ford cost only $2800. The average[5] income was only $3800 per year, and the average house cost $15,000.

The[6] 1960s questioned the way we looked at our old values toward national defense, war, civil rights, and the[7] role of women in our society. The civil rights protests led to legislation that would provide equal[8] opportunities for minorities in education, housing, and employment. One outstanding development[9] of this era, the involvement of youth in bringing about change, had lasting effects. For the first time, the[10] political and social issues were not subjects reserved for elder statesmen. When students in substantial numbers[11] challenged those in authority, allowances for greater individual freedom were fought for and won.

This[12] decade has been described as a time in which men's hair grew long and women's hemlines grew short as young people danced to[13] the rock music of such groups as the Beatles and the Rolling Stones, who incorporated social comment into[14] their songs. (281)

2

Dear Mrs. Smith:

We have reserved an efficiency apartment for you in Long Beach. The apartment has an[1] excellent view of the ocean and all of the facilities you requested.

Since your vacation falls during the[2] busy season, we recommend that you confirm your reservation. It would be wise to call one week in advance.[3]

Please send a $50 deposit now to reserve this apartment. If you wish us to handle all arrangements[4] for you, we will be happy to forward your check. We will also confirm the dates of your stay.

We feel certain[5] that you will enjoy living in this charming apartment on the beach. Thank you for allowing us to assist you[6] in making your travel plans. Cordially yours, (128)

3

Dear Mrs. Baxter:

We would like to remind you that your account is past due. Would you take a minute now to mail[1] us a check?

From time to time, we all overlook a payment. Since you have always paid your bills on time, we are certain[2] this delay must be the result of an oversight. If there is some other reason why we have not heard from[3] you, would you drop us a note of explanation?

Perhaps we should point out again that you will save money by[4] submitting your payments in advance. When your payment arrives late, a fee is charged against the unpaid balance.

Thank you[5] for your attention to this matter. If your payment is already in the mail, please disregard this notice.[6] Sincerely yours, (122)

UNIT 37

Sources of Employment Opportunities

There are many sources of job leads to explore when you are seeking employment. This unit describes several of these sources of employment opportunities.

Help-Wanted Ads. Look in the newspapers for appropriate ads describing jobs that fit your qualifications and interests. Trade magazines sometimes list jobs in particular fields. Libraries are good sources for both local and out-of-town newspapers. Be sure to make notes of the important information regarding these jobs and record all details accurately on index cards.

Employment Services. Register with employment services in your school and city and make sure you have spoken in person with a counselor in these agencies.

Company Personnel Offices. Consult your telephone directory and locate companies of possible interest to you. Libraries frequently have out-of-town directories as well, often on microfiche. Call the companies and ask for the name of the personnel director so that you can write directly to that person.

Civil Service Announcements. Call civil service agencies and request information on upcoming tests. Look for posted announcements in libraries, post offices, and schools. Read all requirements and comply as indicated.

Job Fairs. Look for announcements of job fairs in schools and newspapers. Job fairs usually have a large representation of employers who interview on the spot. Resumés are usually required.

Friends and Relatives. Develop a network of job sources through friends, relatives, neighbors, classmates, and their friends and contacts. Supply them with information on the type of job you are looking for and how you can be contacted. Providing this information typed on index cards is especially helpful.

Former Employers. Contact former employers and let them know you are available for work. Also let them know about any additional education and skills you have acquired since working for them.

Temporary Help Organizations. There are numerous temporary help organizations listed in the yellow pages under *Employment Agencies*. Some of these organizations provide training in specific job skills as well as place people in appropriate employment positions.

Private Employment Agencies. These organizations charge a substantial fee for their services, but they do have a good track record of bringing employees and employers together. Use this avenue after others have been thoroughly explored.

SPEEDWRITING PRINCIPLES

1. Write v for the medial or final sound of *tive*.

active, a-k-tive	acv	relative, r-l-tive	rlv
effective, e-f-k-tive	efcv	objective, o-b-j-k-tive	objcv
selective, s-l-k-tive	slcv	positive, p-z-tive	pzv

Write these additional words:

actively	acvl	relatively	rlvl
activity	acv^{t}	effectiveness	efcv'

BRIEF FORMS

usual	uz	manufacture	⁀f
work, world	⁀o	signature, significant, significance	sig

BRIEF FORM DEVELOPMENT

usually	uzl	manufacturer	⁀fr
unusual	uuz	manufacturing	⁀f-
working	⁀o-		

PHRASES

I appreciate	iap	that I	tai
to work	t⁀o		

USE COMMAS WITH PARENTHETICAL EXPRESSIONS.

PUNCTUATION STUDY

A parenthetical expression is a word or group of words that interrupts the natural flow of the sentence. These expressions are often used to add emphasis or show contrast. When removed from the sentence, such expressions do not change the meaning of the sentence.

When the word or phrase occurs in the middle of the sentence, place a comma before and after the expression. If the expression occurs at the beginning or end of the sentence, use only one comma. Some common examples of parenthetical expressions are as follows:

as a rule	furthermore
in other words	for instance
for example	of course
on the other hand	in fact
therefore	however
naturally	nevertheless

□ We will be happy, *however*, to send you the fabric we have in stock.
□ We do not, *as a rule*, accept cash payments for merchandise.
□ Trust funds offer excellent tax benefits, *for example*.

In following units, parenthetical expressions will be highlighted by the abbreviation **Paren**.

VOCABULARY STUDY

job satisfaction — Degree of contentment an employee feels toward his or her employment position.

jb saly

PRINCIPLES SUMMARY

1. Write v for the medial or final sound of *tive*: active, a-k-tive acv .

WORD DEVELOPMENT

Write the following related words in *Speedwriting* in your notebook.

object objc	-ed	-s	-tive
effect efc	-s	-tive	-tively
act ac	-ed	-tion	-tive
work 	-s	-ed	-er

collect clc   -s   -tion   -tive

WORD CONSTRUCTION

Practice writing these words in *Speedwriting* in your notebook.

productivity, pro-d-k-tive-ity

protective, pro-t-k-tive

activities, a-k-tive-ity-s

defective, d-f-k-tive

effectiveness, e-f-k-tive-ness

sensitive, s-nse-tive

informative, in-for-m-tive

worldly, world-ly

attractive, a-t-r-k-tive

workshop, work-ish-p

WRITING ASSIGNMENT

Self-dictate the following letter as you write it in *Speedwriting*.

Dear Mrs. Gibson:

Our shipments have been arriving after the due date. Our May package was due on the 3rd but[1] was received on the 9th. Our June and July shipments arrived nearly two weeks late.

This problem may have been caused by[2] our recent move. Our letter of April 2 asked you to delay the May shipment while we were getting situated[3] in the new building. Perhaps we did not say when to resume shipping at the regular date. You have our[4] apologies for the misleading message.

We now wish to return to the old schedule. Yours truly, (98)

READING AND WRITING EXERCISES

1

Shared Home Management

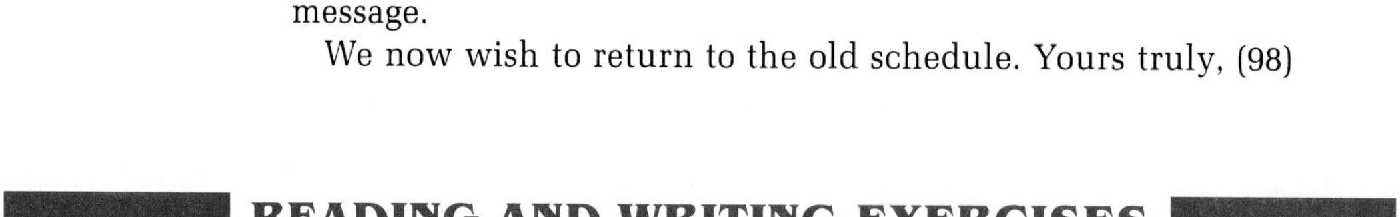

w ym v a h. f me jnrys
d Sc dles — Sl (rspB v f
Paren
+ ldr. z . rl, (flr z (Cf y
ernr + ldr uzl cr- f Cldrn +
Paren
hn. nvrls, du WWII me m —
hr- f f. jbs la cpl r eco Srq
ull a m cd rel f abrd, eco
+ ssl Cnjs v 1960s d /
prclcl f m l lc olsd jbs l splm
Ap
(fl nk. "o drs," . ln la
Ap
hs bk . kn frz, hs h . gr pc
Series Series
o pllcl, ssl, + eco isus v ld. f
Paren
ex, d cr f Cldrn hs bk . nyl ksrn
v gvl + dse v fd n Ppr- fs
hs dv- nl . sSnsl bs. no r r (
Paren Paren
Cnjs b flt l ne grs lN, hoE,
ln w h. z o cpls Srv lglr
Intro DC
l blN (fl bjl — efsNe + efcv,
"sr- h ym" a bk . v pplr
slgn.

2

mo l A dpl yrs
Paren
z uz, eC vu lb asc-
l Ppr . Pf M rpl o
Paren
Nv pes. hoE, ls
yrs rpl lb dfrN.
z uc se f c alC-
Intro DC
cpe, el asc pes lr
Series
opns re lr o Pdcv',
Series
jb saly, + crr gls, p
ncry u ppl l kp lz
rpls z acrll z psB.
b Stn la E, USNs
c Pps v rpl=la s
l hlp eC Psn aCv
, or hr gls, c rzlts
v lz rpls l v . sig
efc o fCr pln. b
o lglr el ncrs c
efsNe vr ogz.

3

dr srp i Stnl
Ap
nyy- rd c mS,
nu dvms n rd
Pss. lqf alo e
lse c Sde n AvN.
n p- lofr i opns
o s efcv', i ks ls
o lb . sig kbj l
c fld. r evns
gvs s . uuz lc S
fCr + s pc o ofs
Psyrs. z h Sa- n
Intro DC
frS Cplr, , objcvs
s l Sva Sd eqpm
n us ld + dS Pdcs
sn lb avlB, r
evns , slcv n , Cys
v exs + brf n , dSys.
Series
i foN c ri lb clr,
Series
Paren
l oq-, + efcv, aq,

iap r opl Lo _ u
n rvu ls Sde. p cl
o _e ef icb v frls
hlp. cu

KEY

WRITING ASSIGNMENT

d _rs gbsn r sms
vb arv af r du da.
r Ma pcj z du 6
3d b z rsv- 6 9l.
r Jn + Jl sms arv-
nrl 2 _cs la, ls
Pbl _a vb cz- b
r rsN _v. r L
v Ap 2 asc- u l

dla r Ma sm l
e _ gl sil- n
nu bld. Ph e dd
n sa _n l rz_
s f rglr da.
uv r aplyes f
Mld _sj, e no
_s l rel l r old
scjl. ul

READING AND WRITING EXERCISES

1

Shared Home Management

Since the end of World War I, we have experienced many social changes. Perhaps one of the most significant[1] changes has been in the management of the American home. For many generations domestic duties[2] were mostly the responsibility of the wife and mother. As a rule, the father was the chief wage earner,[3] and the mother usually cared for the children and the home. Nevertheless, during World War II many[4] women were hired for manufacturing jobs that kept our economy strong until American men could[5] return from abroad.

Economic and social changes of the 1960s made it more practical for women[6] to take outside jobs to supplement the family income. "Working mothers," a term that has become a[7] common phrase, has had a great impact on the political, social, and economic issues of today. For[8] example, day care for children has become a national concern of government, and the merchandising of[9] food in prepared forms has developed into a substantial business. Nowhere are the changes being felt to[10] any greater extent, however, than in the home. As working couples strive together to balance the family[11] budget with efficiency and effectiveness, "shared home management" may become a very popular[12] slogan. (241)

2

MEMO TO: All Department Managers

As usual, each of you will be asked to prepare a performance report[1] on individual employees. However, this year's report will be different. As you can see from the[2] attached copy, we will ask employees their opinions regarding their work productivity, job satisfaction,[3] and career goals.

Please encourage your people to complete these reports as accurately as possible. Be[4] certain that everyone understands the purpose of the report—that it is to help each person achieve his[5] or her goals.

The results of these reports will have a significant effect on future planning. By working[6] together we will increase the efficiency of our organization. (133)

3

Dear Mr. Sharp:

I certainly enjoyed reading the manuscript, *New Developments in Word Processing*. Thank you[1] for allowing me to see the study in advance. I am pleased to offer my opinions on its effectiveness.[2]

I consider this work to be a significant contribution to the field. Mr. Evans gives us an[3] unusual look at the future and its impact on office procedures. As he stated in the first chapter,[4] his objectives are to survey standard equipment in use today and describe products soon to be available.[5]

Mr. Evans is selective in his choice of examples and brief in his descriptions. I found the writing[6] to be clear, well organized, and effective.

Again, I appreciate the opportunity to work with you[7] in reviewing this study. Please call on me if I can be of further help. Cordially yours, (157)

UNIT 38 Preparing Job Application Forms

Completing job application forms to present yourself most advantageously requires careful forethought and advance planning. One of the main goals of an application form is to attract favorable attention and obtain a job interview. There are many similarities in application forms, and they are designed for all age groups with all types of experiences. Job application blanks must be read carefully, and all information that pertains to you should be completed fully and accurately. If an item does not apply to you, write *NA* (not applicable) or draw a line in the blank space to indicate you have read the item.

It is essential to follow directions carefully on an application form. If directions say *Print*, then print neatly. If directions ask for last name, first name, and middle initial in that order, complete the blanks as requested. It is a good idea to work through the application form slowly and do it right the first time.

Be prepared with the following information before you begin filling out an application.

1. Your name, address, telephone number, and how long you have lived at your present address.
2. Your social security number.
3. Your citizenship status.
4. Personal health information.
5. Contact person or persons in case of an emergency (name, address, and telephone number).
6. Education (schools attended, major sequence of study, degrees held, and specialized training, giving dates for all applicable items).
7. Previous work experience (name of organization, address, phone number, your specific duties and contributions, dates of service).
8. Volunteer experience (name of organization, address, phone number, your specific duties and contributions, dates of service).

9. References (state full name, address, phone number, occupation, and relationship to you). Teachers, counselors, employers, or people who know you well in an official capacity are good choices for references. An individual who knows you both personally and professionally would also be a good reference.

SPEEDWRITING PRINCIPLES

1. Write *f* for the word ending *ful.*

useful, u-s-ful *usf*
careful, k-r-ful *crf*
carefully, k-r-ful-ly *crfl*
wonderful, w-nd-r-ful *‿Nrf*
helpful, h-l-p-ful *hlpf*
thankful, ith-ank-ful *Lqf*

Write *f* also for the word ending *ify* (pronounced *uh-fi*).

certify, cer-t-ify *Slf*
justify, j-st-ify *jSf*
qualify, q-l-ify *qlf*
classify, k-l-s-ify *clsf*

2. Write *f1* for the word ending *ification.*

classification, k-l-s-ification *clsf1*
identification, i-d-nt-ification *idNf1*
qualification, q-l-ification *qlf1*
modifications, m-d-ification-s *‿dfjs*

BRIEF FORM DEVELOPMENT

Use these principles to form new words from brief forms:

successful *sucf*
notification *nlf1*
notify *nlf*
grateful *grf*

COMMONLY MISSPELLED WORDS

cannot *cn*
benefited *bnfl-*

VOCABULARY STUDY

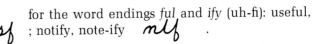

deductible ddcB In reference to insurance policies, a set amount of money to be paid by the policyholder toward the total amount of damages on any claim.

PRINCIPLES SUMMARY

1. Write f for the word endings *ful* and *ify* (uh-fi): useful, u-s-ful usf; notify, note-ify ntf.
2. Write f1 for the word ending *ification*: qualification, q-l-ification qlf1.

WORD DEVELOPMENT

Write the following related words in *Speedwriting* in your notebook.

wonder Nr	-ed	-ing	-ful
use us	-less	-ful	-fulness
help hlp	-ing	-ful	-fulness
class cls	-ify	-ified	-ification
just jS	-ify	-ifies	-ification

WORD CONSTRUCTION

Practice writing these words in *Speedwriting* in your notebook.

identify, i-d-nt-ify	certification, cer-t-ification
qualified, q-l-ify-duh	forgetful, for-guh-t-ful
verify, v-r-ify	verification, v-r-ification
modify, m-d-ify	clarification, k-l-r-ification
unlawful, un-l-aw-ful	hopefully, h-p-ful-ly

WRITING ASSIGNMENT

Self-dictate the following letter as you write it in *Speedwriting*.

Dear Mrs. Billings:

Our nation's banks handle billions of dollars each year for millions of customers, but there is[1] no customer at our bank whom we value more than you. Enclosed is your bank receipt for the money you have asked[2] us to manage for you.

According to our agreement, we will make all your monthly payments while you are out of[3] town. When you return, we will provide you with a report indicating which bills we have paid. The report will also[4] show any earnings on your deposit here at our bank.

If you make arrangements to lease your apartment while[5] traveling, please be sure to send us a copy of the lease agreement. Please include the name of your attorney.[6] We want to be certain we have all the information we may need to manage your money well. Yours truly,[7] (140)

READING AND WRITING EXERCISES

1

Planning for the Golden Years

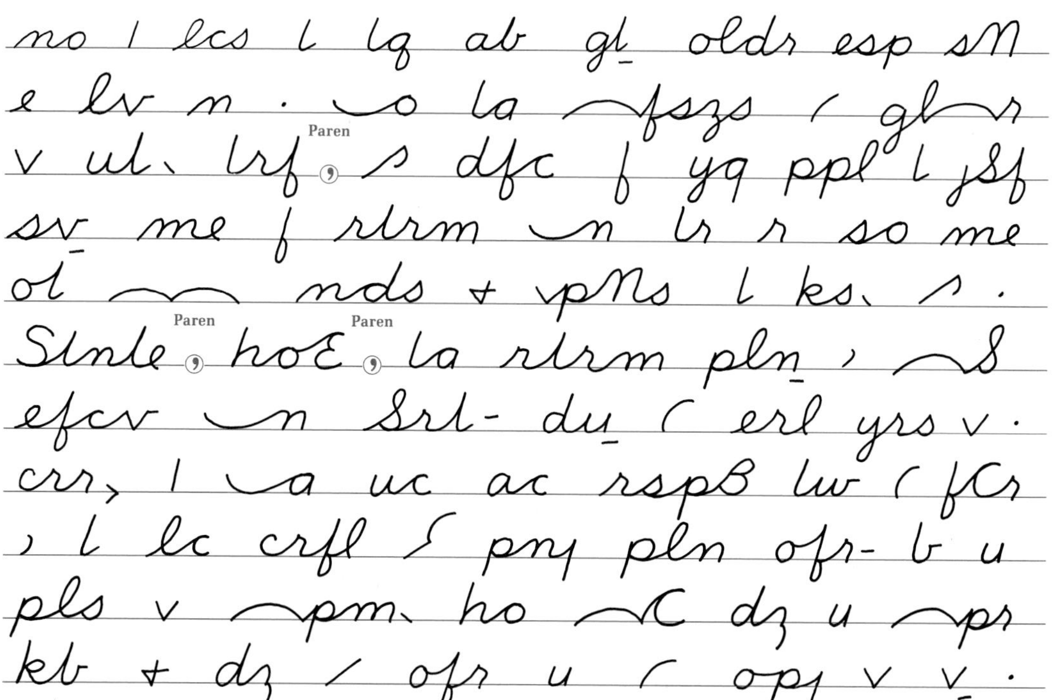

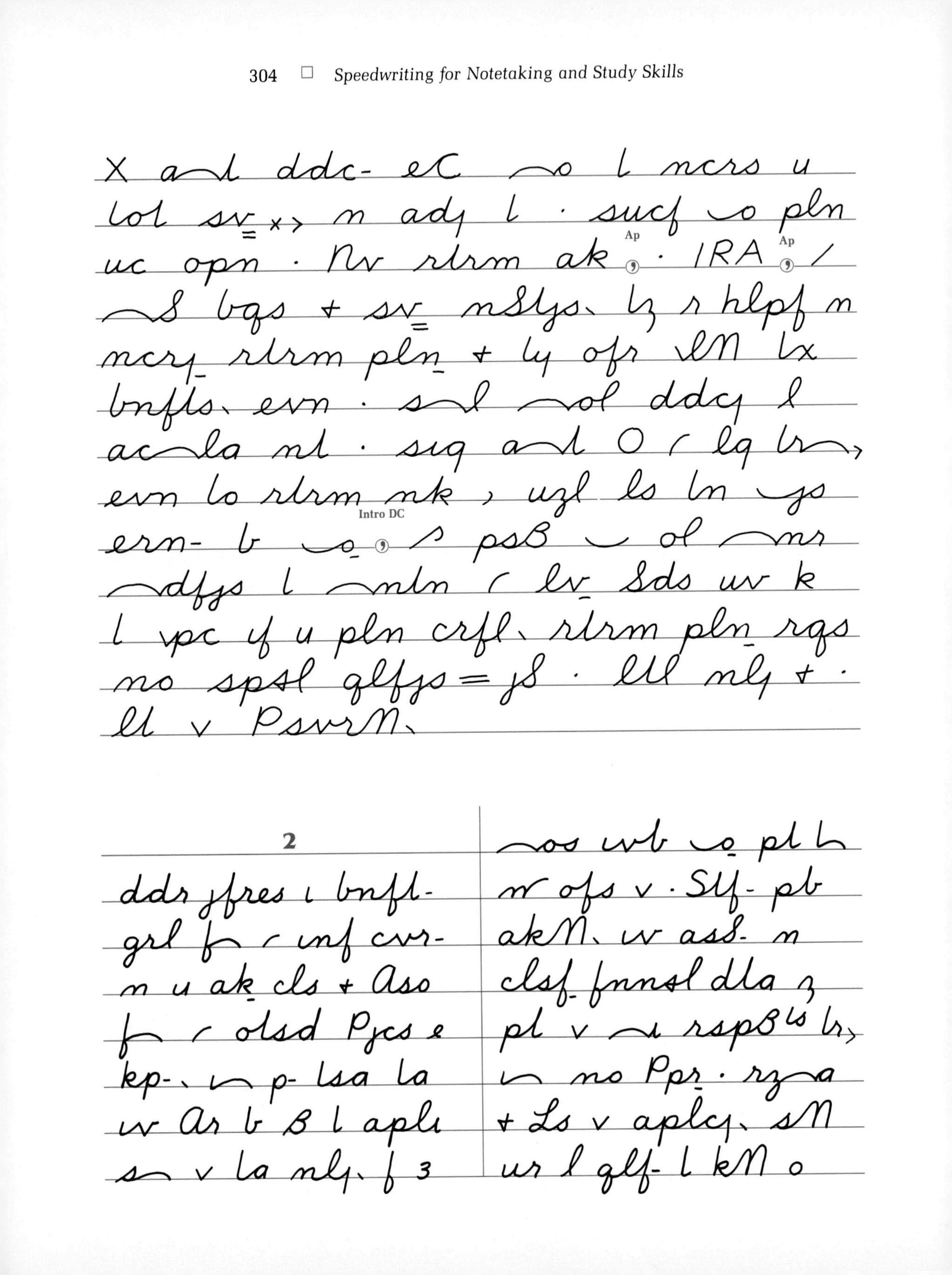

X a l ddc- eC o l ncrs u
tol sv= x> n ady l . sucf o pln
uc opn . Nv rlrm ak Ap , . IRA Ap , /
S bqs + sv= nSlys. lz r hlpf n
ncry rlrm pln + ly ofr vlN lx
bnfts. evn . sl ol ddcy l
acla nl . sig al O r lq lr,
evn lo rlrm nk , uzl ls ln js
Intro DC
ern- b o , r psB ol nr
dfjs l nln r lv Sds uv k
l vpc y u pln crfl. rlrm pln rqs
no spsl qlfjs=jS . lll nly + .
ll v PsvrN.

2

ddr jfres i bnfl-
grl f r inf cvr-
n u ak cls + Aso
f r olsd Pjcs e
kp-. n p- lsa la
w Ar b B l apli
s v la nly. f 3

os wb o pl L
n ofs v . Slf- pb
akN. w asS- n
clsf fnnsl dla z
pl v rspBls lr,
n no Ppr . rz a
+ Ls v aplcy. sN
ur l qlf- l kN o

~i ejcyl bcgroN, (Intro DC)
~a i lS u ~ z
. rfN. u rcmj
db v hlpf. vlu

3

d nu ~pe lk l ~o
elncs. w enc-env
ulfN 3 ~s v vlu
ou nu jb, c frS, u
~pe idNf crd. p
A u sig + cre c crd
du rglr ~o hrs. b
Ppr-l so u crd ~n

u k nl or lv c bld,
c sec ~, u hll
bnfls bcll. rd c
crfl. f uv ne qs
re u hsp or dNl
cvrj, (Intro DC) cl r Psnl ofs
~l, c 3d ~, (Ap) u
~pe hNbc, (Ap) Pvds .
kp gd l r cos Svss
+ plses. p bk f ~lr
~ r Psjrs du u frS
~c ou nu jb, f uv
ne qs, (Intro DC) dN hzla lcl
o s c ne ~. su

KEY

WRITING ASSIGNMENT

d~rs bl r njs
bqs hNl Bs v $
eC yr f Ms v Ks
b lr, no K c r
bq h~ e vlu ~

ln u. enc-, u
bq rse f me uv
asc-s l ~ fu,
acrd l r agrem
el ~c A u ~ol

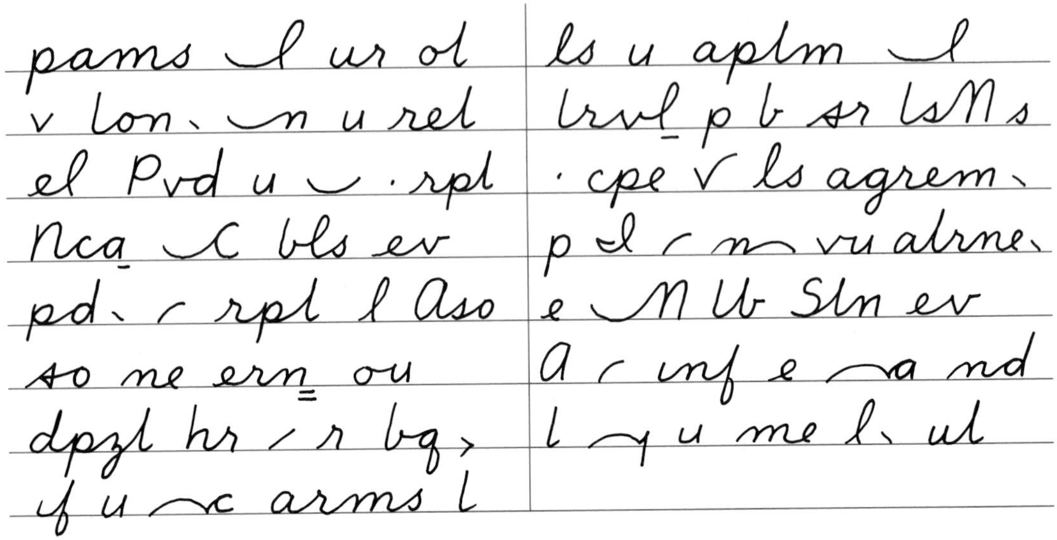

READING AND WRITING EXERCISES

1

Planning for the Golden Years

No one likes to think about getting older, especially since we live in a world that emphasizes the glamor[1] of youth. Therefore, it is difficult for young people to justify saving money for retirement when there[2] are so many other immediate needs and expenses to consider. It is a certainty, however,[3] that retirement planning is most effective when started during the early years of a career.

One way you can[4] act responsibly toward the future is to look carefully at the pension plan offered by your place of[5] employment. How much does your employer contribute, and does it offer you the option of having an extra[6] amount deducted each month to increase your total savings?

In addition to a successful work plan, you can[7] open an individual retirement account, an IRA, at most banks and savings institutions. These are[8] helpful in encouraging retirement planning, and they offer excellent tax benefits. Even a small[9] monthly deduction will accumulate into a significant amount over the long term.

Even though[10] retirement income is usually less than wages earned by working, it is possible with only minor[11] modifications to maintain the living standards you have come to expect if you plan carefully. Retirement[12] planning requires no special qualifications—just a little knowledge and a lot of perseverance. (258)

2

Dear Dr. Jeffries:

I benefited greatly from the information covered in your accounting class and[1] also from the outside projects we completed. I am pleased to say that I have already been able to apply[2] some of that knowledge. For three months I have been working part time in the office of a certified public accountant.[3] I have assisted in classifying financial data as part of my responsibilities there.

I[4] am now preparing a resumé and letters of application. Since you are well qualified to comment on[5] my educational background, may I list your name as a reference? Your recommendation would be very[6] helpful. Very truly yours, (125)

3

Dear New Employee:

Welcome to World Electronics. In the enclosed envelope you will find three items of value[1] on your new job.

The first is your employee identification card. Please add your signature and carry[2] the card during regular working hours. Be prepared to show your card when you come into or leave the building.[3]

The second item is your health benefits booklet. Read it carefully. If you have any questions regarding[4] your hospital or dental coverage, call our personnel office immediately.

The third item, your[5] employee handbook, provides a complete guide to our company's services and policies. Please become familiar[6] with our procedures during your first week on your new job.

If you have any questions, don't hesitate to call on[7] us at any time. Sincerely yours, (147)

UNIT 39

Preparing a Resumé

A resumé is a one-page summary of important facts about you—your personal information, job objectives, work experience, education, and references. The purpose of the resumé is to attract the attention of an employer and gain you an interview. The resumé should be neatly keyed and printed on good quality white, buff, or gray paper. It is a good idea to save your resumé on a disk and update it as you acquire experience, education, and special skills or accomplishments.

The material you have gathered for interviewing and have developed for your job application form will be useful in preparing your resumé. There is no standard format for a resumé, but the following information should be included.

1. Personal information (name, address, telephone where you can be reached or a message can be left for you).
2. Job objective (clearly defined and stated in a positive manner. Avoid the use of *I* and *my*).
3. Education and training (start with the most recent).
4. Experience (work and volunteer; start with the most recent. If you don't have work experience, note your specific skills developed from classroom work or through extracurricular activities).
5. References (give three names, with addresses, titles, and telephone numbers, or indicate: *References available upon request*).

For samples of resumés, consult books and brochures on resumé writing that are available in any library.

A cover letter always accompanies a resumé when it is mailed to a prospective employer. This letter gives you an opportunity to explain your reason for contacting the prospective employer and why you are interested in a particular job or in working for the company. Try to relate your education and experience to the needs of the job and, in the final paragraph, be sure to ask for an interview.

Make notes on the points you want to emphasize in your letter. Write the cover letter in a positive manner. When it is finished, read it aloud to determine whether you have presented the information clearly and accurately and in the tone you want to convey. Finally, proofread both the resumé and the cover letter for any possible errors. Both must be free of errors in order to make a favorable impression.

SPEEDWRITING PRINCIPLES

1. Write a capital N for the word beginnings *enter, inter,* and *intro.*

enterprise, enter-p-r-z	Nprz	international, inter-n-tion-l	Nnyl
interest, inter-st	Ns	introduced, intro-d-s-duh	Nds-
interview, inter-v-u	Nvu	introductory, intro-d-k-t-r-e	Ndctre

2. Write sf for the word beginning and ending *self.*

self-addressed, self-a-d-r-s-duh	sfadrs-	himself, him-self	hsf
self-made, self-m-d	sf‒d	herself, h-r-self	hrsf
self-confidence, self-con-f-d-nce	sfkfdN	yourself, your-self	usf
self-assurance, self-a-ish-r-nce	sfashrN	itself, it-self	sf

3. Write svs for the word ending *selves.*

ourselves, our-selves	rsvs	yourselves, your-selves	usvs

themselves, ith-m-selves hsvs

ABBREVIATIONS	establish esl	superintendent S
BRIEF FORMS	circumstance Sk	once oN
	particular plc	administrate am
	control kl	sample sa
BRIEF FORM DEVELOPMENT	circumstances Sks	particularly plcl
	circumstantial Skal	administration amj
	controlled kl-	samples sas

PUNCTUATION STUDY

USE A COMMA TO SET OFF DATES IN SENTENCES.

When naming a day of the week, followed by the date, place a comma after the day of the week and the date. If the date falls at the end of the sentence, place a comma only after the day of the week.

- □ The meeting scheduled for Wednesday, April 2, has been postponed.
- □ The next board meeting will be held on Tuesday, March 7.

In following units, commas around dates will be highlighted in your Reading and Writing Exercises by the word **Date**.

VOCABULARY STUDY

international Nnjl	Having to do with activities that extend across national boundaries.
academic programs acdc Pgs	Specialized areas of study within a school curriculum.

PRINCIPLES SUMMARY

1. Write a capital N for the word beginnings *enter, inter,* and *intro*: interest, inter-st N8.
2. Write sf for the word beginning and ending *self*: herself, h-r-self hrsf.

3. Write  for the word ending *selves*: yourselves, your-selves  .

WORD DEVELOPMENT

Write the following related words in *Speedwriting* in your notebook.

entertain 	-ed	-er	-ment
interest 	-ed	-s	-ing
introduce 	-d	-s	-ing
interview 	-s	-ed	-ing
establish 	-ed	-es	-ment

---

WORD CONSTRUCTION

Practice writing these words in *Speedwriting* in your notebook.

interfere, inter-f-r

intervening, inter-v-n-ing

introduction, intro-d-k-tion

self-improvement, self-im-prove-ment

self-defense, self-d-f-nse

self-control, self-control

interval, inter-v-l

sampling, sample-ing

administrator, administrate-r

controller, control-r

WRITING ASSIGNMENT

Self-dictate the following letter as you write it in *Speedwriting*.

Dear Mrs. James:

Your new credit card is enclosed, and we are pleased to welcome you as a charge customer. Your credit[1] limit is shown at the top of this letter.

The attached brochure gives the information you requested about[2] our rose bushes and other plants that would be appropriate for a warm climate. It also refers you to[3] a local dealer to whom you may go for help with your specific landscaping situation. Our dealers are[4] glad to cooperate with our mail-order customers.

You may order either by telephone or by mail,[5] whichever is more convenient. To ensure prompt delivery, we ship by air freight as soon as we receive your[6] order.

If you should have any questions about your new account, please give us a call. Cordially yours, (137)

READING AND WRITING EXERCISES

1

Hamburgers and Economics

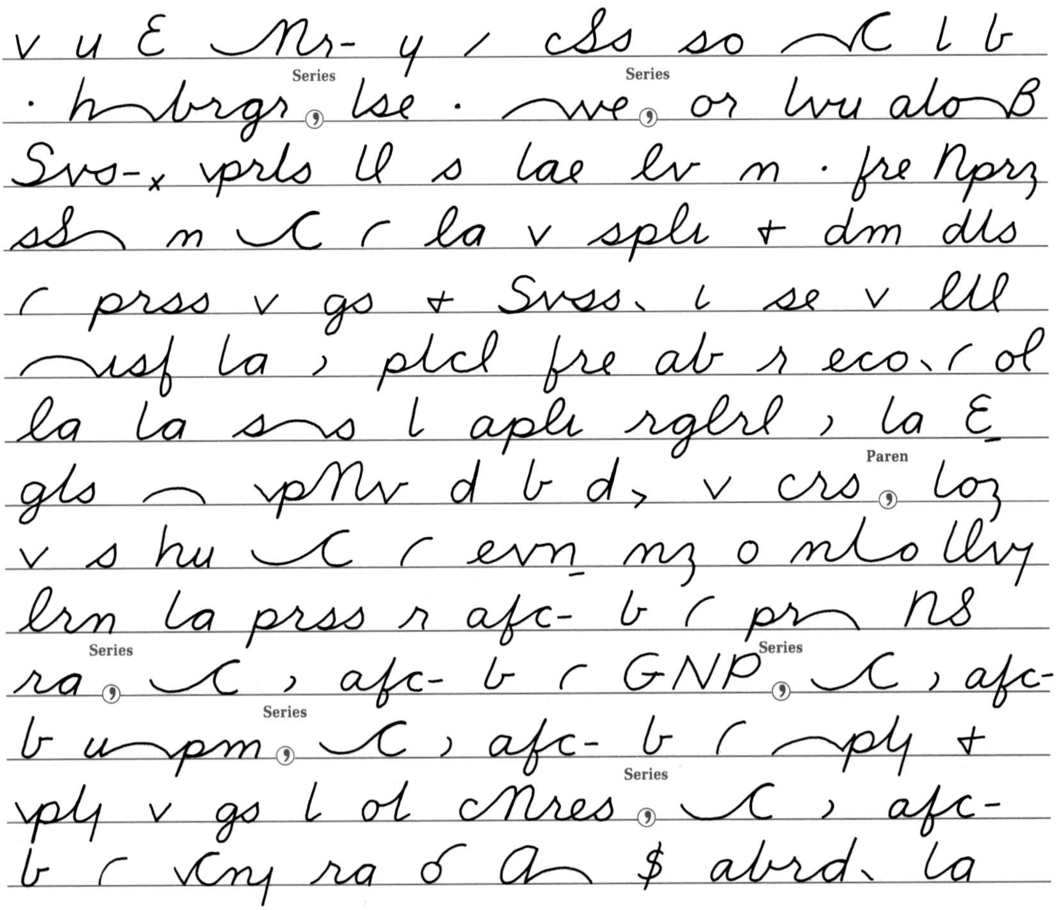

Slnl clrs p E dzN / x> oN ·
h-brgr ks of r grl fu l sa-, (Intro DC)
-l dls -lr / Ad cS 10¢ or 10$ x
Alo r Sks la kl r eco r l kplx
f -S v s l fl USN, (Intro DC) edu nd lv
· USN v bsc eco prNpls n od
l fqj - efsNl n r ssi, / -a
ucb rznB Sln v sv me o ·
h-brgr, (Paren) hoE, (Paren) r l cc / usf!

2

dM jnsn dd uno
laur lc r -S
porf cr crd n
A- x> r A- G crd
sn hr, -ln · cr
crd, s u lcl l r
-o v Nnyl bs
lrvl, ulfN / ac-
n -yr eslms A O
r -o, f u -s l
apli f mbrs, (Intro DC)

s-pl kp r enc-
f + rel / w
sfadrs- env, f
u apli b Mn, (Date) Ma6, (Intro DC)
ul rsv · ex lrvl
cs, ls spsl Ndclre
gfl, blefl Sl- l
oq u Psnl -rs,
y n pl u sig o
-S usf crd n
A- x lrvl w sfasr-
-nr v p- bs ppl

Intro DC

3

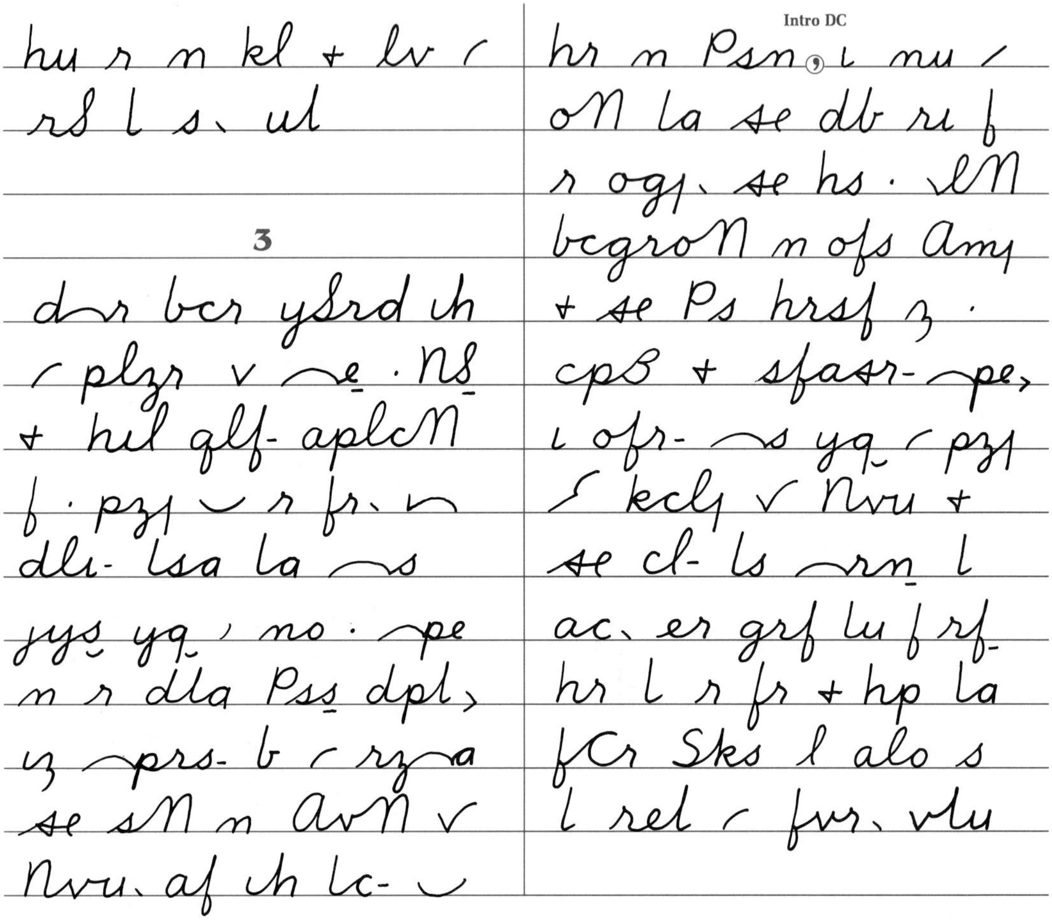

KEY

WRITING ASSIGNMENT

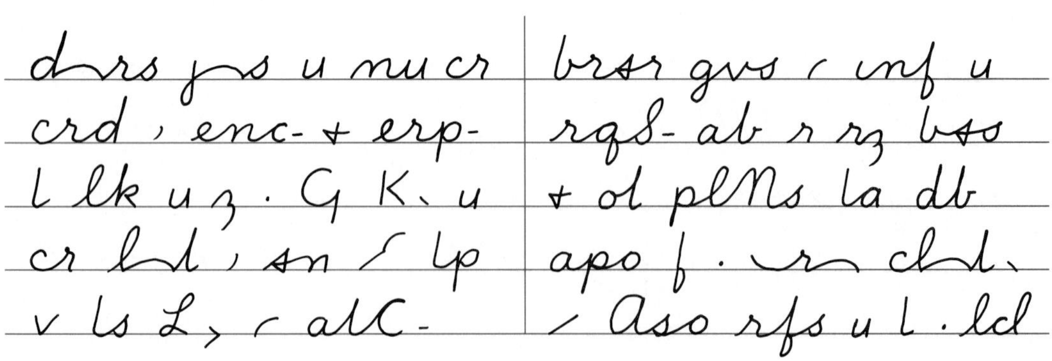

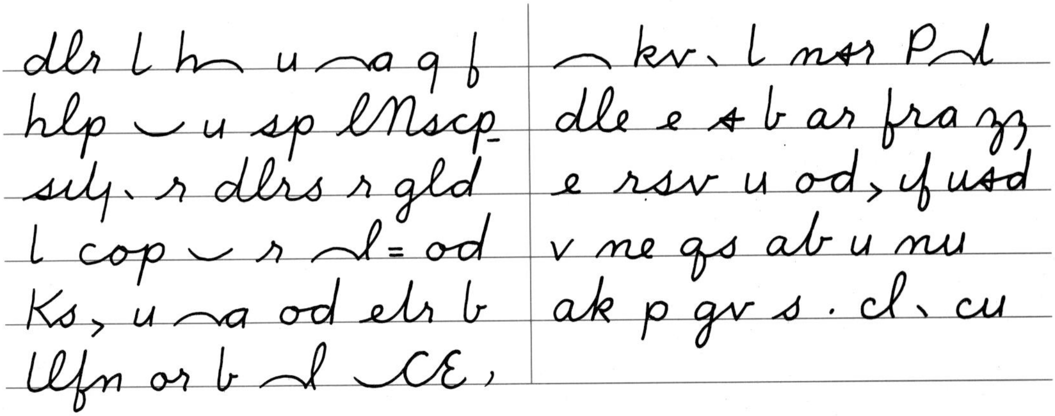

READING AND WRITING EXERCISES

1

Hamburgers and Economics

Have you ever wondered why it costs so much to buy a hamburger, to see a movie, or to have your automobile[1] serviced? Experts tell us that we live in a free enterprise system in which the law of supply and demand[2] determines the prices of goods and services. I see very little myself that is particularly[3] free about our economy. The only law that seems to apply regularly is that everything gets[4] more expensive day by day.

Of course, those of us who watch the evening news on network television learn that prices[5] are affected by the prime interest rate, which is affected by the gross national product, which is affected[6] by unemployment, which is affected by the importation and exportation of goods to other countries,[7] which is affected by the exchange rate on the American dollar abroad. That certainly clears up[8] everything, doesn't it?

Once a hamburger comes off the grill for you to sample, what determines whether it[9] should cost 10¢ or $10? Although the circumstances that control our economy are too complex for[10] most of us to fully understand, we do need to have an understanding of the basic economic[11] principles in order to function more efficiently in our society. One way you can be reasonably[12] certain of saving money on a hamburger, however, is to cook it yourself! (255)

2

Dear Miss Johnson:

Did you know that you are looking at the most powerful credit card in America?

The[1] American Charge Card shown here is more than a credit card. It is your ticket to the world of international[2] business travel. You will find it accepted in major establishments all over the world.

If you wish to apply[3] for membership, simply complete the enclosed form and return it in the self-addressed envelope. If you apply[4] by Monday, May 6, you will receive an executive travel case. This special introductory gift is[5] beautifully styled to organize your personal items.

Why not put your signature on the most useful card[6] in America? Travel in the self-assured manner of experienced business people who are in control[7] and leave the rest to us. Yours truly, (146)

3

Dear Mr. Baker:

Yesterday I had the pleasure of meeting an interesting and highly qualified[1] applicant for a position with our firm. I am delighted to say that Ms. Joyce Young is now an employee in[2] our data processing department.

I was impressed by the resumé she sent in advance of the interview.[3] After I had talked with her in person, I knew at once that she would be right for our organization. She has[4] an excellent background in office administration, and she presents herself as a capable and self-assured[5] employee.

I offered Ms. Young the position at the conclusion of the interview, and she called this morning[6] to accept. We are grateful to you for referring her to our firm and hope that future circumstances will[7] allow us to return the favor. Very truly yours, (150)

UNIT

40

Preparing for a Job Interview

A job interview has two goals: to inform the interviewer about you in order to make a decision about hiring, and to inform you about the job and the possibilities for a successful match of interests, qualifications, and needs. Thorough preparation is the key to a successful job interview. A good way to prepare for an interview is to formulate answers to these frequently asked questions.

1. What are your short-range and long-range goals?
2. How are you preparing yourself to achieve these goals?
3. In what type of position are you most interested?
4. What do you see yourself doing five years from now?
5. Why do you think you might like to work for our company?
6. What are your salary expectations?
7. How much money do you expect to be earning five years from now?
8. What do you consider to be your greatest strengths? Your greatest weaknesses?
9. What jobs have you previously held, how long did you work at each of the jobs, and why did you leave them?
10. How would you describe yourself?
11. What motivated you to choose your field?
12. What subjects did you like best in school? Least? Why?
13. Do you have plans for advanced study?
14. What extracurricular activities did you participate in?
15. In what ways do you think you can make a positive contribution to our company?

The impression you make during an interview will largely determine whether or not you are chosen for the job you want. Be prepared in these key areas.

Appearance. Wear clean, neatly pressed, conservative clothes that make you look like a serious candidate during the interview.
Handshake. Practice a firm handshake and smile sincerely when introduced.
Preparation. Be prepared to answer questions about yourself. The simple statement, "Tell me about yourself," can be disconcerting, so think about what you would say and relate your comments to the job for which you are applying. Actually, this request gives you a good opportunity to make an effective sales presentation of yourself. Be informative but somewhat brief and be as interesting as possible.
Practice. Ask a family member, teacher, coach, or other adult to conduct a mock interview with you. Interviewing improves with practice. Have an adult ask you some or all of the 15 questions in this unit, or even ask additional questions to allow for your spontaneous replies. Ask for suggestions for improvement in your answers and presentation. Be sure to practice eye contact, clear speech without hesitation, and a good choice of language. Remember that family and friends can be very helpful in the practice interview phase; however, they should never accompany you to the actual interview.

SPEEDWRITING PRINCIPLES

1. When a word contains two medial, consecutively pronounced vowels, write the first vowel.

trial, t-r-i-l *trl*

client, k-l-i-nt *cliN*

annual, an-u-l *aul*

material, m-t-r-e-l *—trel*

premium, pre-m-e-m *P—e—*

actually, a-k-chay-u-l-ly *acCull*

previous, pre-v-e-s *Pves*

diagram, d-i-gram *dig*

various, v-r-e-s *vres*

period, p-r-e-d *pred*

2. When a word ends in two consecutively pronounced vowel sounds, write only the last vowel.

area, a-r-a *ara*

audio, aw-d-o *ado*

radio, r-d-o rdo   create, k-r-ate cra

idea, i-d-a ida   media, m-d-a mda

PUNCTUATION STUDY

USE A COMMA BEFORE A COORDINATE CONJUNCTION THAT CONNECTS TWO INDEPENDENT CLAUSES.

The words *and, or, but, for, nor* are conjunctions. When one of these words connects two complete thoughts, place a comma before it. Make certain that the conjunction is connecting two complete thoughts—that is, either thought can stand alone without the rest of the sentence.

- □ David will type the report, and Susan will distribute it.
- □ I will be gone on Tuesday, but Ms. Hamilton will be glad to help you.
- □ Do you wish to pay for the item now, or shall we charge it to your account?

In your Reading and Writing Exercises, commas before conjunctions will be highlighted with the term **Conj**.

VOCABULARY STUDY

audio-visual
ado = vzul

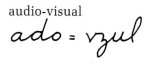

Educational materials (such as filmstrips, movies, videotape programs, and slide/tape programs) that can be seen and heard.

PRINCIPLES SUMMARY

1. When a word contains two medial, consecutively pronounced vowels, write the first vowel: trial, t-r-i-l tril .
2. When a word ends in two consecutively pronounced vowel sounds, write only the last vowel: area, a-r-a ara .

WORD DEVELOPMENT

Write the following related words in *Speedwriting* in your notebook.

diagram dig	-s	-med	-ming
realize relz	-d	-s	-ing
create cra	-d	-s	-ing
evaluate evla	-s	-d	-ing
graduate grja	-d	-s	-ing

WORD CONSTRUCTION

Practice writing these words in *Speedwriting* in your notebook.

ideas, i-d-a-s

manual, m-n-u-l

mutual, m-chay-u-l

renewal, re-n-u-l

science, s-i-nce

valuation, v-l-u-tion

appliance, a-p-l-i-nce

beyond, b-e-nd

serious, s-r-e-s

liability, l-i-bil-ity

WRITING ASSIGNMENT

Self-dictate the following letter as you write it in *Speedwriting*.

Dear Mr. Harvey:

I want to compliment you on the completion of your new building situated on Park[1] Drive. Our city can be proud of this new addition to our community.

The members of the city council[2] are planning a ribbon-cutting ceremony on the date you requested. The public is invited, and[3] music will be provided by a local high school band. The president of the city council will officially[4] open the ceremony. After he speaks, you will be presented with a key to the city.

Perhaps you have[5] considered conducting tours of the building. While tours are generally not planned, this is no ordinary building.[6] Its special characteristics should be seen to be fully appreciated.

Let us know if we can help[7] make necessary arrangements for the tour.

Sincerely, (150)

READING AND WRITING EXERCISES

1

Healthy Eating

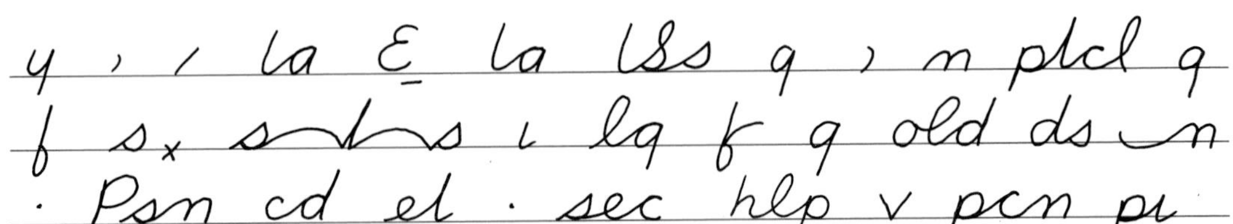

_ _p- cr_ _ol no la / kln-
_ ln (rcm- dl aloN v clSrl, Series
Sgr, Series + hr_f Avs, no ev Dcvr-
la s_ fds v (uuz prp v acCull
rds clSrl lvls. vprls nr siN v
nlrj sa la lr r c_dls n brn, Series
egplN, Series olv yl, Series sc_ _lc, Series fS, Series
ygrl, Series + vres lps v bns la lor u
clSrl lvl. vres frus sC z apls +
grpfru r Aso efcv nr s_ _a,
b esl q el hbls + flo . hlle dil
ec grl rds (rsc v sres il', Conj +
el ld hper + _ Pdcv lvs. (nx
l_ ur l_l- l sa_ . jse Sc or
. X scp v is cr_, Intro DC lq v ho _C
blr / db l od nve bns nSd. Ph
ulb _C _ sucf ln i_ n cra
. pzv ida f . l_l vjlB snc.

2

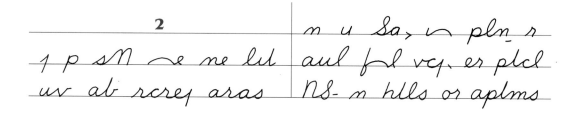

1 p sN _e ne lil
uv ab rcrej aras
n u Sa, i_ pln r
aul fl vcj. er plcl
NS- n hlls or aplms

lca- o bC. du uv
brsrs lS r ns
avlB n . dl prs
rnj×> ev Aso hrd
me q lgs ab u Sa
prcs. p I . cal
Series Series
dS (prcs, lr fsl ls,
& acv ls Pvd- b
eC 1> r lr spsl
Sks esd no ab×
r kdjs n u ara
suB f cp× l, (
bze szn fu prcs×>
edb grf f ne Avs
uv lw hlp s pln
. sucf vcj. e lc
fw lhr f u. su

3

dns An f ur lc
Intro DC
Shrcrs, u
spN C vu d

Ppr ls. sdN uv
(bS psB rels
Lo × e lq usd.
La, y e cra- r nu
ln v cc r, er so
kvN- v gl' vr
Pdc Lae c ls
me=bc grnle. od
u spsl Ndclre sl
& uz / o . lril bss.
c u dsj S N v
. 30=d pred. f ur
Intro DC
n kpl sal-, u a
rel (sl. el ln rel
u me> l cs s
so sr ul lv r
cc r× evb f- fn
Conj
Pdcs f O 40 yrs, &
eno l q ccs lc
f. oN u lri ls plc
Intro DC
sl, ul nvr N luz
ne els> pv / l usf.

lre usf l s_ spsl
nr cCn, cu

KEY

WRITING ASSIGNMENT

dr s hrve l M
l kplm u o kpj
vu nu bld sil-
o prc drv, s sle
cb prod v ls nu
adj l s kn, ,
mbrs v sle ksl
s pln . rbn = cl
srme o da u
rqs- , pb , nvi-
+ zc lb Pvd- b .
lcl hi scl bN ,

P v sle ksl l
ofsll opn , srme.
af h spcs ulb P-
. ce l , sle, Ph
uv ks- kdc lrs v
bld, l lrs s jnl
n pln- ls , no
ord bld, s spsl
crcs sdb sn lb
fl ap-, ll s no
if ec hlp c
nes arms f lr, s

READING AND WRITING EXERCISES

1

Healthy Eating

Why is it that everything that tastes good is not particularly good for us? Sometimes I long for the good[1] old days when a person could eat a second helping of pecan pie with whipped cream without knowing that it contained[2] more than the recommended daily allowance of cholesterol, sugar, and harmful additives.

Now we have[3] discovered that some foods have the unusual property of actually reducing cholesterol levels.[4] Experts in the science of nutrition say that there are chemicals in bran, eggplant, olive oil, skim milk, fish,[5] yogurt, and various types of beans that lower your cholesterol level. Various fruits such as apples and[6] grapefruit are also effective in the same way.

By establishing good eating habits and following a healthy[7] diet, we can greatly reduce the risk of serious illness, and we will lead happier and more productive[8] lives. The next time you are tempted to sample a juicy steak or an extra scoop of ice cream, think of how much[9] better it would be to order navy beans instead. Perhaps you will be much more successful than I am in[10] creating a positive idea for a tempting vegetable snack. (213)

2

Gentlemen:

Please send me any literature you have about recreation areas in your state.

I am[1] planning our annual family vacation. We are particularly interested in hotels or[2] apartments located on the beach. Do you have brochures listing rooms available in a middle price range?

We have[3] also heard many good things about your state parks. Please include a catalog describing the parks, their facilities,[4] and the activities provided by each one.

Are there special circumstances we should know about? Are[5] conditions in your area suitable for camping? What is the busy season for your parks?

We would be grateful[6] for any advice you have toward helping us plan a successful vacation. We look forward to hearing from you.[7] Sincerely yours, (144)

3

Dear Ms. Allen:

If you are like most homemakers, you spend much of your day preparing meals. Shouldn't you have the best[1] possible materials to work with? We think you should. That is why we created our new line of cookware.

We[2] are so convinced of the quality of our product that we make this money-back guarantee. Order your special[3] introductory set and use it on a trial basis. Make your decision at the end of a 30-day[4] period. If you are not completely satisfied, you may return the set. We will then return your money.

What[5] makes us so sure you will love our cookware? We have been manufacturing fine products for over 40 years, and[6] we know what good cooks look for. Once you try this particular set, you will never want to use anything else.

Prove[7] it to yourself. Treat yourself to something special in the kitchen. Cordially yours, (154)

UNIT
41 Job Interview Follow-up

For each interview that you have, keep a record of contacts, addresses, telephone numbers, sources of contact, date and status of interview, and any important facts about each situation. An index card for each contact is an efficient way to keep your notes. The information will help you evaluate the advantages and disadvantages of each job situation and complete the needed follow-up. For example, you may have agreed to telephone the prospective employer at an exact time and date. Such important follow-up can easily be confused or forgotten unless promptly recorded.

The following are post-interview activities that are important for a successful job search.

Review Your Performance. Take time after an interview to review your performance. Answer these questions honestly: *What parts of the interview went well? What parts of the interview did not go well? How can I improve my presentation?* Use this information to strengthen your next interview opportunity.

Keep Up the Search. After a job interview, don't sit back and wait for a job offer. Keep sending out other applications and resumés. Schedule other interviews. You can expect to interview several times before being offered the job you want. The job search is often frustrating, but it is just what the word implies—a *search*. You will sharpen your interview skills with practice and increase your knowledge about different companies and job opportunities, so the interview experience will have value whether you immediately receive a job offer or not.

Follow Up the Interview. If you are interested in a particular job, write a follow-up letter thanking the interviewer and expressing your desire to work for the company. A thank you letter to the interviewer is always important, even if you decide the position is not right for you. You should express your appreciation for the time and interest given you during the interview. Remember, you are not obligated to accept a job offer simply because you had an interview. If the job does not appear to be what you are interested in, it would probably be in your best interest and the company's best interest for you not to accept the job offer.

When you do accept a job, write a brief letter to the companies that may still be considering your application, notifying them that you have obtained a job elsewhere but that you do appreciate their consideration of you as a candidate for a job with their company. Matching your interests with a company's needs can take time, but it is time well spent when done conscientiously.

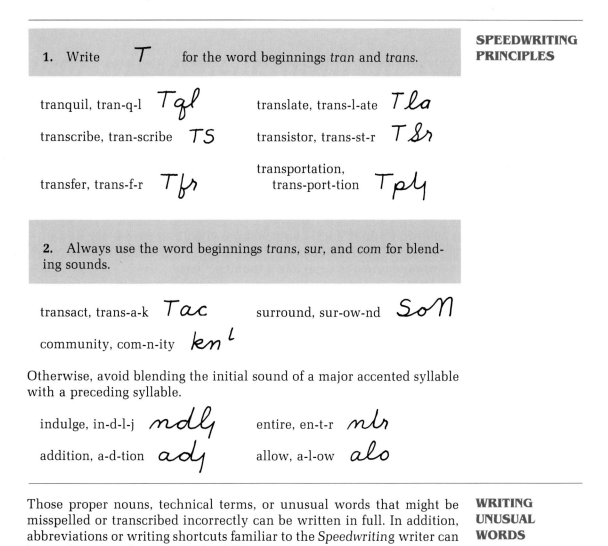

SPEEDWRITING PRINCIPLES

1. Write T for the word beginnings *tran* and *trans*.

tranquil, tran-q-l	Tql	translate, trans-l-ate	Tla
transcribe, tran-scribe	TS	transistor, trans-st-r	TSr
transfer, trans-f-r	Tfr	transportation, trans-port-tion	Tply

2. Always use the word beginnings *trans, sur,* and *com* for blending sounds.

transact, trans-a-k	Tac	surround, sur-ow-nd	Sōn̄
community, com-n-ity	kn		

Otherwise, avoid blending the initial sound of a major accented syllable with a preceding syllable.

indulge, in-d-l-j	ndlj	entire, en-t-r	ntr
addition, a-d-tion	adj	allow, a-l-ow	alo

WRITING UNUSUAL WORDS

Those proper nouns, technical terms, or unusual words that might be misspelled or transcribed incorrectly can be written in full. In addition, abbreviations or writing shortcuts familiar to the *Speedwriting* writer can be used in recording notes. The following sentence is an example.

Mr. Aillet is head of the word processing department at Yazoo Industries.

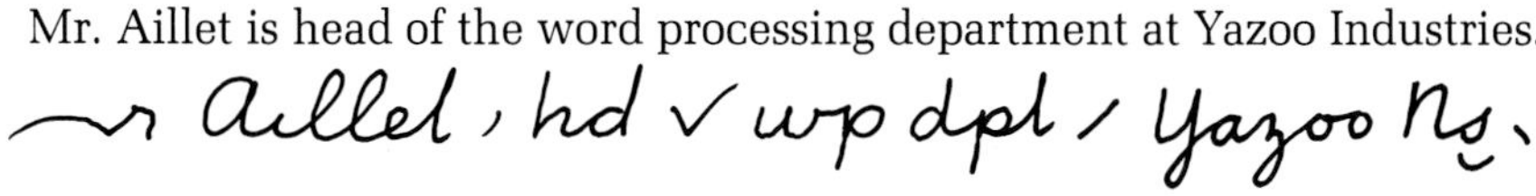

PUNCTUATION STUDY

USE COMMAS WITH INTRODUCTORY PHRASES.

An introductory infinitive phrase (a verb preceded by *to*) is followed by a comma.

□ To get our proposal completed, we had to work for three months after closing hours.

An introductory participial phrase (a verb form used as an adjective) is followed by a comma.

□ Leaving her umbrella at the office, the secretary got wet while running to catch her bus.

An introductory prepositional phrase or phrases consisting of five or more words, or an introductory prepositional phrase containing a verb form is followed by a comma.

□ In two or three days, I will be finished with the inventory.
□ At the beginning of our employment with Brown and Company, we were required to complete a training course.
□ After giving considerable thought to your suggestion, we have decided to adopt the proposal.

In the Reading and Writing Exercises, the abbreviation **Intro P** will be used to highlight introductory phrases.

VOCABULARY STUDY

transaction  The completion or carrying out of an exchange of things of value, frequently preceded by negotiation.

premiums  In reference to insurance, the payments on an insurance policy.

PRINCIPLES SUMMARY

1. Write T for the word beginnings *tran* and *trans*: transfer, trans-f-r Tfr
2. Always use the word beginnings *trans*, *sur*, and *com* for blending sounds; otherwise, avoid blending the initial sound of a major accented syllable with a preceding syllable.

WORD DEVELOPMENT

Write the following related words in *Speedwriting* in your notebook.

act ac	-ed	-ing	trans-
plant pln	-s	-ed	trans-
late la	re-	-ly	trans-
form 	re-	con-	trans-
port pt	im-	ex-	trans-

WORD CONSTRUCTION

Practice writing these words in *Speedwriting* in your notebook.

transmit, trans-m-t

transforming, trans-for-m-ing

transcript, tran-script

transferred, trans-f-r-duh

transaction, trans-a-k-tion

tranquilize, tran-q-l-z

transistors, trans-st-r-s

transpose, trans-p-z

tranquility, tran-q-l-ity

transmission, trans-m-sion

WRITING ASSIGNMENT

Self-dictate the following letter as you write it in *Speedwriting*.

Dear Mrs. Lee:

In the event of an accident involving someone in your family, you would want help to[1] arrive immediately. Our city is in need of new emergency equipment, and we are asking you[2] to contribute to our fund drive.

We want our equipment to correspond to the standards characteristic of[3] other cities the size of ours. With increased demands for the use of our tax dollars, money for new equipment[4] is just not available. We think we can overcome this difficult situation by gaining the support[5] of concerned citizens like you in our various neighborhoods.

Our current goal is to raise enough money for[6] one new ambulance. Won't you send us a donation in the enclosed envelope? Then you, too, will help in fulfilling[7] a vital need in our community. Sincerely yours, (151)

READING AND WRITING EXERCISES

1

From the Wheel to the Heart

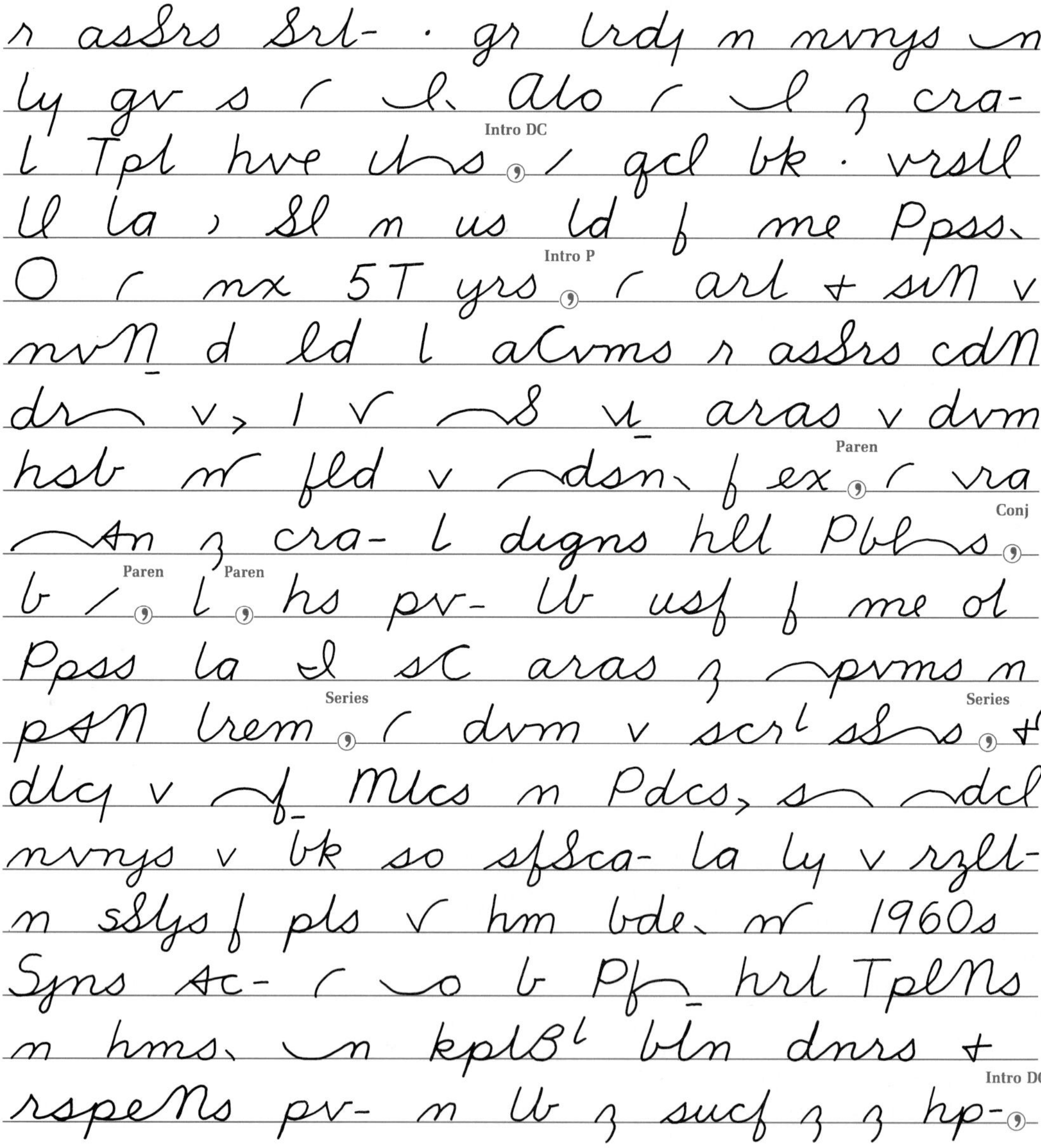

sinlSs Psu- (nvny v arlfsl pls.
opn p nu hrzns n hrl TplN opjs, Intro P
. Sjn sucfl Pf- (frS hrl TplN
uz . kpl arlfsl hrl n 1982. alo (
arlfsl hrl dd n fqj zlz alspa-, (Intro DC
fCr l no dol brq avNs n sinlfc
nvnys ed fN dfc l yn ld.

2

dr as lqf
nqe ab Tfr u
crN aloB ins
l . dfrN cr. (Pss
, qi spl. n od
ldu so, jS gv e Intro P
(dl, yr, c, + Series Series Series
rjSry No vu nucr.
il lc cr v E els,
lr lb . sli ncrs
n u aul Pe.
(ad v ncrs l
dpN o cN v nu
cr u PCs. p nlf

e zz u b u nu
cr. bk efcv d, Intro P
(Cnj n u nu
plse l Pvd u
ku- cvrj. il d
u . cpe v rvz-
plse fu siq, hr
, q nz. efcv Ju, Date
Jl 1, ul rsv . rds- Paren
ra rzrv-f drvrs
hu vn vp- . vdN O
. 5=yr pred. ls ,
r a v rw sf
drv hbls, er A
rde lb v Svs. vlu

3

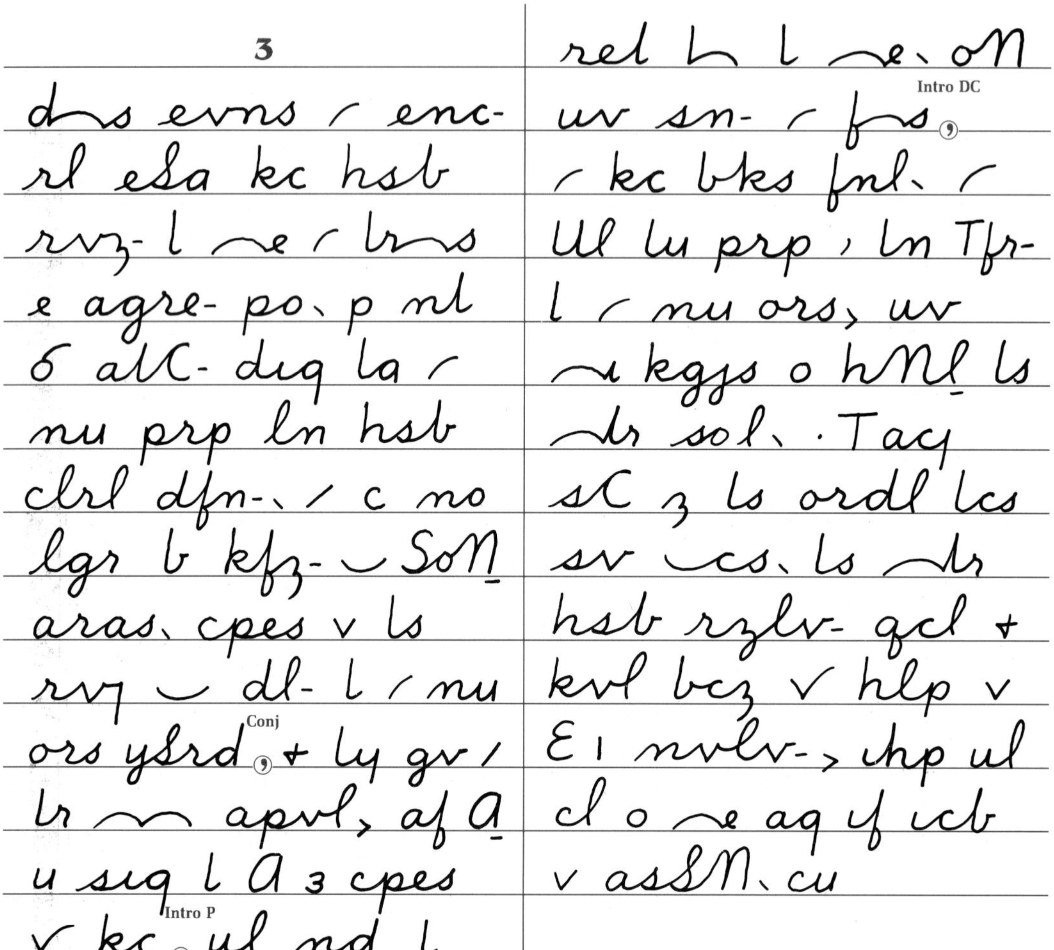

KEY

WRITING ASSIGNMENT

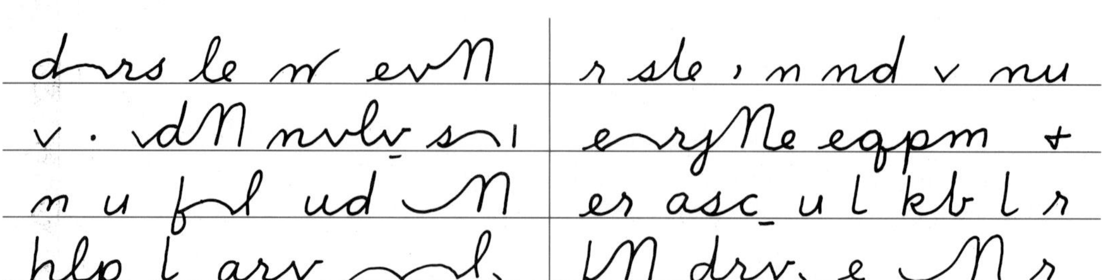

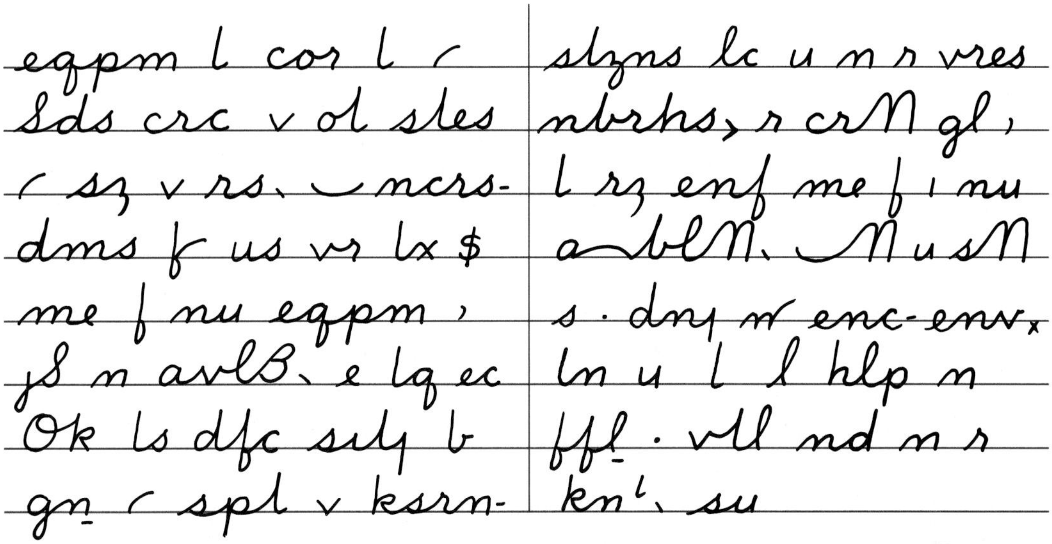

READING AND WRITING EXERCISES

1

From the Wheel to the Heart

Our ancestors started a great tradition in inventions when they gave us the wheel. Although the wheel was created[1] to transport heavy items, it quickly became a versatile tool that is still in use today for many[2] purposes. Over the next 5,000 years, the art and science of inventing would lead to achievements our[3] ancestors couldn't dream of.

One of the most exciting areas of development has been in the field of[4] medicine. For example, the x-ray machine was created to diagnose health problems, but it, too, has proved[5] to be useful for many other purposes that include such areas as improvements in patient treatment,[6] the development of security systems, and the detection of manufacturing mistakes in products.[7]

Some medical inventions have become so sophisticated that they have resulted in substitutions for[8] parts of the human body. In the 1960s surgeons shocked the world by performing heart transplants in humans.[9] When compatibility between donors and recipients proved not to be as successful as was hoped,[10] scientists pursued the invention of artificial parts. Opening up new horizons in heart transplant[11] operations, a surgeon successfully performed the first heart transplant using a completely artificial heart[12] in 1982. Although the artificial heart did not function as well as anticipated, the[13] future will no doubt bring advances in scientific inventions we would find difficult to imagine today.[14] (280)

2

Dear Mr. Ames:

Thank you for your inquiry about transferring your current automobile insurance to a[1] different car. The process is quite simple. In order to do so, just give me the model, year, make, and registration[2] number of your new car. I will take care of everything else.

There will be a slight increase in your annual[3] premium. The amount of the increase will depend on the kind of new car you purchase. Please notify me[4] as soon as you buy your new car. Becoming effective immediately, the change in your new policy will[5] provide you with continued coverage. I will mail you a copy of the revised policy for your signature.[6]

Here is good news. Effective Tuesday, July 1, you will receive a reduced rate reserved for drivers who have[7] not experienced an accident over a five-year period. This is our way of rewarding safe driving[8] habits.

We are always ready to be of service. Very truly yours, (173)

3

Dear Ms. Evans:

The enclosed real estate contract has been revised to meet the terms we agreed upon. Please note on[1] the attached diagram that the new property line has been clearly defined. It can no longer be confused with[2] surrounding areas. Copies of this revision were delivered to the new owners yesterday, and they gave[3] it their immediate approval.

After adding your signature to all three copies of the contract, you will[4] need to return them to me. Once you have signed the forms, the contract becomes final. The title to your property[5] is then transferred to the new owners.

You have my congratulations on handling this matter so well. A[6] transaction such as this ordinarily takes several weeks. This matter has been resolved quickly and conveniently[7] because of the help of everyone involved.

I hope you will call on me again if I can be of assistance.[8] Cordially yours, (163)

UNIT **42**

Review and Reinforcement

1. You learned to write the following word beginnings in Units 36–41:

sub	S	tran, trans	T
enter, inter, intro	N	self	sf

2. You also learned these word endings:

ful	f	self	sf
ify	f	selves	svs
ification	fl		

3. Write these words that illustrate all of the new principles you studied in Units 36–41:

effective, e-f-k-tive	efcv	himself, him-self	hsf
grateful, grate-ful	grf	ourselves, our-selves	rsvs
qualify, q-l-ify	qlf	trial, t-r-i-l	tril
qualification, q-l-ification	qlfl	idea, i-d-a	ida
interview, inter-v-u	Nvu	transcribe, tran-scribe	TS
self-addressed, self-a-d-r-s-duh	sfadrs-	since, s-nce	sN

4. Transcribe the following abbreviations in your notebook:

esl S

5. How quickly can you write these brief forms in your notebook?

usual	once	work
circumstance	manufacture	administrate
world	significance	signature
significant	particular	sample
control		

READING AND WRITING EXERCISES

1

The Age of Titles

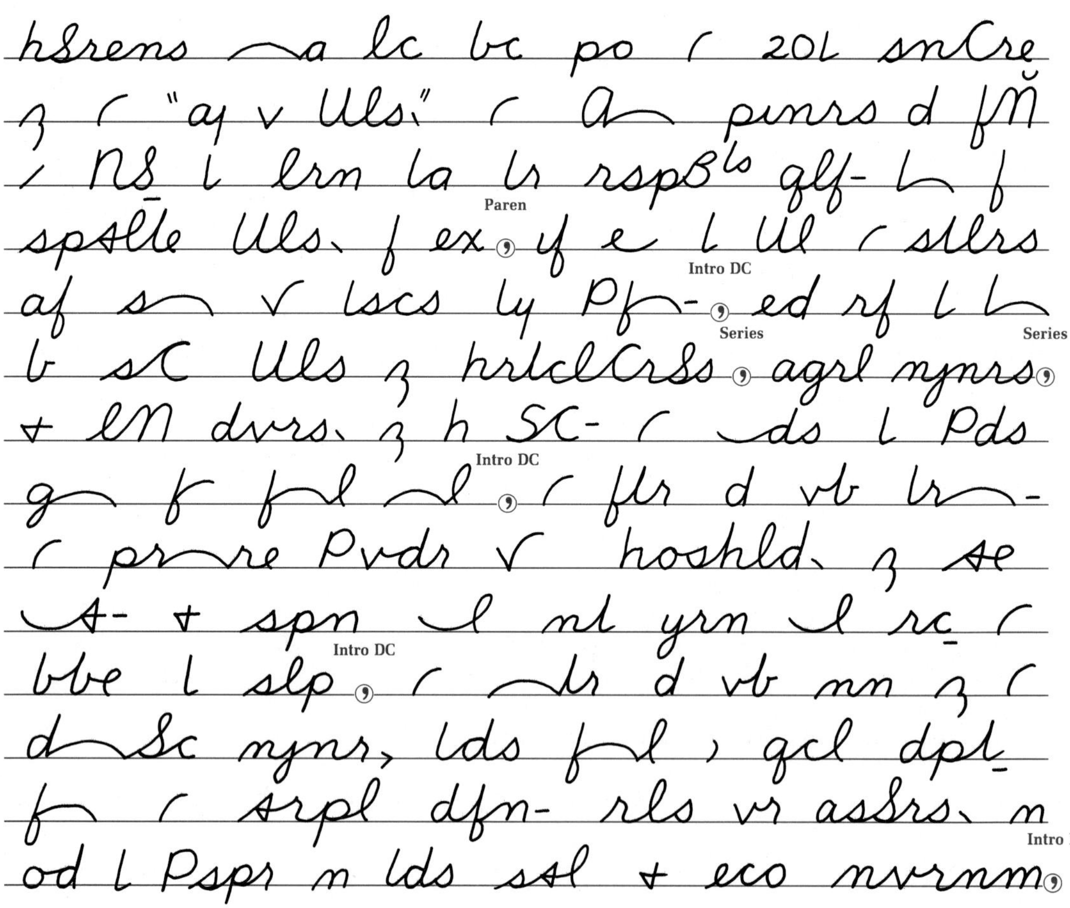

S lrs kb l (hoshld nk b o
olsd (h , & d Sc rl , D-
eqll a q ol mbrs v fl, ls Tfr
v rspBls , Sl bfl l oldr jnrys +
PpnNs v lrdyl vupys, b Ar d Sc
rspBls alos f grr ullzj v nlr fls
rsrsss v l + nk. ls cN v Ar
apol adrss (klprre fl.

Conj

Conj

2

ds jcsn r rqS
f fNs hsb apv-.
l Sv r sle + SoN
ara, ec no esl
r Ppz- ldr& Pq.
Ar u USN (ssl
sig v ls Pq. cliNs
Czn l pp lb lrn-
n ldr& lds.
oN (cliNs v
kp- r crs, ly lb
ncrj- l dr ol

Intro P

Intro DC

sls Pgs n r knl,
r objcv no , l
lca . vp- Psn l ld
r lrn sjs. eblv
u lb (S glf- Psn
bcz vu aCvms n
vlnlr o. d ub
l l Sv z Px, v
crs, ul & lgv
ls dr crf ksj.p
alo e l assr ne
qs u a v / ls
l. s

Paren

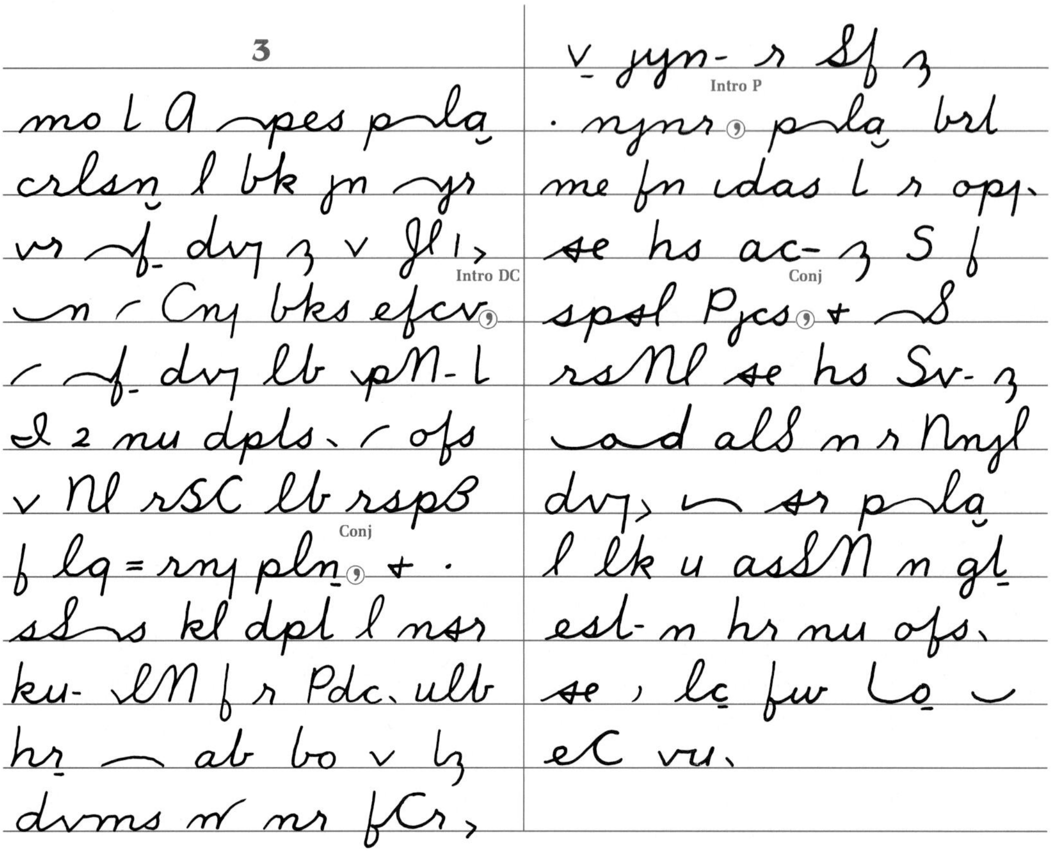

KEY

ABBREVIATIONS establish superintendent

BRIEF FORMS

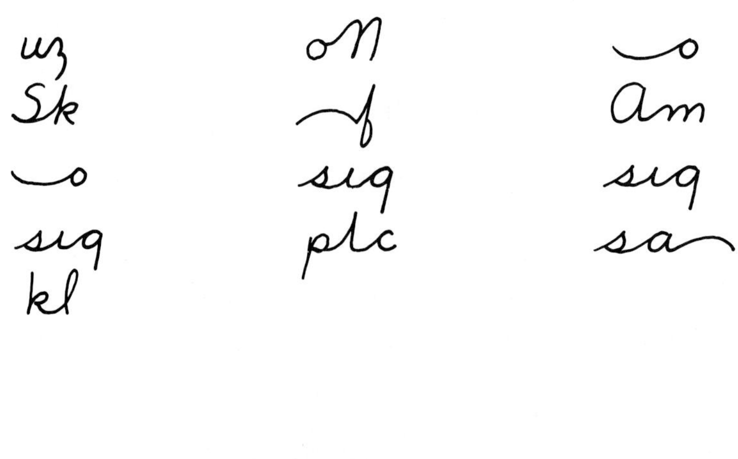

READING AND WRITING EXERCISES

1

The Age of Titles

Historians may look back upon the 20th Century as the "Age of Titles." The American[1] pioneers would find it interesting to learn that their responsibilities qualified them for specialty[2] titles. For example, if we were to title the settlers after some of the tasks they performed, we would refer[3] to them by such titles as horticulturists, agricultural engineers, and land developers. As he[4] searched the woods to produce game for the family meal, the father would have been termed the primary provider[5] of the household. As she washed and spun wool into yarn while rocking the baby to sleep, the mother would have been known[6] as the domestic engineer.

Today's family is quickly departing from the sharply defined roles of our[7] ancestors. In order to prosper in today's social and economic environment, most mothers contribute[8] to the household income by working outside the home, and the domestic role is distributed more equally[9] among other members of the family.

This transfer of responsibilities is still baffling to older[10] generations and proponents of traditional viewpoints, but sharing domestic responsibilities[11] allows for greater utilization of the entire family's resources of time and income. This kind of[12] sharing more appropriately addresses the contemporary family. (254)

2

Dear Ms. Jackson:

Our request for funds has been approved. To serve our city and surrounding area, we can now[1] establish our proposed leadership program. I am sure you understand the social significance of this program.[2] Clients chosen to participate will be trained in leadership methods. Once the clients have completed our course,[3] they will be encouraged to direct other similar programs in our community.

Our objective now is[4] to locate an experienced person to lead our training sessions. We believe you to be the most qualified[5] person because of your achievements in volunteer work. Would you be willing to serve as president?

Of course, you[6] will wish to give this matter careful consideration. Please allow me to answer any questions you may have[7] at this time. Sincerely, (145)

3

MEMO TO: All Employees

Pamela Carlson will become general manager of our manufacturing[1] division as of July 1.

When the change becomes effective, the manufacturing division will be[2] expanded to include two new departments. The office of industrial research will be responsible for[3] long-range planning, and a systems control department will ensure continued excellence for our product. You will be[4] hearing more about both of these developments in the near future.

Having joined our staff as an engineer,[5] Pamela brought many fine ideas to our operation. She has acted as superintendent for special[6] projects, and most recently she has served as worldwide analyst in our international division.

I am[7] sure Pamela will welcome your assistance in getting established in her new office. She is looking forward[8] to working with each of you. (165)

BRIEF FORMS BY ORDER OF PRESENTATION

The numeral in the upper left corner of a box indicates the unit in which the brief forms were introduced. To use the table as a reference for brief forms in the order of their presentation, read from left to right across each numbered row.

	A	B	C	D	E	F	G	H
1	1 .	/	)	m	r	l	e	l
2	2 r	c	b	v	s	4 fr	f	L
3	⌒y	⌒r	o	pl	Ph	d	u	6 ac
4	af	apo	b	dl	du	nes	y	9 ar
5	3	jn	gr	hsp	la	⌣	11 bln	op
6	pp	py	prp	rf	rsp	s	sil	sug
7	loz	13 ⌒	G	dr	q	h	ly	16 ap
8	cor	D	p	P	sp	18 ab	K	hs
9	el	od	O	U	20 avj	aq	bs	sv
10	22 crc	E	N	ol	sal	24 ak	k	kp
11	ku	kb	kv	dl	opl	26 bo	⌒pl	Nv
12	pb	27 a	ks	nl	ord	pv	30 Ar	apx
13	vp	⌒	nx	32 B	kc	dfc	⌒p	opn
14	34 acj	aso	kq	dv	oq	Sd	suc	37 ⌒f
15	sig	uz	⌣o	39 Am	Sk	kl	oN	plc
16	sa⌒							

ABBREVIATIONS BY ORDER OF PRESENTATION

The numeral in the upper left corner of a box indicates the unit in which the abbreviations were introduced. To use the table as a reference for abbreviations in the order of their presentation, read from left to right across each numbered row.

	A	B	C	D	E	F	G	H
1	2 +	cal	co	inf	P	rel	VP	4 M
2	~r	~rs	~s	6 corp	E	enc	N	S
3	W	9 ad	all	cr	No	%	lol	11 dpl
4	env	ins	inv	re	13 jr	sec	sr	16 ave
5	blvd	d	ex	hr	~o	rec	18 B	¢
6	$	H	in	M	oz	lb	T	20 agr
7	eco	fl	sq	yd	22 esp	elc	~dse	gl
8	g	U	24 fed	gvt	inc	ok	rep	S
9	27 Av	Xs	34 a	ltl	vol	39 esl	S	

PHRASES BY ORDER OF PRESENTATION

The numeral in the upper left corner of a box indicates the unit in which the phrases were introduced. To use the table as a reference for phrases in the order of their presentation, read from left to right across each numbered row.

	A	B	C	D	E	F	G	H
1	13 [illegible]	ic	ih	iv	il	ilb	er	ec
2	ev	ehp	ed	edb	ur	uc	uv	uno
3	ul	ud	lb	lq	lv	lvu	lvu	lno
4	lpa	lqf	lqf	lqfL	15 icd	ihp	lse	f
5	v	lau	lau	lb	db	s	16 id	idap
6	idb	esd	el	edap	ucb	udlc	+v	s
7	lae	17 iblv	udu	usd	lcp	cdb	fu	fu
8	nv	vu	vu	lu	lu	18 edu	efl	und
9	[illegible]	vb	vr	lu	lu	19 eap	eh	e
10	u	luz	vh	6	20 ino	ern	elb	ulb
11	lgl	lhr	lsN	cb	22 ivb	isd	iz	eblv
12	eno	zlz	23 idlc	erp-	ucn	ucd	lrsv	lsa
13	24 ifl	udb	zz	ze	25 ilc	ecd	evb	edlc
14	ldu	lgv	lvzl	26 lk	lofr	ldl	29 ulfN	lcl
15	zu	zu	ou	ou	31 zl	hsb	sdb	lqu
16	dlc	33 nvrls	nnls	[illegible]	pda	36 laur	laul	37 iap
17	Lo	lai	appendix icb	icn	idu	ivh	isl	ecb
18	ecn	evh	esl	uh	uvb	uvh	zl	fcla
19	vn	vu	vu					

KEY TO BRIEF FORMS

	A	B	C	D	E	F	G	H
1	1 a an	it at	is his	in not	the	to too	we	will well
2	2 are our	can	for full	of have very	us	4 firm	from	letter
3	manage	market	on own	part port	perhaps	would	your	6 accept
4	after	appropriate	be, but, been buy, by	determine	during	necessary	why	9 arrange
5	as was	general	great grate	hospital	that	were with	11 between	operate
6	participate	point	property	refer	respond response	ship	situate	suggest
7	those	13 am more	charge	doctor direct	go good	he had him	they	16 appreciate
8	correspond correspon- dence	distribute	please up	present	specific specify	18 about	customer	has
9	include	order	over	under	20 advantage	again against	business	several
10	22 character characteristic	ever every	industry	other	satisfy satisfactory	24 accomplish	come came committee	complete
11	continue	contribute	convenient convenience	deliver	opportunity	26 both	important importance	individual
12	public	27 always	consider	note	ordinary	prove	30 already	approximate
13	experience	immediate	next	32 able	contract	difficult	employ	opinion
14	34 acknowledge	associate	congratulate	develop	organize	standard	success	37 manufacture
15	signature significant significance	usual	work world	39 administrate	circumstance	control	once	particular
16	sample							

KEY TO ABBREVIATIONS

	A	B	C	D	E	F	G	H
1	[2] and	catalog	company	information	president	return	vice president	[4] Miss
2	Mr.	Mrs.	Ms.	[6] corporation	east	enclose enclosure	north	south
3	west	[9] amount	attention	credit	number	percent	total	[11] department
4	envelope	insurance	invoice	regard	[13] junior	second secretary	senior	[16] avenue
5	boulevard	day	example executive	hour	month	record	[18] billion	cent cents
6	dollar dollars	hundred	inch	million	ounce	pound	thousand	[20] agriculture
7	economic economy	feet	square	yard	[22] especially	et cetera	merchandise	quart
8	question	university	[24] federal	government	incorporate incorporated	okay	represent representative	street
9	[27] advertise	Christmas	[34] America American	literature	volume	[39] establish	superintendent	

KEY TO PHRASES

	A	B	C	D	E	F	G	H
1	[13] I am	I can	I had	I have	I will	I will be	we are	we can
2	we have	we hope	we would	we would be	you are	you can	you have	you know
3	you will	you would	to be	to go	to have	to have you	to have your	to know
4	to pay	thank you for	thank you for your	thank you for your letter	[15] I could	I hope	to see	for the
5	of the	that you	that your	will be	would be	it is	[16] I would	I would appreciate
6	I would be	we should	we will	we would appreciate	you can be	you would like	and the	at the
7	that we	[17] I believe	you do	you should	to keep	could be	for you	for your
8	in the	of you	of your	will you	will your	[18] we do	we feel	you need
9	to make	have been	of our	to you	to your	[19] we appreciate	we had	we were
10	you were	to use	have had	on the	[20] I know	we are not	we will be	you will be
11	to get	to hear	to send	can be	[22] I have been	I should	I was	we believe
12	we know	as well as	[23] I would like	we are pleased	you cannot	you could	to receive	to say
13	[24] I feel	you would be	as soon as	as we	[25] I look	we could	we have been	we would like
14	to do	to give	to visit	[26] to come	to offer	to determine	[29] you will find	to call
15	as you	as your	on you	on your	[31] as I	has been	should be	thank you
16	would like	[33] nevertheless	nonetheless	time to time	up to date	[36] that you are	that you will	[37] I appreciate
17	to work	that I	[appendix] I can be	I cannot	I do	I have had	I shall	we can be
18	we cannot	we have had	we shall	you had	you have been	you have had	as to	fact that
19	have not	have you	have your					

BRIEF FORMS BY ALPHABETICAL ORDER

a (an)	·
able	B
about	ab
accept	ac
accomplish	ak
acknowledge	acj
administrate	Am
advantage	Avj
after	af
again (against)	aq
against (again)	aq
already	Ar
always	a
am (more)	⌒
an (a)	·
appreciate	ap
appropriate	apo
approximate	apx
are (our)	r
arrange	ar
as (was)	z

associate	aso
at (it)	/
be (been, but, buy, by)	b
been (be, but, buy, by)	b
between	bln
both	bo
business	bs
but (be, been, buy, by)	b
buy (be, been, but, by)	b
by (be, been, but, buy)	b
came (come, committee)	k
can	c
character (characteristic)	crc
characteristic (character)	crc
charge	Cj
circumstance	Sk
come (came, committee)	k
committee (came, come)	k
complete	kp
congratulate	kq
consider	ks

continue ku
contract kc
contribute kb
control kl
convenience (convenient) kv
convenient (convenience) kv
correspond (correspondence) cor
correspondence (correspond) cor
customer K
deliver dl
determine dl
develop dv
difficult dfc
direct (doctor) dr
distribute D
doctor (direct) dr
during du̲
employ -p
ever (every) E
every (ever) E
experience vp
firm fr
for (full) f
from f
full (for) f
general jn
go (good) g
good (go) g
grate (great) gr
great (grate) gr
had (he, him) h
has hs
have (of, very) v
he (had, him) h
him (had, he) h
his (is))
hospital hsp
immediate ⌒
importance (important) -pl
important (importance) -pl
in (not) n
include -l
individual Nv
industry N
is (his))
it (at) /

letter	*L*
manage	
manufacture	
market	
more (am)	
necessary	*nes*
next	*nx*
not (in)	*n*
note	*nl*
of (have, very)	*v*
on (own)	*o*
once	*oN*
operate	*op*
opinion	*opn*
opportunity	*opl*
order	*od*
ordinary	*ord*
organize	*og*
other	*ol*
our (are)	*r*
over	*O*
own (on)	*o*
part (port)	*pl*
participate	*pp*
particular	*plc*
perhaps	*Ph*
please (up)	*p*
point	*py*
port (part)	*pl*
present	*P*
property	*prp*
prove	*pv*
public	*pb*
refer	*rf*
respond (response)	*rsp*
response (respond)	*rsp*
sample	
satisfactory (satisfy)	*sal*
satisfy (satisfactory)	*sal*
several	*sv*
ship	
signature (significance, significant)	*sig*
significance (signature, significant)	*sig*
significant (signature, significance)	*sig*

situate	sit
specific (specify)	sp
specify (specific)	sp
standard	Sd
success	suc
suggest	sug
that	ta
the	
they	ty
those	toz
to (too)	t
too (to)	t
under	U
up (please)	p
us	s
usual	uz
very (have, of)	V
was (as)	z
we	e
well (will)	l
were (with)	
why	y
will (well)	l
with (were)	
work (world)	
world (work)	
would	d
your	u

ABBREVIATIONS BY ALPHABETICAL ORDER

advertise *av*
agriculture *agr*
America (American) *Am*
American (America) *Am*
amount *amt*
and +
attention *att*
avenue *ave*
billion *B*
boulevard *blvd*
catalog *cat*
cent (cents) ¢
cents (cent) ¢
Christmas *Xmas*
company *co*
corporation *corp*
credit *cr*
day *d*
department *dept*
dollar (dollars) $
dollars (dollar) $
east *E*
economic (economy) *eco*
economy (economic) *eco*
enclose (enclosure) *enc*
enclosure (enclose) *enc*
envelope *env*
especially *esp*
establish *est*
et cetera *etc*
example (executive) *ex*
executive (example) *ex*
federal *fed*
feet *ft*
government *govt*
hour *hr*
hundred *H*
inch *in*
incorporate (incorporated) *inc*
incorporated (incorporate) *inc*
information *inf*
insurance *ins*

invoice	inv
junior	jr
literature	lil
merchandise	—dse
million	M
Miss	M
month	—o
Mr.	—r
Mrs.	—rs
Ms.	—s
north	N
number	No
okay	ok
ounce	oz
percent	%
pound	lb
president	P
quart	ql
question	q
record	rec
regard	re
represent (representative)	rep
representative (represent)	rep
return	rel
second (secretary)	sec
secretary (second)	sec
senior	sr
south	S
square	sq
street	S
superintendent	S
thousand	T
total	lol
university	U
vice president	VP
volume	vol
west	W
yard	yd

PHRASES BY ORDER OF CATEGORY

The following phrases are presented in alphabetical segments beginning with the pronouns *I*, *we*, and *you* plus a verb, followed by infinitive phrases (*to* plus a verb), high-frequency word combinations, and word combinations with words omitted.

I am	im
I appreciate	iap
I believe	iblv
I can	ic
I can be	icb
I cannot	icn
I could	icd
I do	idu
I feel	ifl
I had	ih
I have	iv
I have been	ivb
I have had	ivh
I hope	ihp
I know	ino
I look	ilc
I shall	ishl
I should	ishd
I was	iz
I will	il
I will be	ilb
I would	id
I would appreciate	idap
I would be	idb
I would like	idlc
we appreciate	eap
we are	er
we are not	ern
we are pleased	erp-
we believe	eblv
we can	ec
we can be	ecb
we cannot	ecn
we could	ecd
we do	edu
we feel	efl
we had	eh
we have	ev

we have been	evb
we have had	evh
we hope	ehp
we know	eno
we shall	esl
we should	esd
we were	e—
we will	el
we will be	elb
we would	ed
we would appreciate	edap
we would be	edb
we would like	edlc
you are	ur
you can	uc
you cannot	ucn
you can be	ucb
you could	ucd
you do	udu
you had	uh
you have	uv
you have been	uvb
you have had	uvh

you know	uno
you need	und
you should	usd
you were	u—
you will	ul
you will be	ulb
you will find	ulfN
you would	ud
you would be	udb
you would like	udlc
to be	lb
to call	lcl
to come	lk
to determine	ldl
to do	ldu
to get	lgl
to give	lgv
to go	lg
to have	lv
to have you	lvu
to have your	lvu
to hear	lhr
to keep	lcp

to know lno
to make Lc
to offer lofr
to pay lpa
to receive lrsv
to say lsa
to see lse
to send lsN
to use luz
to visit lvzl
to work Lo
and the +
as I zi
as to zl
as we ze
as well as zlz
as you zu
as your zu
at the s
can be cb
could be cdb
fact that fcla
for the f

for you fu
for your fu
has been hsb
have been vb
have had vh
have not vn
have you vu
have your vu
in the n
it is s
of our vr
of the v
of you vu
of your vu
on the o
on you ou
on your ou
should be Adb
thank you lqu
that I lai
that we lae
that you lau
that you are laur

that you will laul
that your lau
to you lu
to your lu
will be lb
will you lu
will your lu
would be db
would like dlc

as soon as 33
nevertheless nvrls
nonetheless nnls
thank you for lqf
thank you for your lqf
thank you for your letter lqfL
time to time t t
up to date pda

IDENTIFICATION INITIALS FOR UNITED STATES AND TERRITORIES

Alabama (AL) AL

Alaska (AK) AK

Arizona (AZ) AZ

Arkansas (AR) AR

California (CA) CA

Colorado (CO) CO

Connecticut (CT) CT

Delaware (DE) DE

District of Columbia (DC) DC

Florida (FL) FL

Georgia (GA) GA

Hawaii (HI) HI

Idaho (ID) ID

Illinois (IL) IL

Indiana (IN) IN

Iowa (IA) IA

Kansas (KS) KS

Kentucky (KY) KY

Louisiana (LA) LA

Maine (ME) ME

Maryland (MD) MD

Massachusetts (MA) MA

Michigan (MI) MI

Minnesota (MN) MN

Mississippi (MS) MS

Missouri (MO) MO

Montana (MT) MT

Nebraska (NE) NE

Nevada (NV) NV

New Hampshire (NH) NH

New Jersey (NJ) NJ

New Mexico (NM) NM

New York (NY) NY

North Carolina (NC) NC

North Dakota (ND) ND

Ohio (OH) OH

Oklahoma (OK) OK

Oregon (OR) OR

Pennsylvania (PA) PA

Rhode Island (RI) RI

South Carolina (SC) SC

South Dakota (SD) SD

Tennessee (TN) TN

Texas (TX) TX

Utah (UT) UT

Vermont (VT) VT

Virginia (VA) VA

Washington (WA) WA

West Virginia (WV) WV

Wisconsin (WI) WI

Wyoming (WY) WY

Guam (GU) GU

Puerto Rico (PR) PR

Virgin Islands (VI) VI

CANADIAN PROVINCES AND TERRITORIES

Alberta (AB) AB

British Columbia (BC) BC

Labrador (LB) LB

Manitoba (MB) MB

New Brunswick (NB) NB

Newfoundland (NF) NF

Northwest Territories (NT) NT

Nova Scotia (NS) NS

Ontario (ON) ON

Prince Edward Island (PE) PE

Quebec (PQ) PQ

Saskatchewan (SK) SK

Yukon Territory (YT) YT

METRIC TERMS

	meter m (length)	liter l (capacity)	gram g (weight)
kilo	km	kl	kg
hecto	hm	hl	hg
deca	dam	dal	dag
deci	dm	dl	dg
centi	cm	cl	cg
milli	mm	ml	mg
micro	⌒crm	⌒crl	⌒crg
nano	nm	nl	ng

SPELLING STUDY

All individuals who write, whether it be for school assignments or for professional communications, need to spell correctly frequently used words. In fact, the ability to spell well consistently ranks among the traits most desired by employers and is an important tool for expressing your ideas in written examinations, reports, and essays.

Surprisingly, a large number of spelling errors occurs from a relatively small number of words. Each of the six Spelling Checks that follow consists of 100 common words that tend to cause spelling problems. Mastery of the words in the Spelling Checks will enable you to spell correctly most of the words in which spelling errors frequently occur. Although the lists are not long, time devoted to the spelling study of the words on each list will certainly be time well spent.

SPELLING CHECK NUMBER 1

1. ability
2. access
3. accounting
4. acknowledgment
5. adaptable
6. admissible
7. advise
8. allotted
9. alternative
10. analyze
11. applicants
12. approximate
13. ascertain
14. assure
15. audit
16. ballot
17. believable
18. brilliant
19. calendar
20. capacity
21. categories
22. changeable
23. clients
24. commitment
25. competitor
26. congratulations
27. consumer
28. cooperation
29. counseling
30. curriculum
31. definitely
32. determine
33. disappoint
34. distribution
35. edition
36. eligible
37. enrollment
38. especially
39. exaggerate
40. executive
41. expenses
42. facilities
43. fascinate
44. filed
45. foreign
46. general
47. growth
48. human
49. incidentally
50. installation
51. interest
52. irrelevant
53. lease
54. liability
55. lose
56. marriage
57. meant
58. merge
59. modifications
60. necessary
61. objectives
62. offered
63. opinion
64. organization
65. parallel
66. participation
67. percentage
68. personally
69. physical
70. possibility
71. preliminary
72. presently
73. prior
74. professional
75. proprietary
76. pursuant
77. questionnaire
78. receipts
79. recommend
80. referring
81. repetition
82. restaurant
83. salary
84. security
85. sewer
86. sincerely
87. software
88. stationary
89. subject
90. sufficient
91. surprise
92. taxable
93. termination
94. through
95. transmitted
96. truly
97. union
98. usually
99. valve
100. versus

SPELLING CHECK NUMBER 2

1. abrupt
2. accessible
3. accrual
4. acquaintance
5. addition
6. admittance
7. advisory
8. allowable
9. among
10. anxious
11. appointment
12. aptitude
13. assessed
14. athlete
15. authorization
16. bankruptcy
17. believe
18. brochure
19. campus
20. capital
21. category
22. choose
23. closing
24. committee
25. complaint
26. conscientious
27. continuing
28. coordinator
29. courses
30. customer
31. delegate
32. develop
33. disastrous
34. district
35. education
36. embarrass
37. entered
38. essential
39. exceed
40. exhibit
41. experience
42. facility
43. field
44. forty
45. generally
46. guarantee
47. imagine
48. incompatible
49. institution
50. internal
51. issue
52. juvenile
53. led
54. library
55. mailable
56. material
57. media
58. microcomputer
59. monitoring
60. nickel
61. obsolete
62. officer
63. opponent
64. orientation
65. parcel
66. particularly
67. perform
68. personnel
69. plausible
70. practical
71. premises
72. prevalent
73. privilege
74. professor
75. provided
76. pursue
77. quotient
78. receive
79. recommendations
80. registration
81. replacement
82. retrieval
83. schedules
84. seize
85. shining
86. specifically
87. stationery
88. subsequent
89. suggested
90. survey
91. technical
92. than
93. throughout
94. transportation
95. university
96. utilization
97. variable
98. vice
99. warranty
100. whose

SPELLING CHECK NUMBER 3

1. absence
2. accidentally
3. accumulate
4. acquire
5. address
6. adolescent
7. affect
8. allowed
9. amounts
10. apologies
11. appraisal
12. argued
13. assessment
14. attendance
15. authorized
16. banquet
17. beneficial
18. brought
19. cancellation
20. carried
21. ceiling
22. chose
23. collateral
24. committees
25. compliance
26. conscious
27. continuous
28. corporate
29. courteous
30. debatable
31. delinquent
32. development
33. discuss
34. divide
35. effect
36. emphasis
37. entitled
38. established
39. excellence
40. existence
41. explanation
42. facsimile
43. finally
44. friend
45. government
46. handicapped
47. immediately
48. increase

49. instruction
50. international
51. issued
52. knowledge
53. ledger
54. license
55. maintenance
56. mathematics
57. medical
58. miniature
59. moral
60. ninth
61. occasion
62. omission
63. opportunity
64. original
65. parity
66. passed
67. performance
68. persuade
69. pleasant
70. practice
71. premium
72. previously
73. probably
74. projects
75. providing
76. pursuing
77. rapport
78. received
79. recommended
80. relieve
81. representative
82. rhythm
83. scheduling
84. sense
85. similar
86. specifications
87. stockholder
88. substantial
89. suggestions
90. surveyor
91. techniques
92. their
93. together
94. treasurer
95. unnecessary
96. utilized
97. varies
98. video
99. weather
100. withdrawal

SPELLING CHECK NUMBER 4

1. abundance
2. accommodate
3. accurate
4. acquisition
5. adequate
6. advantageous
7. affluent
8. almost
9. analyses
10. apologize
11. appreciable
12. arguing
13. assistance
14. attention
15. available
16. basis
17. benefited
18. bureaus
19. candidate
20. cashier
21. census
22. cite
23. column
24. communications
25. conceive
26. consensus
27. contractors
28. correspondence
29. criteria
30. decision
31. describe
32. different
33. discussed
34. divine
35. efficient
36. employee
37. entry
38. estate
39. excellent
40. exists
41. extension
42. faculty
43. financial
44. fulfill
45. governor
46. hardware
47. implementation
48. indicates
49. insurance
50. interpret
51. it's
52. labeling
53. legible
54. limited
55. manageable
56. matrix
57. medicine
58. minimum
59. morale
60. nominal
61. occasionally
62. omit
63. opposite
64. paid
65. partial
66. password
67. permanent
68. persuasive
69. plotter
70. precede
71. preparation
72. primitive
73. procedures
74. prominent
75. provisions
76. pursuit
77. realize
78. receiving
79. reconcile
80. reluctant
81. required
82. ridiculous
83. secretaries
84. separate
85. specified
86. strength
87. substantially
88. summary
89. susceptible
90. technology
91. then
92. toward
93. tries
94. until
95. validate
96. variety
97. villain
98. warehouse
99. weird
100. writing

SPELLING CHECK NUMBER 5

1. academic
2. accomplish
3. achieve
4. across
5. adjournment
6. advertisement
7. all right
8. already
9. analysis
10. apparent
11. appreciated
12. argument
13. associated
14. attorneys
15. beginning
16. benefits
17. business
18. cannot
19. cassette
20. certainly
21. claimants
22. coming
23. comparative
24. concern
25. consistent
26. controlled
27. council
28. criticism
29. deductible
30. description
31. disability
32. disease
33. division
34. either
35. employees
36. environment
37. estimated
38. except
39. expenditure
40. extraordinary
41. familiar
42. fiscal
43. function
44. grammar
45. height
46. implemented
47. industrial
48. integrated
49. interrupt
50. itinerary
51. laboratory
52. leisure
53. loneliness
54. manufacturing
55. maximum
56. mentioned
57. miscellaneous
58. mortgage
59. noticeable
60. occurred
61. omitted
62. optical
63. participant
64. pamphlet
65. past
66. permissible
67. pertinent
68. position
69. preferred
70. prepared
71. principal
72. proceed
73. property
74. psychology
75. quantity
76. reason
77. recent
78. reference
79. remittance
80. requirement
81. role
82. secretary
83. sequential
84. site
85. speech
86. studies
87. succeed
88. supersede
89. system
90. temporary
91. there
92. tragedy
93. useful
94. valuable
95. various
96. visible
97. whether
98. wholly
99. written
100. yield

SPELLING CHECK NUMBER 6

1. accelerate
2. accordance
3. achievement
4. activities
5. administrative
6. advisable
7. allotment
8. alter
9. analyst
10. appearance
11. appropriate
12. arrangement
13. assumption
14. audio
15. balance
16. behavior
17. binary
18. businesslike
19. capabilities
20. casualty
21. certificate
22. clientele
23. commission
24. competitive
25. conference
26. consultant
27. convenience
28. counsel
29. currently
30. defendant
31. despair
32. disappear
33. diskette
34. dissatisfied
35. document
36. electrical
37. enclosing
38. equipped
39. evaluate
40. excess
41. expense
42. extremely
43. family
44. follows
45. further
46. grateful
47. heroes
48. important
49. initial
50. intelligence
51. inventories
52. its
53. laid
54. letterhead
55. loose
56. marketable

57. means
58. menu
59. misspell
60. notify
61. occurrence
62. operating
63. optimism
64. paragraph
65. participate
66. patient
67. personal
68. phase
69. possession
70. prejudiced
71. prescription
72. principle
73. production
74. proposal
75. purpose
76. quarter
77. reasonable
78. recognize
79. referred
80. renewable
81. resolution
82. safety
83. sector
84. services
85. situation
86. station
87. studying
88. successful
89. supervisor
90. tariff
91. terminal
92. thorough
93. transferred
94. undoubtedly
95. using
96. valuation
97. vendor
98. volume
99. while
100. wholesale

READING-RATE CHART

The ability to read *Speedwriting* notes rapidly will help you to record and transcribe those notes more efficiently. To develop your reading ability most effectively, set a reading-rate goal. As a general rule, you should be able to read from *Speedwriting* notes at approximately twice your dictation-recording goal. That is, if you are striving to write in *Speedwriting* at a minimum of 80 words per minute, the reading-rate goal (from material you have practiced) should be at least 160 words per minute. The reading-rate chart on the following pages has been designed to assist you in measuring your ability to read from any document in the text.

Reading rates in words per minute are indicated horizontally across the top of the chart. The number of words in a letter is indicated vertically down the left side of the chart. The body of the table gives the amount of time required to read a certain length of document at a given rate. For example, a 130-word document would need to be read in 49 seconds to achieve a reading rate of 160 words per minute.

The reading-rate chart can be used in two ways:

1. You can determine the number of minutes and seconds needed to reach a specified reading-rate goal.
2. You can read a document, determine the amount of time elapsed, and then determine the rate at which you read the document.

When you are reading for practice and hesitate over a word, follow these three steps:

1. Immediately sound-spell the word.
2. If sound-spelling does not reveal the word, read a few words ahead to see if the word can be determined by context. (This skill will prove extremely valuable in transcription.)
3. Consult the printed key to determine the correct word.

Words in Document	Reading Rate (words per minute)												
	40	50	60	70	80	90	100	110	120	130	140	150	160
62	1:33	1:14	1:02	0:53	0:47	0:41	0:37	0:34	0:31	0:29	0:27	0:25	0:23
64	1:36	1:17	1:04	0:55	0:48	0:43	0:38	0:35	0:32	0:30	0:27	0:26	0:24
66	1:39	1:19	1:06	0:57	0:50	0:44	0:40	0:36	0:33	0:30	0:28	0:26	0:25
68	1:42	1:22	1:08	0:58	0:51	0:45	0:41	0:37	0:34	0:31	0:29	0:27	0:26
70	1:45	1:24	1:10	1:00	0:53	0:47	0:42	0:38	0:35	0:32	0:30	0:28	0:26
72	1:48	1:26	1:12	1:02	0:54	0:48	0:43	0:39	0:36	0:33	0:31	0:29	0:27
74	1:51	1:29	1:14	1:03	0:56	0:49	0:44	0:40	0:37	0:34	0:32	0:30	0:28
76	1:54	1:31	1:16	1:05	0:57	0:51	0:46	0:41	0:38	0:35	0:33	0:30	0:29
78	1:57	1:34	1:18	1:07	0:59	0:52	0:47	0:43	0:39	0:36	0:33	0:31	0:29
80	2:00	1:36	1:20	1:09	1:00	0:53	0:48	0:44	0:40	0:37	0:34	0:32	0:30
82	2:03	1:38	1:22	1:10	1:02	0:55	0:49	0:45	0:41	0:38	0:35	0:33	0:31
84	2:06	1:41	1:24	1:12	1:03	0:56	0:50	0:46	0:42	0:39	0:36	0:34	0:32
86	2:09	1:43	1:26	1:14	1:05	0:57	0:52	0:47	0:43	0:40	0:37	0:34	0:32
88	2:12	1:46	1:28	1:15	1:06	0:59	0:53	0:48	0:44	0:41	0:38	0:35	0:33
90	2:15	1:48	1:30	1:17	1:08	1:00	0:54	0:49	0:45	0:42	0:39	0:36	0:34
92	2:18	1:50	1:32	1:19	1:09	1:01	0:55	0:50	0:46	0:42	0:39	0:37	0:35
94	2:21	1:53	1:34	1:21	1:11	1:03	0:56	0:51	0:47	0:43	0:40	0:38	0:35
96	2:24	1:55	1:36	1:22	1:12	1:04	0:58	0:52	0:48	0:44	0:41	0:38	0:36
98	2:27	1:58	1:38	1:24	1:14	1:05	0:59	0:53	0:49	0:45	0:42	0:39	0:37
100	2:30	2:00	1:40	1:26	1:15	1:07	1:00	0:55	0:50	0:46	0:43	0:40	0:38
102	2:33	2:02	1:42	1:27	1:17	1:08	1:01	0:56	0:51	0:47	0:44	0:41	0:38
104	2:36	2:05	1:44	1:29	1:18	1:09	1:02	0:57	0:52	0:48	0:45	0:42	0:39
106	2:39	2:07	1:46	1:31	1:20	1:11	1:04	0:58	0:53	0:49	0:45	0:42	0:40
108	2:42	2:10	1:48	1:33	1:21	1:12	1:05	0:59	0:54	0:50	0:46	0:43	0:41
110	2:45	2:12	1:50	1:34	1:23	1:13	1:06	1:00	0:55	0:51	0:47	0:44	0:41
112	2:48	2:14	1:52	1:36	1:24	1:15	1:07	1:01	0:56	0:52	0:48	0:45	0:42
114	2:51	2:17	1:54	1:38	1:26	1:16	1:08	1:02	0:57	0:53	0:49	0:46	0:43
116	2:54	2:19	1:56	1:39	1:27	1:17	1:10	1:03	0:58	0:54	0:50	0:46	0:44
118	2:57	2:22	1:58	1:41	1:29	1:19	1:11	1:04	0:59	0:54	0:51	0:47	0:44
120	3:00	2:24	2:00	1:43	1:30	1:20	1:12	1:05	1:00	0:55	0:51	0:48	0:45

(Chart is continued on next page.)

Words in Document	Reading Rate (words per minute)												
	40	50	60	70	80	90	100	110	120	130	140	150	160
122	3:03	2:26	2:02	1:45	1:32	1:21	1:13	1:07	1:01	0:56	0:52	0:49	0:46
124	3:06	2:29	2:04	1:46	1:33	1:23	1:14	1:08	1:02	0:57	0:53	0:50	0:47
126	3:09	2:31	2:06	1:48	1:35	1:24	1:16	1:09	1:03	0:58	0:54	0:50	0:47
128	3:12	2:34	2:08	1:50	1:36	1:25	1:17	1:10	1:04	0:59	0:55	0:51	0:48
130	3:15	2:36	2:10	1:51	1:38	1:27	1:18	1:11	1:05	1:00	0:56	0:52	0:49
132	3:18	2:38	2:12	1:53	1:39	1:28	1:19	1:12	1:06	1:01	0:57	0:53	0:50
134	3:21	2:41	2:14	1:55	1:41	1:29	1:20	1:13	1:07	1:02	0:57	0:54	0:50
136	3:24	2:43	2:16	1:57	1:42	1:31	1:22	1:14	1:08	1:03	0:58	0:54	0:51
138	3:27	2:46	2:18	1:58	1:44	1:32	1:23	1:15	1:09	1:04	0:59	0:55	0:52
140	3:30	2:48	2:20	2:00	1:45	1:33	1:24	1:16	1:10	1:05	1:00	0:56	0:53
142	3:33	2:50	2:22	2:02	1:47	1:35	1:25	1:17	1:11	1:06	1:01	0:57	0:53
144	3:36	2:53	2:24	2:03	1:48	1:36	1:26	1:19	1:12	1:06	1:02	0:58	0:54
146	3:39	2:55	2:26	2:05	1:50	1:37	1:28	1:20	1:13	1:07	1:03	0:58	0:55
148	3:42	2:58	2:28	2:07	1:51	1:39	1:29	1:21	1:14	1:08	1:03	0:59	0:56
150	3:45	3:00	2:30	2:09	1:53	1:40	1:30	1:22	1:15	1:09	1:04	1:00	0:56
152	3:48	3:02	2:32	2:10	1:54	1:41	1:31	1:23	1:16	1:10	1:05	1:01	0:57
154	3:51	3:05	2:34	2:12	1:56	1:43	1:32	1:24	1:17	1:11	1:06	1:02	0:58
156	3:54	3:07	2:36	2:14	1:57	1:44	1:34	1:25	1:18	1:12	1:07	1:02	0:59
158	3:57	3:10	2:38	2:15	1:59	1:45	1:35	1:26	1:19	1:13	1:08	1:03	0:59
160	4:00	3:12	2:40	2:17	2:00	1:46	1:36	1:27	1:20	1:14	1:09	1:04	1:00
162	4:03	3:14	2:42	2:19	2:02	1:48	1:37	1:28	1:21	1:15	1:10	1:05	1:01
164	4:06	3:17	2:44	2:21	2:03	1:49	1:38	1:29	1:22	1:16	1:10	1:06	1:02
166	4:09	3:19	2:46	2:22	2:05	1:51	1:40	1:31	1:23	1:17	1:11	1:06	1:02
168	4:12	3:22	2:48	2:24	2:06	1:52	1:41	1:32	1:24	1:18	1:12	1:07	1:03
170	4:15	3:24	2:50	2:26	2:08	1:53	1:42	1:33	1:25	1:18	1:13	1:08	1:04
172	4:18	3:26	2:52	2:27	2:09	1:55	1:43	1:34	1:26	1:19	1:14	1:09	1:05
174	4:21	3:29	2:54	2:29	2:11	1:56	1:44	1:35	1:27	1:20	1:15	1:10	1:05
176	4:24	3:31	2:56	2:31	2:12	1:57	1:46	1:36	1:28	1:21	1:15	1:10	1:06
178	4:27	3:34	2:58	2:33	2:14	1:59	1:47	1:37	1:29	1:22	1:16	1:11	1:07
180	4:30	3:36	3:00	2:34	2:15	2:00	1:48	1:38	1:30	1:23	1:17	1:12	1:08

(Chart is continued on next page.)

Words in Document	Reading Rate (words per minute)												
	80	90	100	110	120	130	140	150	160	170	180	190	200
82	1:01	0:55	0:49	0:45	0:41	0:38	0:35	0:33	0:31	0:29	0:28	0:26	0:25
84	1:03	0:56	0:50	0:46	0:42	0:39	0:36	0:34	0:31	0:29	0:28	0:27	0:25
86	1:04	0:57	0:52	0:47	0:43	0:40	0:37	0:34	0:32	0:31	0:29	0:27	0:26
88	1:06	0:59	0:53	0:48	0:44	0:41	0:38	0:35	0:33	0:31	0:29	0:28	0:26
90	1:08	1:00	0:54	0:49	0:45	0:42	0:39	0:36	0:34	0:32	0:30	0:28	0:27
92	1:09	1:01	0:55	0:50	0:46	0:42	0:39	0:37	0:34	0:32	0:31	0:29	0:28
94	1:10	1:03	0:56	0:51	0:47	0:43	0:40	0:38	0:35	0:33	0:31	0:30	0:28
96	1:12	1:04	0:58	0:52	0:48	0:44	0:41	0:38	0:36	0:34	0:32	0:30	0:29
98	1:13	1:05	0:59	0:53	0:49	0:45	0:42	0:39	0:37	0:35	0:32	0:31	0:29
100	1:15	1:07	1:00	0:55	0:50	0:46	0:43	0:40	0:38	0:35	0:34	0:32	0:30
102	1:16	1:08	1:01	0:56	0:51	0:47	0:44	0:41	0:38	0:36	0:34	0:32	0:31
104	1:18	1:09	1:02	0:57	0:52	0:48	0:45	0:42	0:39	0:37	0:35	0:33	0:31
106	1:19	1:11	1:04	0:58	0:53	0:49	0:45	0:42	0:40	0:37	0:35	0:33	0:32
108	1:21	1:12	1:05	0:59	0:54	0:50	0:46	0:43	0:40	0:38	0:36	0:34	0:32
110	1:23	1:13	1:06	1:00	0:55	0:51	0:47	0:44	0:41	0:39	0:37	0:35	0:33
112	1:24	1:15	1:07	1:01	0:56	0:52	0:48	0:45	0:42	0:40	0:37	0:35	0:34
114	1:25	1:16	1:08	1:02	0:57	0:53	0:49	0:46	0:43	0:40	0:38	0:36	0:34
116	1:27	1:17	1:10	1:03	0:58	0:54	0:50	0:46	0:43	0:41	0:38	0:37	0:35
118	1:28	1:19	1:11	1:04	0:59	0:54	0:51	0:47	0:44	0:41	0:40	0:37	0:35
120	1:30	1:20	1:12	1:05	1:00	0:55	0:51	0:48	0:45	0:43	0:40	0:38	0:36
122	1:31	1:21	1:13	1:07	1:01	0:56	0:52	0:49	0:46	0:43	0:41	0:39	0:37
124	1:33	1:23	1:14	1:08	1:02	0:57	0:53	0:50	0:46	0:44	0:41	0:39	0:37
126	1:34	1:24	1:16	1:09	1:03	0:58	0:54	0:50	0:47	0:44	0:42	0:40	0:38
128	1:36	1:25	1:17	1:10	1:04	0:59	0:55	0:51	0:48	0:45	0:43	0:40	0:38
130	1:38	1:27	1:18	1:11	1:05	1:00	0:56	0:52	0:49	0:46	0:43	0:41	0:39
132	1:39	1:28	1:19	1:12	1:06	1:01	0:57	0:53	0:49	0:47	0:44	0:42	0:40
134	1:40	1:29	1:20	1:13	1:07	1:02	0:57	0:54	0:50	0:47	0:44	0:42	0:40
136	1:42	1:31	1:22	1:14	1:08	1:03	0:58	0:54	0:51	0:48	0:46	0:43	0:41
138	1:43	1:32	1:23	1:15	1:09	1:04	0:59	0:55	0:52	0:49	0:46	0:44	0:41
140	1:45	1:33	1:24	1:16	1:10	1:05	1:00	0:56	0:53	0:49	0:47	0:44	0:42

(Chart is continued on next page.)

Words in Document	Reading Rate (words per minute)												
	80	90	100	110	120	130	140	150	160	170	180	190	200
142	1:47	1:35	1:25	1:17	1:11	1:06	1:01	0:57	0:53	0:50	0:47	0:45	0:43
144	1:48	1:36	1:26	1:19	1:12	1:06	1:02	0:58	0:54	0:51	0:48	0:45	0:43
146	1:50	1:37	1:28	1:20	1:13	1:07	1:03	0:58	0:55	0:52	0:49	0:46	0:44
148	1:51	1:39	1:29	1:21	1:14	1:08	1:03	0:59	0:56	0:52	0:49	0:47	0:44
150	1:53	1:40	1:30	1:22	1:15	1:09	1:04	1:00	0:56	0:53	0:50	0:47	0:45
152	1:54	1:41	1:31	1:23	1:16	1:10	1:05	1:01	0:57	0:54	0:51	0:48	0:46
154	1:56	1:43	1:32	1:24	1:17	1:11	1:06	1:02	0:58	0:54	0:51	0:49	0:46
156	1:57	1:44	1:34	1:25	1:18	1:12	1:07	1:02	0:59	0:55	0:52	0:49	0:47
158	1:59	1:45	1:35	1:26	1:19	1:13	1:08	1:03	0:59	0:56	0:53	0:50	0:47
160	2:00	1:47	1:36	1:27	1:20	1:14	1:09	1:04	1:00	0:56	0:53	0:51	0:48
162	2:02	1:48	1:37	1:28	1:21	1:15	1:09	1:05	1:01	0:57	0:54	0:51	0:49
164	2:03	1:49	1:38	1:29	1:22	1:16	1:10	1:06	1:02	0:58	0:55	0:52	0:49
166	2:05	1:51	1:40	1:31	1:23	1:17	1:11	1:06	1:02	0:59	0:55	0:52	0:50
168	2:06	1:52	1:41	1:32	1:24	1:18	1:12	1:07	1:03	0:59	0:56	0:53	0:50
170	2:08	1:53	1:42	1:33	1:25	1:18	1:13	1:08	1:04	1:00	0:57	0:54	0:51
172	2:09	1:55	1:43	1:34	1:26	1:19	1:14	1:09	1:05	1:01	0:57	0:54	0:52
174	2:11	1:56	1:44	1:35	1:27	1:20	1:15	1:10	1:05	1:01	0:58	0:55	0:52
176	2:12	1:57	1:46	1:36	1:28	1:21	1:15	1:10	1:06	1:02	0:59	0:56	0:53
178	2:14	1:59	1:47	1:37	1:29	1:22	1:16	1:11	1:07	1:03	0:59	0:56	0:54
180	2:15	2:00	1:48	1:38	1:30	1:23	1:17	1:12	1:08	1:04	1:00	0:57	0:54
182	2:17	2:01	1:49	1:39	1:31	1:24	1:18	1:13	1:08	1:04	1:01	0:57	0:55
184	2:18	2:03	1:50	1:40	1:32	1:25	1:19	1:14	1:09	1:05	1:01	0:58	0:55
186	2:20	2:04	1:52	1:41	1:33	1:26	1:20	1:14	1:10	1:06	1:02	0:59	0:56
188	2:21	2:05	1:53	1:43	1:34	1:27	1:21	1:15	1:11	1:06	1:03	0:59	0:56
190	2:23	2:07	1:54	1:44	1:35	1:28	1:21	1:16	1:11	1:07	1:03	1:00	0:57
192	2:24	2:08	1:55	1:45	1:36	1:29	1:22	1:17	1:12	1:08	1:04	1:01	0:58
194	2:26	2:09	1:56	1:46	1:37	1:30	1:23	1:18	1:13	1:08	1:05	1:01	0:58
196	2:27	2:11	1:58	1:47	1:38	1:30	1:24	1:18	1:14	1:09	1:05	1:02	0:59
198	2:29	2:12	1:59	1:48	1:39	1:31	1:25	1:19	1:14	1:10	1:06	1:03	0:59
200	2:30	2:13	2:00	1:49	1:40	1:32	1:26	1:20	1:15	1:11	1:07	1:03	1:00

SPEEDWRITING PRINCIPLES BY ORDER OF PRESENTATION

Principle	Word	Speedwriting	Word	Speedwriting
1. Write what you hear.	high	hi		
2. Drop medial vowels.	build	bld		
3. Write initial and final vowels.	office	ofs	fee	fe
4. Write c for the sound of *k*.	copy	cpe		
5. Write a capital C for the sound of *ch*.	check	Cc		
6. Write ⌒ for the sound of *m*.	may	⌒a		
7. Write ‿ for the sounds of *w* and *wh*.	way	‿a	when	‿n
8. Underscore the last letter of any word to add *ing* or *thing* as a word ending.	billing	bl̲	something	s⌒̲
9. To form the plural of any word ending in a mark of punctuation, double the last mark of punctuation.	savings	sv̳		
10. Write s to form the plural of any word, to show possession, or to add s to a verb.	books	bcs	runs	rns
11. Write m for the sounds of *mem* and *mum*.	memo	mo		
12. Write m for the sounds of *men, min, mon, mun*.	menu	mu	money	me
13. Write m for the word endings *mand, mend, mind, ment*.	demand	dm	amend	am
	remind	rm	payment	pam
14. Write a capital N for the sound of *nt*.	sent	sN		

15. Write ʃ for the sound of *ish* or *sh*.	finish	fnʃ		
16. Write a capital a for the word beginnings *ad, all, al*.	admit	ad	also	aso
17. Write n for the initial sound of *in* or *en*.	indent	ndN		
18. Write o for the sound of *ow*.	allow	alo		
19. Write a printed capital S (joined) for the word beginnings *cer, cir, ser, sur*.	certain	Sln	survey	Sva
20. To form the past tense of a regular verb, write a hyphen after the word.	used	uz-		
21. Write ʟ for the sound of *ith* or *th*.	them	ʟm		
22. Write l for the word ending *ly* or *ily*.	family	fl		
23. Write a capital D for the word beginning *dis*.	discuss	Dcs		
24. Write a capital M for the word beginning *mis*.	misplace	Mpls		
25. Retain beginning or ending vowels when building compound words.	payroll	parl	headache	hdac
26. Retain root-word vowels when adding prefixes and suffixes.	disappear	Dapr	payment	pam
27. Write a capital P (disjoined) for the word beginnings *per, pur, pre, pro, pro* (prah).	person	Psn	prepare	Ppr
	provide	Pvd	problem	Pbl
28. Write g for the word ending *gram*.	telegram	tlg		

29. Write y for the sound of *oi.*	boy	by		
30. For words ending in a long vowel + *t*, omit the *t* and write the vowel.	rate	ra	meet	⌒e
31. Write a for the word beginning *an.*	answer	asr		
32. Write q for the medial or final sound of any vowel + *nk.*	bank	bq	link	lq
33. Write a capital S (disjoined) for the word beginning *super* and for the word endings *scribe* and *script.*	supervise	Svz	describe	dS
	manuscript	⌒nS		
34. Write el for the word beginning *electr.*	electronic	elnc		
35. Write w for the word ending *ward.*	backward	bcw		
36. Write h for the word ending *hood.*	boyhood	byh		
37. Write 1 for the word ending *tion* or *sion.*	vacation	vc1		
38. Write a for the initial and final sound of *aw.*	law	la	audit	adl
39. Write q for the sound of *kw.*	quick	qc		
40. Write a capital N for the sound of *nd.*	friend	frN		
41. Write ⌒ for the initial sound of *em* or *im.*	emphasize	⌒fsz	impress	⌒prs
42. Omit *p* in the sound of *mpt.*	prompt	P⌒l		

43. Write k for the sounds of *com, con, coun, count.*	common	kn	convey	kva
	counsel	ksl	account	ak
44. Write *s* for the sound of *st.*	rest	r*s*		
45. Write q for the word ending *quire.*	require	rq		
46. Write z for the sound of zh.	pleasure	plzr		
47. Write ′ for the word ending *ness.*	kindness	cN′		
48. Write \ for words beginning with the sound of any vowel + x.	explain	\pln	accident	\dN
49. Write x for the medial and final sound of x.	boxes	bxs	relax	rlx
50. Write X for the word beginnings *extr* and *extra.*	extreme	X–		
	extraordinary	Xord		
51. Write q for the medial or final sound of any vowel + ng.	rang	rq	single	sgl
52. Write B for the word endings *bil, ble, bly.*	possible	psB	probably	PbB
53. Omit the final *t* of a root word after the sound of *k.*	act	ac		
54. Write a small, disjoined, and slightly raised *t* ᵗ for the word ending *ity.*	quality	qlᵗ		
55. Write u for the word beginning *un.*	until	ull		

56. Write sl for the word ending *cial* or *tial* (shul, chul).	financial	fnnsl
57. Write N for the sounds of *ance, ence, nce, nse.*	expense	vpN
58. Write s for the word beginning *sub.*	submit	smt
59. Write v for the medial and final sound of *tive.*	effective	efcv
60. Write f for the word endings *ful* and *ify.*	careful	crf
	justify	jsf
61. Write fy for the word ending *ification.*	qualifications	qlfys
62. Write a capital N for the word beginnings *enter, inter, intro.*	enterprise	Nprz
	introduce	Nds
	interest	Ns
63. Write sf for the word beginning and ending *self.*	self-made	sfmd
	myself	msf
64. Write svs for the word ending *selves.*	ourselves	rsvs
65. When a word contains two medial, consecutively pronounced vowels, write the first vowel.	trial	tril
66. When a word ends in two consecutively pronounced vowels, write only the last vowel.	idea	ida
67. Write T for the word beginnings *tran* and *trans.*	transfer	Tfr

SPEEDWRITING PRINCIPLES BY SYSTEM CATEGORY

Simple Sounds

			Unit
1. Write what you hear.	high	hi	1
2. Write c for the sound of k.	copy	cpe	2
3. Write  for the sound of m.	may		2
4. Write  for the sound of w.	way		2
5. Write s to form the plural of any word, to show possession, or to add s to a verb.	books	bcs	
	runs	rns	2
6. Omit *p* in the sound of *mpt*.	empty		22
7. Write x for the medial and final sound of x.	boxes	bxs	
	tax	tx	29
8. Omit the final *t* of a root word after the sound of *k*.	act	ac	31

Vowels

1. Drop medial vowels.	build	bld	1
2. Write initial and final vowels.	office	ofs	
	fee	fe	1
3. Retain beginning or ending vowels when building compound words.	payroll	parl	
	headache	hdac	9

4. Retain root-word vowels when adding prefixes and suffixes.	disappear	Dapr	
	payment	pam	9
5. For words ending in a long vowel + *t*, omit the *t* and write the vowel.	rate	ra	
	meet	⌢e	12
6. When a word contains two medial, consecutively pronounced vowels, write the first vowel.	trial	tril	40
7. When a word ends in two consecutively pronounced vowels, write only the last vowel.	idea	ida	40

Vowel Blends

1. Write o for the sound of *ow*.	allow	alo	5
2. Write y for the sound of *oi*.	boy	by	11
3. Write a for the initial and final sound of *aw*.	law	la	
	audit	adl	19

Consonant Blends

1. Write a capital C for the sound of *ch*.	check	Cc	2
2. Write ‿ for the sound of *wh*.	when	‿n	2
3. Write a capital N for the sound of *nt*.	sent	sN	3
4. Write ⌿ for the sound of *ish* or *sh*.	finish	fn⌿	4

5. Write l for the sound of *ith* or *th*.	them	lm	8
6. Write q for the medial or final sound of any vowel + *nk*.	bank	bq	
	link	lq	13
7. Write q for the sound of *kw*.	quick	qc	19
8. Write a capital N for the sound of *nd*.	friend	frN	20
9. Write S for the sound of *st*.	rest	rS	23
10. Write z for the sound of *zh*.	pleasure	plzr	25
11. Write g for the medial or final sound of any vowel + *ng*.	rang	rg	
	single	sgl	30
12. Write M for the sounds of *ance, ence, nce, nse*.	balance	blM	36

Compound Sounds

1. Write m for the sounds of *mem* and *mum*.	memo	mo	3
2. Write m for the sounds of *men, min, mon, mun*.	menu	mu	
	money	me	3
3. Write k for the sounds of *com, con, coun, count*.	common	kn	
	convey	kva	
	counsel	ksl	
	account	ak	23

Word Beginnings

1. Write a capital A for the word beginnings *ad, all,* and *al.*	admit	Ad	
	also	Aso	4
2. Write n for the initial sound of *in* and *en.*	indent	ndN	4
3. Write a printed capital S (joined) for the word beginnings *cer, cir, ser, sur.*	certain	Sln	
	survey	Sva	5
4. Write a capital D for the word beginning *dis.*	discuss	Dcs	8
5. Write a capital M for the word beginning *mis.*	misplace	Mpls	8
6. Write a capital P (disjoined) for the word beginnings *per, pur, pre, pro, pro* (prah).	person	Psn	
	prepare	Ppr	
	provide	Pvd	
	problem	Pbl	10
7. Write a for the word beginning *an.*	answer	asr	13
8. Write a capital S (disjoined) for the word beginning *super.*	supervise	S vz	15
9. Write el for the word beginning *electr.*	electronic	elnc	15
10. Write ⌒ for the initial sound of *em* or *im.*	emphasize	⌒fsz	
	impress	⌒prs	22
11. Write \ for words beginning with the sound of any vowel + x.	explain	\pln	
	accident	\dN	29

12. Write X for the word beginnings *extr* and *extra*.	extreme	Xm	
	extraordinary	Xord	29
13. Write u for the word beginning *un*.	until	utl	33
14. Write s for the word beginning *sub*.	submit	smt	36
15. Write a capital N for the word beginnings *enter, inter, intro*.	enterprise	Nprz	
	interest	Ns	
	introduce	Nds	39
16. Write sf for the word beginning *self*.	self-made	sfmd	39
17. Write T for the word beginnings *tran* and *trans*.	transfer	Tfr	41

Word Endings

1. Underscore the last letter of the word to add *ing* or *thing* as a word ending.	billing	bl̲	
	something	sm̲	2
2. To form the plural of any word ending in a mark of punctuation, double the last mark of punctuation.	savings	sv̳	2
3. To form the past tense of a regular verb, write a hyphen after the word.	used	uz-	6
4. Write m for the word endings *mand, mend, mind, ment.*	demand	dm	
	amend	am	
	remind	rm	
	payment	pam	3

5. Write l for the word ending *ly* or *ily*.	family	fml	8
6. Write g for the word ending *gram*.	telegram	tlg	10
7. Write a capital S (disjoined) for the word endings *scribe* and *script*.	describe	dS	
	manuscript	mnS	15
8. Write w for the word ending *ward*.	backward	bcw	16
9. Write h for the word ending *hood*.	boyhood	byh	16
10. Write 1 for the word ending *tion* or *sion*.	vacation	vc1	17
11. Write q for the word ending *quire*.	require	rq	25
12. Write ʹ for the word ending *ness*.	kindness	cNʹ	26
13. Write B for the word endings *bil, ble, bly*.	possible	psB	
	probably	PbB	31
14. Write a small, disjoined, and slightly raised *t* for the word ending *ity*.	quality	ql t	32
15. Write sl for the word ending *cial* or *tial* (shul, chul).	financial	fnnsl	34
16. Write v for the medial and final sound of *tive*.	effective	efcv	37
17. Write f for the word endings *ful* and *ify*.	careful	crf	
	justify	jSf	38

18. Write  for the word ending *ification.* — qualifications  — 38

19. Write  for the word ending *self.* — myself  — 39

20. Write  for the word ending *selves.* — ourselves  — 39

Marks of Punctuation

1. Underscore the last letter of the word to add *ing* or *thing* as a word ending. — billing  — something  — 2

2. To form the plural of any word ending in a mark of punctuation, double the last mark of punctuation. — savings  — 2

3. To form the past tense of a regular verb, write a hyphen after the word. — used 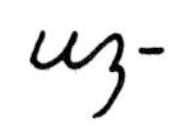 — 6

4. Write / for the word ending *ness.* — kindness  — 26

5. To show capitalization, draw a small curved line under the last letter of the word. — Bill  — 1

6. Write \ to indicate a period at the end of a sentence. — 1

7. Write x to indicate a question mark. — 1

8. Write > to indicate the end of a paragraph. — 1

9. Write ! to indicate an exclamation mark. — 5

10. Write = to indicate a dash. 5

11. Write = to indicate a hyphen. 5

12. To indicate solid capitalization, double the curved line underneath the last letter of the word. 5

13. To indicate an underlined title, draw a solid line under the word. 5

14. Write 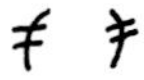 to indicate parentheses. 32

Miscellaneous